joan of arc
at the university

edited by

Mary Elizabeth Tallon

Library of Congress Cataloging-in-Publication Data

Joan of Arc at the University /
edited and with a preface by Mary Elizabeth Tallon.
   p. cm.
  Includes bibliographical references and index.
   ISBN 0-87462-005-8   1. Joan, of Arc, Saint, 1412-1431—Influence. 2. Women
soldiers-France-Public opinion. 3. Public opinion—France—History—Sources.
4. Christian women saints—France—Biography—History and criticism. 5.
Hundred Years' War, 1339-1453. 6. France—History—Charles VII, 1422-1461—
Historiography. 7. Personality and history. I. Tallon, Mary Elizabeth, 1941-
  DC103 .J63 1997
  944'.025—dc21   97-33758

MARQUETTE UNIVERSITY PRESS
MILWAUKEE

The Association of Jesuit University Presses

Cover and book design, and photos
(unless otherwise indicated) by Andrew J. Tallon

Special thanks to Olivier Bouzy and the staff of the Centre Jeanne d'Arc in
Orléans; the staff of the Musée de Vaucouleurs; Jacquie Bablet; Alain Préaux of
the Musée Jeanne d'Arc in Rouen; Gaël Leroux; the staff of the Cathedral of St.
Rémi in Reims; and Lisa Remby.

∾:∾

The lectures for *Joan of Arc at the University*
were supported by a grant from
the Wisconsin Humanities Council and
the National Endowment for the Humanities

∾:∾

The cover photo is of a statue in the Hôtel
Groslot, Orléans, by Marie d'Orléans.

O Jeanne, sans sépulchre,
sans portrait, toi qui savais
que le tombeau des héros est
le cœur des vivants.
— *Malraux*

Contents

---

*given before performances of *The Lark*

Joan of Arc at the University

Mary Elizabeth Tallon

Joan of Arc was the focus of a three week celebration that took place at Marquette University in the fall of 1996. This book, the fruit of a series of lectures which anchored that celebration, includes essays on Joan's life and the history of medieval Europe as she helped to shape it; essays on her spirituality; on the legal, political, and theological issues raised in her trial; on art works and films inspired by her; on French Gothic architecture; on adolescent psychology and feminism as they relate to Joan. These studies represent the University at work: outstanding teacher-scholars who bring their unique reflections and common understandings to see Joan in fresh perspective.

It was first of all a wish to celebrate university that inspired the Joan of Arc project. We wanted to explore potential diversity of approaches to a single topic, to ignite interdisciplinary dialogue, to cause the "collision of mind with mind, and knowledge with knowledge"[1] that characterizes the process of liberal education. In *The Idea of a University*, John Henry Newman recommends a full range of studies whose dynamic mutual existence provides an access to truth unavailable to each in isolation. Individual disciplines ask questions which sometimes can only be answered by correcting to a larger perspective—one provided by the aggregate of liberal studies. When these questions remain unanswered, students and teachers alike risk becoming, in Newman's words, "narrow-minded biggots."[2] At a university, scholars

---

Dr. Tallon teaches English at Marquette University.

are "kept from extravagance by the very rivalry of other studies," from which they gain "a special illumination and largeness of mind."[3]

While a university community may have many things in common—a public ethos, a core curriculum, a central campus, for example—Newman implies a more dynamic sharing, a "communication and circulation of thought,"[4] that extends beyond individual classes. Where does this happen? When do the ideas of separate disciplines "collide?" Where do scholars "adjust together the claims and relations of their respective subjects of investigation?"[5] At Marquette, team taught courses, dissertation boards, and special seminars sometimes cross department boundaries. Recently, the theology, history, philosophy, and physics departments shared responsibility for a seminar on "The Origins of the Universe." Another, "Ideas for a University," began as a national conference and continued as an inter-disciplinary seminar. The Honors program and a proposed Residential College aim specifically to overcome insularity among subjects, between students and faculty, and between social and classroom learning. But formal cross-pollination of studies is uncommon. Generally ideas come together in one place: the intellectual experience of those students who are mature enough to relate, compare, and integrate them. What if such students—and teachers—hungry to learn and to express resonances among ideas, are challenged at some given time by a single, highly focused topic? What if each department and school at the university is encouraged to participate? What if the topic is set before us in some kind of an open forum? Ideally, in the process of "viewing many things at once as one whole,... referring them severally to their true place in the universal system,...understanding their respective values, and determining their mutual dependence,"[6] we would truly become a university at work.

Cardinal Newman's description of such an event, even if more than a century early, spoke our hopes for the Joan of Arc celebration.

A fine time of the year is chosen, when days are long, skies are bright, the earth smiles, and all nature rejoices; [a location is chosen] where buildings are spacious and hospitality hearty. The novelty of place and circumstance, the excitement of strange, or the refreshment of well-known faces, the majesty of rank or of genius, the amiable charities of [those] pleased both with themselves and with each other; the elevated spirits, the circulation of thought, the curiosity; the morning sections, the outdoor exercise, the well-furnished, well-earned board, the not ungraceful hilarity, the evening circle; the brilliant lecture, the discussions or collisions or guesses of [the great,] one with another, the narratives of [scholarly] processes, of hopes, disappointments, conflicts and successes, the splendid eulogistic orations; these and the like constituents of the annual celebration are considered to do something real and substantial for the advance of knowledge which can be done in no other way.[7]

Marquette University, a Jesuit, Catholic university, which maintains a wealth of courses in the Liberal Arts and a mandatory core curriculum, is an ideal place for such a celebration. Joan of Arc was an obvious choice: she is a Catholic saint, of college age during her public life and at her death. She is an accessible model for young people who seek the courage of their convictions. Moreover, the Joan of Arc chapel,* the only medieval structure in North America dedicated to its original purpose, stands on Marquette's central campus.

More than obvious, Joan of Arc was a splendid choice. By virtue of her special character and rich context, Joan provided the University with an excellent focus to draw different realms of study together. The several disciplines represented in these essays—theology, history, political science, spirituality, art history, film studies, theatre, psychology, sociology, and legal studies (ecclesiastical and civil)—each claims her as a legitimate subject of study. Ronald Zupko, in his research, has found "a Joan who can be classified in any category that any author has an inclination to pursue." Dr. Zupko emphasizes the "Many Faces of Joan," Linda Seidel the "Changing Images of Joan of Arc," Dominic Paul Noth the variety of Joan images in film. Joan travels a continuum between polar opposites: "Right or Left: Who Own's Joan of Arc" (Brigitte Coste), "Joan of Arc: Saint or Terrorist?" (Joseph Perry and Michael Gillick); while she is described as a goad (Tom Hughson) and a witch (Dan Maguire), George Tavard names her "*the* daughter of God"; Dr. Zupko commends her as a dauntless warrior and yet John McCabe praises her prudence; Phillip Naylor compares her to de Gaulle, Sherri Coe-Perkins to contemporary students; she is at once a traditional young woman and a feminist (Helen Sterk). A study of Joan of Arc brings to us the late Middle Ages in western Europe. She was embroiled in its central political turmoil, she prayed in its great cathedrals, she was tried by the Inquisition.

The striking diversity of visual images of Joan is usually explained by the fact that no one knows exactly what she looked like; no true portrait of her is known. However, the similarly diverse notions of who or what she was cannot be explained analogously. In fact, although Joan was a fifteenth century peasant girl, we know a great deal about her. During her long Inquisitional trial in 1430-1431, Joan painted a detailed picture of her life which was fleshed out during her Rehabilitation trial in 1455-1456 by many who had personally known her.[8] So we conclude that the various treatment of her is not for lack of concrete information but because she was so truly multifaceted. She defies classification.

---

* The Joan of Arc chapel is described here in Curtis Carter's essay, "Her Spirit in Stone."

Joan raised issues that are relevant to us: the rights of the individual in monolothic systems (political, ecclesiastical, legal, penal) and the place of the woman in a male dominated world. She challenged the Church to honor the role of individual conscience and to rethink the relationship of the Church militant and triumphant. Taking her prayer to the battlefield, she struck a balance between the mystical and active life.

Saint Joan is a hero for us now, when we yearn for heroes of more substance than those who flicker on our video screens. She is courageous, astute, steadfast—full of ginger, love of life, and simple faith. She is a politician who doesn't vacillate, a military strategist who knows the value of honor, a self-taught lawyer who keeps her eye on the truth. Joan is a young woman with a purpose who would not stoop to dissemble or sell her integrity to achieve it. She is a girl who listens to her inner voices and is true to them.

Did the Joan of Arc celebration succeed in provoking argument or producing new understanding? Did it bring the University together? In many ways, yes. After the lectures (and after the polite questions) there was discussion and often dispute between traditionalists and revisionists and between those who think of Joan as a saint and those whose view of her is more humanistic. The campus was transformed with banners and faerie trees, trumpet fanfares and songs, students and faculty—and horses—in medieval garb. We were surrounded for three weeks with events of all kinds having to do with Joan and her world (see Appendix II); Joan of Arc emerged from the mist of legend through the wealth of the University's diverse offerings. Significantly, the event succeeded in the remarkably full-hearted response to the planning and work of the project at all levels of the University, which seemed to suggest a need to celebrate community.

While this book is only one part of the Joan of Arc celebration, it expresses the whole. There is in each essay fresh questioning and insight—and among them new understanding. In offering its inspired best, the University gives Joan here a new voice.

*   *   *

I would like to dedicate this book to all of those who took part in the Joan of Arc celebration and especially to Deb Krajec, my colleague and friend, who co-imagined the event, and to my wonderful family, Andy, Andrew and Clare, who were directly involved in the project, both at Marquette and at home.

Notes

1 John Henry Newman, "What is a University," in *Essays English and American* (New York: P. F. Collier & Son, 1910), 38.

2 John Henry Newman, *The Idea of a University*, ed. I. T. Kerr (London: Oxford University Press, 1976), 63.

3 Newman, *The Idea of a University*, 146.

4 Newman, "What is a University," 31.

5 Newman, *The Idea of a University*, 95.

6 Newman, *The Idea of a University*, 122-123.

7 Newman, "What is a University," 35-36.

8 See Raymond Oursel, *Le procès de condamnation et le procès de réhabilitation de Jeanne d'Arc* (Paris: Editions Denoëls, 1959).

Introduction to the Joan of Arc celebration
A Sense of History

Thomas Hachey

Of all the things one might name as being essential to a graduate of Marquette University's College of Arts and Sciences, a solid sense of history has always seemed to me a critical necessity. I do not say this because I am a historian or because I still harbor the desire to return to teaching Western Civilization to a thousand Marquette undergraduates in a former movie house. *Historia magister vitae suae:* history is the great teacher of human life. This maxim was reminding educators of a responsibility to the past long before the rise of modern historiography. I am proud that the College of Arts and Sciences insists upon it.

Lately, however, one might reasonably wonder how this great teacher acquires her credentials. In the past few months, the media have made us aware of a number of controversies surrounding history and how it finds its way into the public mind. Think of the arguments over placing the Enola Gay on display to commemorate the end of World War Two. The din of political argument quickly drowned out a more reasoned discussion on the meanings of the proposed display. The Disney Corporation eventually gave up with a plan to put mechanized reenactments of American history on display in a theme park near Washington, D.C. And most recently, a virtual-reality attraction near Dealy Plaza in Dallas has offered to let ordinary people experience the sounds and sensations of riding in the limousine of President Kennedy the moment he was assassinated.

Dr. Hachey is dean of Arts and Sciences at Marquette University.

To be sure, these are very different types of "historical" presentations. But one thing they do have in common is a simplistic notion of how the past teaches, and what its inherent power is.

This is why I am so pleased to have the opportunity to be part of the opening of the Joan of Arc Celebration. The wonderful program of events brings into focus for me one important quality of the past as teacher, a quality that is forgotten if we think of history only as making the past available to be heard, or seen, or touched.

Think for a moment of why Joan of Arc appeals today, especially to young people, despite the fact that the historical record is unable to provide much in the way of concrete detail. If the one element of history that has been under suspicion for some time is the way in which it tells stories, it is something of a surprise that what appeals to a person concerning Joan of Arc is her story.

And it appeals to young people for good reason, I might add, because this is a story of a person at the threshold of adulthood. A young person at this age is coming into what we can recognize as a true sense of herself as an independent, thinking, imagining individual, who is beginning to recognize horizons beyond family, school, community. She is like so many others at this point in life: awakening to intellectual and ethical independence, and growing aware of the responsibilities of true individuals.

However mysterious she might remain to academic historians, Joan emerges in the story as a young woman who has somehow become aware of the presence of God, whose strength is based on a higher authority, who acts with urgency for the greater good.

Without help from academic historians—without debate over the correctness of historical portrayal or the physical sensations of her travails—one recognizes in her a human being acting with courage.

Andrew Jackson is supposed to have said, "One man with courage makes a majority." What one can agree upon about Joan of Arc is quite simple: she recognized the right thing and acted on it. Joan offers us a young person who—completely without political savvy or machinations —becomes a genuine leader, aware of a mission, and acting with decisiveness. And by acting with courage, she was reflecting what is best in the human being. She becomes a model of what is possible.

What appeals about Joan of Arc is the truth that it illuminates in our present situation. Robert F. Kennedy, writing just a few weeks after the death of his brother, John, said, "What happens to the country, to the world, depends on what we do with what others have left us."

This, I believe, is the moral charge of the historian. To teach new generations not only the facts of their own past, but to recognize the contours of the moral landscape they have inherited from the past and to find their way in that landscape.

The past—when it is allowed to also be simply a story—touches us more profoundly than would the mere sensations of times past. It makes us more at home in the present. It shows to our inner eye the complexities that embrace us.

Like the Kennedys of a generation ago, I am convinced that "the courage of those who went before us in this land exists in the present generation of Americans." It is as necessary now as before, and I commend to you the story of courage that will emerge in the coming weeks of celebration.

The Many Faces of Joan

Ronald Edward Zupko

Hôtel Groslot, Orléans

Joan of Arc or Jeanne d'Arc, known under a variety of other names and appellations throughout history—such as la Pucelle, the Maid, the Maiden, Princesse Royale, and l'enfant de France—has been the subject of an incredible number of publications since the fifteenth century. In France alone there were more than 20,000 manuscripts, books, scholarly articles, plays, poems, and newspaper and magazine items dealing with the events of her life through the year 1920, the date of her canonization by Pope Benedict XV. If one then totals the accumulated bibliography on Joan in just the rest of Europe and the Americas, from her own era to the last decade of the twentieth century (running well over 50,000 publications), one can easily see that she is among the most researched personalities in European civilization. Very few individuals in history can claim such a remarkable record. Perhaps very few hereafter ever will.

It is not my intent today to capsulize for you this prodigious outpouring of interest over the last six centuries—such a goal is unattainable. Also, I do not intend to state categorically or otherwise who she was, which interpretation is correct, or where research in the future might lead us. I have four principal aims in this address. First,

Dr. Zupko teaches History at Marquette University.

it is necessary to trace the major episodes or phases of The Hundred Years' War to provide you with the historical backdrop during which Joan rose to prominence and gained her reputation. Second, I shall present the figure of Joan as she emerges from the pages of the most important traditional historical scholarship and literature, those sources which are most methodologically trusted and verifiable. Third, I shall examine Joan at the hands of her detractors, who have grown increasingly more evident and vocal during the twentieth century. Some of these conclusions may shock or at least alarm those who attach themselves to the more traditional interpretations, but they must be stated since they constitute an integral part of the historical record. Last, since most of us live in a computer literate world, I shall detail for you my own investigations over the last year of "surfing" the Internet. Joan is one of the liveliest topics on it. Perhaps nothing is a more fitting tribute to her timeless appeal. Along the way, I trust that you gain a greater understanding of Joan, her life, her mission, her death, her meaning.

The Hundred Years' War Before the Emergence of Joan

The Hundred Years' War is a misnomer. There were actually two of them—the first beginning in 1066 when William of Normandy won the celebrated Battle of Hastings, and, after a five-year scorched-earth policy in the southeastern shires, declared himself and the Normans heirs to Anglo-Saxon history. From then until the thirteenth century, the English and the French waged intermittent warfare which saw the tide of battle sway between the early successes of Henry II and Richard the Lion Heart on the English side and Philip Augustus and St. Louis on the French side. It is crucial to note that, by 1199, England (with its French-speaking monarchy) controlled two thirds of France, while the French kings held only one third of the remaining one third. The thirteenth century witnessed a remarkable reversal of fortunes for the French, especially during the reign of Philip Augustus, when he totally humiliated King John of England after 1204. Much French territory, save for Aquitaine and certain remote spots, was returned to France at that time and during the remaining decades of that century. This era is known currently in some scholarly circles as "The First Hundred Years' War."

We are concerned here today with "The Second Hundred Years' War"—the more famous of the two—which I shall refer to hereafter simply as "The War." The latter French and English engagement, often cited as the longest continuous military action of either country in history, officially running from 1337 to 1453, would witness revolutionary changes in military operations, the decline of feudalism, the rise of citizen armies, nascent nationalism, the bitterest church-state conflict of the Middle

Ages (which would not be resolved until the Council of Constance that sat between 1414 and 1418), the ravages of the worst famines and plagues in European history, a French civil war, and a host of other massive upheavals.

The War began unofficially in 1294 in what might be labeled "The Prelude," and it lasted a mere four years until 1298. The causes for this initial hostility were the same as those which would drag both countries into war after 1337—the lingering debates over Gascony, Aquitaine, and Flanders, and the question of succession to the French throne. The Gascony debate involved the attempt by King Philip IV to take this province in southwestern France from the English and Edward III's resolution that only a full-scale war could prevent a French takeover. The Aquitaine and Flanders debates were much older. Aquitaine became part of English possessions in 1152 after the marriage of Eleanor, heiress to the Duchy of Aquitaine, to Henry of Anjou who became Henry II of England in 1154. This area, held by the English as a fief from the French crown, was the largest producer of wine in Europe and the enormous profits accrued mainly to England. France wanted a more equitable distribution of the financial gains. The county of Flanders, a French fiefdom, was the industrial heartland of Europe; it produced the majority of woolen cloth for European markets. Since the raw material came mainly from England and the finished cloth was distributed throughout Europe by English ships and sold by English merchants, the French felt cheated out of its rightful share. Finally, Edward III's conflict with the French encouraged him to assert his claim to the French throne. The French Capetian dynasty had died out following the deaths without heirs of the three sons of Philip IV. Philip IV's daughter, Isabelle, was the mother of Edward III. As the grandson of Philip IV, Edward was, in fact, the closest living male heir to the French throne. The French courts, however, had invalidated Edward's claim by citing Salic Law, which barred inheritance through the female line, and had awarded the crown to Philip's nephew, Philip of Valois, who became Philip VI in 1328, the first king of the Valois dynasty.

Phase I of the War began in 1337, but no significant hostilities ensued until three years later. To wage war in France, the English needed control of the seas leading to the French and Flemish coasts. To thwart this and to prevent an English invasion, a French fleet consisting of Norman, Genoese, and Spanish ships (190 in all) gathered at Sluys, the harbor of Bruges. In June of 1340, however, it was almost totally destroyed by an English fleet of 150 ships, giving England mastery over the Channel for the next three decades. Only twenty of France's ships survived while England won one of its greatest naval victories in history, of which there would be many more in the centuries to come.

Five years later, an urban revolution in Flanders led to the reestablishment of French influence in the Flemish cities. Consequently, England had to seek another port of entry into France at Calais, the siege of which began in 1346. Raids had already begun on French territory from Aquitaine, and a large expedition was gathered for an invasion of northern France in the winter of 1345-1346. Because the French troops were concentrated in Poitou to meet the expected attack from Aquitaine, Edward III landed without resistance in Normandy in July of 1346 and started a scorched-earth policy. He was forced to take a stand at Crécy, where French troops, hurriedly summoned from Poitou, finally caught up with him. The result was devastating for the French. The English had cannons at Crécy and a large number of bowmen, and although the cannons were only powerful enough to make horrendously loud noises which caused the steeds of the French knights to buck, the archers decisively destroyed the Genoese crossbowmen employed by the French. The French knights were then slaughtered and suffocated by the English infantry forces.

More decisive still was the final capture of Calais in August 1347; it proved to be the most permanent English conquest of the war and it was held until 1558. French citizens were expelled from the town and replaced by English colonists. England now had an open door into France, which more than compensated for its loss of influence in Flanders.

Soon thereafter, all military activities temporarily ceased due to the destruction wrought by the Black Death which ravaged all of Europe. Before the first wave of bubonic and other strains of plague had taken their toll in this dreaded century, approximately one third of Europe would succumb—a total conservatively estimated at twenty-five million people.

The war resumed in the summer of 1356 with the Black Prince, Edward's eldest son, harrowing the cities of the Loire valley and the provinces of Berry, Touraine, and Anjou. Only in mid-September did a large French army make its appearance and force the Black Prince to fight when it might have starved him into submission. The unfortunate result of this miscalculation was that the English won again, this time at Poitiers, with an even more overwhelming victory than before. King John the Good of France, three of his sons, two marshals, and a large number of aristocratic French knights who were unable to flee were captured and held for ransom. The number of other prisoners was so great that the Black Prince, fearing a mutiny, had them slaughtered. He wintered in Bordeaux with much feasting and merriment, returning to England in the spring of 1357 with his catch. Not the most responsible king in French annals, John had a marvelous time in England where he was treated more as a guest than as a prisoner—he was lodged in the Savoy Palace with many servants, he received a liberal spending allowance, he hunted in the royal forests, and he loathed to return to his war-torn country. France needed more of its royal leader at this juncture of the war.

By this point, France had suffered embarrassing losses, considerable government expense, devastation of agricultural lands, domestic misery, taxation abuses, and loss of honor. It is not surprising that a revolt, known as the Jacquerie, began in northern France, led by a Parisian revolutionary named Etienne Marcel. Harassed by demands for money to pay the ransom demands of the Black Prince and beset by well-organized companies of plundering mercenaries, the peasants and their urban brethren rose up against the government. The dauphin, John's eldest son and the heir apparent, luckily escaped Paris and Marcel; through a series of intricate manipulations, he was able to summon a meeting of loyalist forces in Compiègne, where he was granted additional war funds. He then advanced on Paris in July of 1358 and restored order. This heroic action saved France for the moment.

The first phase of this war ended in 1360 with the signing of the Treaty of Bretigny or Calais even though important events precipatory to renewed military action would drag out until 1369, the beginning of the next phase. The treaty gave Guienne, Gascony, and Poitou to Edward III without feudal obligation. Several northern counties were also ceded to him, which increased English holdings substantially. The ransom for King John, converted from French gold crowns to English monetary pounds, came to the astronomical figure of approximately 30,000,000 pounds, an almost incomprehensible figure given that the usual English government's yearly expense during the period were around forty thousand pounds. Very little of this amount would ever be forthcoming, however, as it depended on Edward's willingness to relinquish his claim to the French throne—a modest concession indeed. Even though a partial payment was made on the ransom, the self-indulgent John enjoyed himself in England until his death in 1364.

In the lull before the renewal of hostilities, Philip the Bold emerged as a powerful leader in Burgundy, and France acquired its best monarch during the entire war. A new chapter was about to begin.

Phase II began in 1369 when the awkward and sickly Charles V, known as "The Wise," ascended the French throne. In the next eleven years, this gifted king, with the aid of Bertrand du Guesclin—the tough Breton constable and renowned military genius—not only reduced English holdings in France to Calais, Cherbourg, and Brest in the north and a strip extending from Bordeaux to Bayonne in the southwest, but they virtually freed France from the ravages of mercenary companies. Charles created a royal navy that won back the Channel from the English; he reorganized the finances with France's first attempts at sales and income taxes; he introduced effective infantry, archery, and artillery dimensions to the armed forces; and he convinced the French citizenry that the monarchy was the savior of France. Unfortunately, Charles's health would not stand up to the rigors of war; he died in 1380, before his task was completed. France would pay dearly.

The third phase of the war began with Charles's successor and continued until 1420, with the tide of battle reversing itself dramatically to the advantage of the English—especially in the later stages. In four decades, France sank to its lowest level of the entire war. The most important reason for France's demise was Charles's son and successor, Charles VI. As a minor, the new king was under the tutelage of three uncles, the dukes of Berry, Anjou, and Burgundy, who were quick to rob the treasury and to powerbroke for their own selfish interests. While this was transpiring, Philip the Bold used French troops to put down renewed Flemish revolts. In 1384, entering into the rich inheritance of his wife, Philip became Count of Flanders. A Burgundian-Flemish monolith could only spell trouble for the French crown. After Charles reached majority, he ruled for a while with several of his father's ablest ministers. In 1392, however, he became violently insane. There immediately ensued a struggle between Philip the Bold and the king's brother, Louis of Orléans, for control of the government. Philip died in 1404, but the rivalry continued with Philip's son, John the Fearless. Then disaster happened. On an evening in November, 1407, while riding on his mule from a visit with the queen and reported to be contentedly humming a tune, Louis of Orléans was murdered in cold blood by hired assassins of John the Fearless, who confessed to the deed quite openly and got away with it.

The murder produced a civil war between the Burgundian faction of northern and northeastern France and the Orleanist or Armagnac faction (so-called from the father-in-law of the new Duke of Orléans, Count Bernard of Armagnac) of southern and southeastern France. The two parties were not only struggling for the control of the government of a mad king, but they were divided over the question of the war and over which pope to support in the schism between the pope in Avignon and his rival in Rome (which began when the Babylonian Captivity of the Church ended in 1377—a period that saw the seat of Roman Catholicism absent from Rome for seventy years). Burgundy sided with the new Lancastrian dynasty in England and was neutral in the matter of the schism; the Armagnacs half-heartedly supported the Crown and the French pope. It was the perfect situation for the English to reopen the war vigorously.

Henry V was king of England at this juncture and his hold on the throne was shaky; a glorious victory over the French would help him to secure it. After renewing his claim to the French throne, one which had less validity than Edward's, the war was reopened vigorously in 1415 with the English in possession of a loose kind of alliance with the Burgundians. Henry's aim was to open up another port of entry on the continent at Harfleur, to provide plunder for his army by marching north through Normandy, and then to embark at Calais for England. The original aim was accomplished, but on the march northward, the English were forced by an Armagnac army to take a stand at Agincourt. England's finest hour in the war was about to begin.

The Battle of Agincourt was a complete disaster for the French. While the Burgundians resisted military action on either side, English forces scored a slaughter even greater than at Crécy and Poitiers. The French apparently forgot all of the military reforms initiated by Charles V, since their army was composed overwhelmingly of heavily armored cavalry without the support of the necessary auxiliary troops. The English repeated their traditional tactics. The result was that more French knights were slain or suffocated than there were men in the English army. There was now little to prevent the English occupation of practically all of northern France, which was begun in 1418 with the important and successful siege of Rouen.

In the same year, John the Fearless took control of Paris and the royal government. Those Armagnacs who were left in the city, after a terrible massacre, managed to escape south of the Loire with the dauphin, the future Charles VII; here a rival government was subsequently set up for all Armagnac territory. The dauphin was now the virtual head of the Armagnac faction.

Despite his alliance with the English, John the Fearless began negotiations with the Armagnacs, looking towards a cessation of the civil war and a common front against the English. Ostensibly, blood and common bonds ran deeper than diplomatic loyalty. But did they? The final conference was arranged for September 10, 1419, at the Bridge of Montereau. It ended in the murder of John with an axe. This crime made all further attempts to come to terms with the Armagnac party impossible. Philip the Good, John's son, immediately turned to the English and by Christmas had concluded a truce with them. Philip, in charge of the French government, finalized the negotiations during the spring months, and the Treaty of Troyes was signed in 1420.

This famous treaty amounted to the realization of the most opportunistic of English dreams. The dauphin was cast aside in favor of Henry V, who was declared by some unbiological contrivance to be Charles VI's son and heir to the French kingdom. During the lifetime of Charles VII, Henry was to act as regent with the cooperation of John the Good. He was to retain all his conquests in full sovereignty, but he promised on oath to return them to France when he succeeded Charles. To seal this pact, Henry married Catherine, Charles VI's daughter. In a manner of speaking, England believed it had set into reverse the events of 1066.

The exuberant English soon afterwards began to spread their conquests north of the Loire and to consolidate their enviable position. But the fates intervened once more. In 1422, both Henry V and Charles VI died. This was a catastrophe for the English. The infant English king, Henry VI, was now King of France north of the Loire; he was represented in regency by his uncle John, Duke of Bedford, with the support of John the Good. History may or may not repeat itself, but the English should have been wary of their Burgundian allies. South of the Loire ruled the former dauphin, Charles VII, king but without benefit of coronation and consecration in Rheims Cathedral.

France was now in its most perilous and desperate predicament. Fortunately for French interests, the next several years of the war witnessed no more significant battles and the theater of operations remained at a virtual standstill. It was then, amid all of this gloom and depression, that the fates smiled on France. Joan of Arc emerged to carve her indelible niche in French history.

What follows is an examination of her life, her role in this war, and her death according to traditionally accepted historical records and scholarship. In the next three decades, she would play a considerable part in France's ascent to victory

Joan and Her Role in Traditional Historical Scholarship

Joan of Arc was born in January, 1412, at Domremy in the Castellany of Vaucouleurs, a region on the northeastern Lorraine frontier that had remained loyal to the Armagnac cause. Her father was Jacques d'Arc, reported to be a highly respected leader of his village; her mother was Isabelle Romée. Like many other young persons of her age, she was devoted to the saints whose images stood in the parish church, and, early on, she became convinced that they were devoted to her. She knew her prayers, was instructed in the faith, went to Mass frequently, and knelt in the fields when she heard the angelus bell. Unlike others, however, she was certain that she heard the voices of the saints speaking directly to her, particularly those of St. Michael, St. Catherine, and St. Margaret; the first saint was of renowned military reputation, while the other two were famous martyrs. These voices announced that they had a mission for her: she must depart her village, seek an audience with the dauphin, and lead him to Rheims to be crowned and anointed. These commands to her were nothing less than direct commands from God, upon which it was imperative to act immediately.

Supposedly upon the advice of an uncle, and accompanied by him, she went to Captain Robert de Baudricourt, commander of the military garrison at Vaucouleurs, to seek an escort to the king's temporary residence at Chinon. Given the extremely unsavory conditions of army camps during the Middle Ages and the personal habits of many of the personnel, it should not appear surprising that Baudricourt was taken aback with the pleading of an innocent, angelic-looking peasant girl telling him of her mission and goals. She professed, he rebuffed, and she returned home. Later in 1428, a raid by Burgundian troops caused her family and others at Domremy to flee for a short time to the nearby village of Neufchâteau. After further urging by her voices, Joan returned with her uncle to Vaucouleurs early in 1429. Perhaps influenced more by her persistence than by his acknowledgement of her divine mission, Baudricourt granted Joan an escort of six men. Somehow, this small ensemble managed to travel through 300 miles of Anglo-Burgundian territory to Chinon where Joan, dressed as a man, presented herself to Charles with the simple announcement that she had come on God's behalf to help him and his kingdom.

At first, Charles was as incredulous as Baudricourt had been and he refused to see her. Although the sources conflict at this point, Joan reportedly revealed things that were only known to the dauphin. The extraordinary character of this incident made her suspect, and, after a cursory local examination by several bishops and theologians that must have been unconvincing, Charles ordered her to be turned over to a commission of theologians at Poitiers who, after a three-week interrogation, pronounced her to be simple, good, honest, and virtuous. In the course of the proceedings she predicted, among other things, that the siege of Orléans would be decided in favor of France, the English would be destroyed, the king would be crowned at Rheims, and Paris would be restored to its time-honored dignity as the capital of France.

In April, Joan, now accepted by the dauphin, was sent to Tours. She was given a horse, a suit of white armor, a banner with the inscription Jesus Maria, and a sword which, after instructions from her voices, she had found buried near the altar of the Church of St. Catherine at Fierbois. At the head of a small militia-type troop, she moved on to Blois, where she joined a force variously estimated at between 3,000 to 12,000 men. They marched on Orléans together, arriving there on April 28. The ensuing military activity took more than a week, but by May 7, an all day battle brought victory to the French; the next day, the English withdrew their forces. Although wounded in the shoulder in the heat of the conflict, Joan found time amid the wild celebrations that broke out in the city to admonish the army on its moral laxity. She tried to get rid of the throng of prostitutes who followed the army (a customary practice in medieval warfare), she forbade her own men to curse, and she repeatedly encouraged them to confess their sins and attend Mass. Soon thereafter, Joan rejoined Charles at Tours.

News of this victory spread throughout France and beyond. The blow to English prestige and the resulting elevation of French morale was considerable. The French, or at least some of them, believed that they were accompanied by a saint. She made up for her apparent ignorance of military affairs with a reckless abandon that inspired the troops. A flurry of slogans was invented—one of the most popular was that before her appearance, two hundred Englishmen could repel five hundred Frenchmen; after Joan appeared, two hundred Frenchmen could repel five hundred Englishmen. She also received accolades from some distinguished French churchmen and celebrated intellectuals, one of whom, John Gerson, a former Chancellor of the University of Paris, wrote a treatise supporting and praising her valiant efforts. This treatise would resurface as part of her rehabilitation some twenty five years later.

Joan spent most of the rest of May with Charles while he pondered laboriously over what the next course of action should be, even proposing that French troops concentrate their efforts on an invasion of Normandy. All Joan wanted to do was to get to Rheims where Charles could be properly crowned and anointed with the holy oil that had supposedly been sent from heaven initially to be used on the Merovingian king, Clovis, the father of France, in the late fifth century. In June, she received royal leave to join the government forces engaged in the freeing of the Loire basin. It might have been advantageous had this army headed directly for Paris, but Joan stated over and over that her main mission was to lead Charles to Rheims for his coronation, and her perseverance won the day.

It should not be surmised that Joan was ever in command of the army. In an important victory at Patay, for example, she was in the rear; in others, such as Jargeau, Meung, and Beaugency, her whereabouts are open to dispute. But she was with the army, and in the popular imagination that was sufficient. Essentially, she had official command only over the handful of men who started out with her and who formed her military household, although others frequently rallied to her standard in battle. There is also a dispute over her official title, but "Captain" seems closest to historical reality. Only once in the months before her capture is she ever referred to in any document as one of the commanders, and that may be an overstatement.

By the end of June, Joan had caught up with Charles. After additional victories at Auxerre, Troyes, and Châlons in the first two weeks of July, she and the king were received joyously at Rheims. On July 17, 1429, Charles was crowned in the cathedral with a crown of no special importance since he had apparently forgotten to bring his own. Joan and her banner stood behind the king during the ceremonies.

At this particular point, Joan's role was really ended. She had been instrumental in securing the relief of Orléans, the king had been crowned, and she had revived hopes for the ultimate victory of the French dominion. That was a spectacular success. Had Joan retired here, her fate may have been radically different, but she was convinced that her mission was only half-completed—the English were not yet driven out of France. Her wish to continue the war, however, did not conform to the wishes of Charles. The king was anxious to get back to his comfortable chateau in the Loire valley, and his advisors preferred to negotiate with the English and the Burgundians rather than continue the struggle. But Joan's voices drove her on. She refused to listen to the advice of government ministers or to take orders that deviated from her course; she had become a nuisance. This may be apocryphal but Charles, in a fit of pique, was said to have wished that she would go and hang herself.

Soon thereafter, events prevented Charles from returning to the Loire, and, regardless of whatever actually happened between them, Joan was permitted to go on with the French army and Charles accompanied her. In August, the French scored victories at Compiègne, Senlis, Beauvais, and St. Denis. But then, in an abortive attack on Paris in early September, Joan was wounded again; this time an arrow pierced her thigh. The French retreated and Joan, much to her chagrin, spent the next few weeks wallowing in idleness with Charles.

In the autumn of 1429, the French seized several additional towns of no great strategic importance and then retired for the winter. Then in March and April of 1430, when Joan became weary from the long period of agonizing inactivity, action resumed. With a significantly smaller military force than she was accustomed to, and without the consort of Charles, she took off once again. In the third week of April, after reinforcements had arrived (perhaps at the request of Charles), she was victorious at Lagny. She then moved on to Senlis. An intricate series of events now transpired which included the news that young King Henry VI and a new English army had landed at Calais, and that the English and Burgundians would concentrate their efforts at capturing Compiègne. This was catastrophic. All of her efforts on behalf of her voices and her God might come to naught if this enemy strategy came to fruition. After receiving word that a large enemy force was threatening this vitally important city, Joan, in her usual haste—and once again equipped with a much smaller force (perhaps fewer than 500 men who were foolish enough to accompany her)—arrived at Compiègne in the dawn hours of May 24. Most of her troops, completely outmatched in manpower and sensing disaster, deserted her. She was eventually dragged from her horse and captured in a swampy meadow by a Burgundian archer. She was turned over to a Burgundian partisan who sold her to the English for ten thousand pounds. The days of The Maid as a war hero were now over. Rumors spread that she was possessed by demons and was, most certainly, a witch. She had but one more year to live. Her fate would be decided by the Inquisition.

Joan was abandoned quickly by Charles, who did nothing, either militarily or diplomatically, to secure her release from the English. Apparently, he never even offered to match the ransom request—a piddling sum by medieval standards of ransom raised for such luminaries as Richard the Lion Heart and St. Louis to free them from their European and Moslem captors during the Crusades. Indeed, Joan was abandoned by everyone, she thought, except her God and her voices.

The English, nervously and impetuously desirous of destroying what they believed to be the abnormal influence that Joan had wielded positively over her own forces and negatively over those of England and its Burgundian allies for almost two years, were resolved to destroy her. They were anxious to have her condemned to death as a witch to prove that England and its fifth column ally in France were being defeated by a person possessed by an insidiously demonic—not divine—power. It should be emphasized that this era was marked by witchcraft trials all over Europe. These occurred regularly during the Middle Ages, almost on a cyclical basis. Joan, unfortunately, happened to be captured at a most inopportune moment. The witch hysteria was at its zenith.

The Church, too, was much concerned over Joan's claim that she was inspired directly by God. According to prevailing medieval dogma, Joan's revelations were impossible. In the course of many centuries, the Church had interposed itself between God and man as the only possible mediator of divine grace. Personal communion with God did away with the necessity of the Church, and any such protestations to the contrary smacked of the heresies of Peter Waldo, John Wyclif, John Hus, and a host of other important religious figures. Joan's fate was sealed almost before the proceedings began.

The trial took place in the city of Rouen where Joan had been incarcerated since being handed over by the English to their inquisitorial commission. It began officially on January 9, 1431, and would end with her burning at the stake on May 31. It was presided over by Pierre Cauchon, the Bishop of Beauvais, in whose diocese Joan had been taken prisoner. It should be noted that Cauchon was one of the many residents who had to flee Beauvais temporarily when French forces stormed the town the preceding August. Time does not permit an intensive examination of the day-to-day deliberations or a recitation of the large number of charges against her, but significant elements of the period of confinement, the day of execution, and the post-trial happenings will comprise the next section devoted to Joan's detractors.

Joan's trial was probably no more unfair than any other trial by inquisition. She was charged essentially with heresy and sorcery, and a large assemblage of legal and theological talent was employed to try her. Joan asserted early on that she was God's messenger, commissioned by Him through the voices of the saints and angels. Her interrogators countered this assertion with the charge that her inspiration came rather from the devil and his demons. They also condemned her supposed knowledge of the exact identities of her voices (who spoke to her in French), her historical prophesies and revelations, her wearing of men's clothing, her use of a cross as well as the names of Jesus and Mary on her banner, and her obstinance in defying Church judgments—especially in matters of faith. To the tribunal the essential question was: Would Joan be willing to leave the determination solely to the Church? If she refused this submission, her guilt was established, for to deny the authority of the Church was the commonest and deadliest of heresies. If she submitted, then the ecclesiastical commission before which she stood was ready to assume the functions of the Church and decide the issue against her.

Hour after hour, day after day, through the long months of the trial, the intrepid Joan foiled her inquisitors by the ingenuous candor of her speech and disarmed them by the shrewdness of her retorts. When asked repeatedly if she was in the state of grace, she would reply that, if she were not, she hoped God would bring her there and if she were, that He would keep her there. She thus avoided presuming on the authority of the Church by answering in the affirmative, and, conversely, avoided convicting herself by a negative response. Joan refused to be browbeaten into declaring anything that was against her convictions or to be forced to acquiesce to the will of her tormentors. She persistently denied the charges levied against her. Her will was indefatigable. The prosecution grew steadily impatient with her obstinence. The Inquisition always pressed for a rapid confession, due mainly to the fact that their judicial dockets were normally filled with a backlog of pending cases. As a result, in May, articles were drawn up convicting her of sorcery and heresy and quickly approved by the theological faculty of the University of Paris, long considered the dominant theological school in Europe.

On the morning of May 24, 1431, Joan was brought to the churchyard of St. Ouen in Rouen to hear the sentence committing her to the flames. She was weary, deserted, heartsick, and homesick. Her body was pained and her mind anguished, both devastated by the long imprisonment after a lifetime spent on the open farm fields of her youth and on the battlefields of her short military career. She was totally worn out by the severe strain of her long trial, some of which occurred during the Lenten fast which she had faithfully kept, even with her meager prison food. She was horrified at the thought that her nice body, as she put it, would be devoured in flames and burned to ashes.

It is for these reasons, perhaps more than any others, that Joan abjured after the sentence was read against her. Although there are conflicting reports at this critical juncture, Joan confessed to a document drawn up in French by Cauchon and his assistants that said, among other things, that she invented her visions and revelations, she practiced superstitious divinations, she blasphemed God and the saints, she transgressed divine and ecclesiastical law, she wore men's clothing as an abhorrence to her sex, she bore arms with the desire of shedding blood, she despised God and the sacraments, she worshipped and invoked spirits, she acted schismatically, and she committed errors against the faith. After her recantation, Cauchon changed her sentence from excommunication and burning to a penance of perpetual imprisonment. She returned to prison, resumed female clothing, and had her head shaved since she had formerly worn it in the custom of the French army of the period.

Once back in prison, however, she realized that she had been untrue to herself, her voices, and her faith. On May 28, only four days into her lifetime sentence, she resumed wearing male clothing since, as she said, she was a soldier of God. She announced that she had confessed to her guilt simply out of fear, that everything that she said in her testimony was absolutely true, and that she did not understand what the implications of her abjuration entailed.

To the Inquisition, this was clearly a relapse into heresy, for which there was no atonement. There could be no more trial deliberations, no more prosecution, and no more defense. She was turned over to the authorities to be sentenced according to the specifications predating her abjuration. On the morning of May 30, 1431, she was led to her final destination, the market square at Rouen, where she was fastened to a stake surrounded by a mass of combustible materials and burned to death as a heretic. A huge throng of spectators from Rouen and the surrounding areas witnessed what we in the twentieth century would label a media event. It was reported that she died with the name of Jesus on her lips.

After Joan's death, the course of the war continued in favor of France. At the Congress of Arras in 1435, the Duke of Burgundy abandoned his English alliance on very generous terms. England was offered both Guienne and Normandy as fiefs of the French crown on the condition that Henry VI renounce all claims to the French throne. The English not only refused this offer, but they demanded that all of France north of the Loire be turned over to them and be free from any feudal obligations. This was a stupid move. It inspired the French government to press forward with the war, and in the next decade, they initiated massive military reorganization and needed tax reform. In a sense, France returned to the sagacious policies of Charles V and they yielded fantastic returns. After the beginning of a total military onslaught in 1449, French armies conquered Rouen, Caen, and Cherbourg in 1449 and 1450 and liberated Normandy. Bordeaux and Bayonne were taken in 1450 and 1451, and Guienne and Gascony were finally added by July, 1453. Although this was not the official end of the war, since none was ever declared and since the English persisted in its claims until 1492, it was, effectively, the real end. France, due to the intercession of Joan of Arc, had turned the tide of battle and won the war.

Three years after the military action ended, Joan got her retribution. In 1456, in order to conciliate Charles VII and free the French monarchy from the charge that it had been assisted in its victory by a convicted sorceress and heretic, the papacy ordered a rehearing of Joan's case. In the extensive rehabilitation proceedings that followed, there was a complete examination of the original trial; of the objectives and methods of operation of the prosecution; of the activities therein of Pierre Cauchon who was responsible for adhering to the letter of inquisitorial law; of the testimony of Joan, her witnesses, and her defense; and all other particulars that pertained to the case. Much of what we now know of the original hearings and the specifics of this famous trial is culled from their deliberations and documentary publications. In the end, the original trial was judged irregular; its verdict was overturned and Joan's punishment was deemed unjustified. Joan was vindicated.

In 1909, slightly more than 450 years after her rehabilitation, Pope Pius X declared her beatified. In 1920, Pope Benedict XV canonized her a saint. As will be seen in the following section, there were many reasons why these events occurred so long after Joan's death (in 1431) and her rehabilitation (in 1456), including serious political and diplomatic considerations. But for now, that is unimportant. In a way, and at last, Joan had joined her voices. She was now one of them.

Joan at the Hands of Her Detractors

The preceding account of Joan's life, travails, and death is the one that, in one form or another, appears in the majority of published historical monographs and scholarly articles. There may be occasional variations in interpretation over certain key episodes of the story, there may be disputes over the precise meaning of some medieval documentary words and phrases, and there may be sincere disagreement over the extent of the contribution made by Joan to the war effort and to French resurgence, but most writers have traditionally followed the main outlines of the story that I have unfolded for you.

However, skepticism in regard to various elements of this story began shortly after the death of Joan, and in the centuries that followed, this took many different forms, both in historical writing and literature. The debate has peaked and ebbed repeatedly in this long period of time, but it has been most intense in the twentieth century, particularly since World War II. Just as it is impossible to cover all of the sources for the traditional interpretation, it is equally too large a task to cover everything at this end of the spectrum since the published corpus of Joan's detractors is very extensive. It is necessary, therefore, to limit the investigation to the major writers and their principal theories and opinions. The last section of this address will deal with four major categories: first, the position taken by Maurice David-Darnac, the most radical reinterpreter of the life and exploits of Joan; second, the claims advanced by Pierre de Sermoise during the 1960s and 1970s; third, the literary Joan of drama, poetry, and the popular imagination; and, finally, Joan as she appears today on the Internet. Along the way, one of the most multidimensional individuals in history will emerge—someone who appears to be everything to everybody.

In 1965, French historian, Maurice David-Darnac, began a massive reinterpretation of the entire Joan saga. In various publications and in interviews with the media, he advanced theories that may be considered the furthest to the left in this debate, if one wants to interject a political dimension. He angered many by his statements and the traditionalists countered with the argument that his views were merely gratuitous claims made to satisfy the modern public's craving for theories that go against the grain of universally held ideas. The basic threads of his argument run as follows. Joan of Arc escaped the burning pyre at Rouen. Rather than being born to a peasant couple, she was the daughter of Isabelle, the wife of Charles VI, and the mad king's brother, Louis, Duke of Orléans. (Remember earlier when I related the visit of Louis to the Queen and his departure upon that mule while singing a tune? This event occurred in 1407, five years before the traditional date of Joan's birth.) As the story continues, when Louis was murdered, Isabelle, fearing for the child's safety, had her secretly spirited out of Paris and taken to Domremy to be raised by the d'Arc family as their own daughter. Because Joan was of royal blood, half sister to Charles VII and to Queen Catherine of England, her death at the stake would have been politically embarrassing to many prominent French and English dignitaries.

To prove these assertions, David-Darnac concentrates briefly on statements made in some medieval accounts, chiefly on the events of the day of execution itself. In these accounts, he noted that, as early as 1431, a citizen of Rouen stated in his personal diary that Joan escaped the execution and that another woman was burned in her place. A second manuscript raised doubts that the victim was Joan and implied that townsfolk were of differing opinions on the matter. In *La Nef des Dames*, published in Lyons in 1503, as well as in several other contemporary sources, similar sentiments were aired.

But David-Darnac relies mainly on the events of May 30, 1431, to buttress his argument. Early on that day, he says, Pierre Cauchon visited Joan in her prison at the Château du Bouvreuil; after she accused him of being responsible for her impending death, he replied that she should be patient, that her predicament was due to her refusal to do what she had promised. Jean Toutmouillé, a Dominican friar, who recounted this episode at Joan's rehabilitation hearings, added that he was not privy to anything else for he had gone outside. There were no other witnesses to what transpired. The *Informatio Post Executionem*, the official document of the rehabilitation process, states that Cauchon, on the pretext of obtaining from Joan the revocation of everything she had abjured days earlier, was alone with her for some time. It was conceivable that Cauchon was able to arrange Joan's escape at this point.

Critics of David-Darnac are especially incensed over his insistence that she then gained her freedom through a secret passageway in the Château, labeling this notion romantic rubbish. But there really was an underground passage at the Château and it is still there today. David-Darnac believes that, in 1431, it must have led to a house belonging to the owner of the Château. So it is reasonable to assume that its exit was in the secondary residence of one of the members of the royal family—probably, he says, the Duke of Bedford. In the remains of the Château today, the entrance of the passage, closed by an iron grating for safety reasons, is in a recess in the ground-floor hall of the keep; this passage exits, oddly enough, at the current address of 102 rue Jeanne d'Arc.

Shortly after Joan's interview with Cauchon, a procession left the Château and rapidly crossed the town. An escort of slightly more than a hundred men-at-arms surrounded a woman prisoner, and no one was allowed to come too close. A far larger force cleared the square and dispersed those who had arrived early onto adjoining streets. The Earl of Warwick had given orders that all the windows overlooking the square were to be shuttered. David-Darnac believes that these security measures were done not only to stifle the danger of revolt, a definite possibility given Joan's reputation and notoriety, but to prevent the citizens, many of whom had seen or talked to Joan, from identifying the woman. Executions in the Middle Ages were popular events, but on this occasion, much was done to shield the victim from the view of the spectators. Moreover, she was clad in a strange fashion. She wore a long black tunic which fell to her feet. It was impossible to make out her features because her head was covered by a large miter that hid her hair and covered virtually her entire face save for her mouth and chin.

To further inhibit a clear view of the prisoner, three wooden platforms had been erected around the pyre. On one of them sat Cauchon, who exhorted the victim for the last time. But she did not answer. After hearing the indictment against her, she was again silent. David-Darnac finds it incredible to think, if the prisoner were in fact Joan, that she not respond to Cauchon's accusations that she was a pernicious seductress, a blasphemer of God, a heretic, a schismatic, and a devil worshipper. In his mind, the deafening silence proves that the woman who was about to be burned was not Joan. Cauchon's last statement was that the civil authorities spare the condemned the usual tortures that normally preceded such executions. Since bodily exposure would have been necessary to carry out such hideous torments, this only further reinforces his view that Joan had indeed escaped.

Most medieval burnings were long and laborious processes that typically lasted for the better part of a day. This particular one, however, was very short. David-Darnac finds irregularities in the incredible haste of the executioners in attaching the woman by iron chains to a stake on top of a pile of stones, in the way the pyre was built to conceal the victim, in the apparent excessive use of sulphur and pitch to render a massive conflagration and excessive heat that prevented identification of the body as it rapidly decomposed, and other such unusual events of that tragic day. A substitute, perhaps someone in an adjoining cell who had been convicted of witchcraft, died instead. Within approximately four hours, the ordeal was over and the ashes were thrown into the Seine. Nothing remained of the victim's body. No official record of the application of Cauchon's sentence was drawn up. No one, not even the official executioners, signed any document attesting to the event.

David-Darnac believes that Joan was subsequently imprisoned for a short period and then released. He insists that she returned to Lorraine, where she was recognized by the d'Arcs and some citizens of Metz. After a last visit to Orléans, where she was received with certain honors by the townsfolk, she resigned herself to living as a private citizen. She married an aristocrat named Robert des Armoises and lived mainly at the Château de Jaulny in Metz until she died, childless, in 1449. Controversy continues to swirl around this interpretation.

Count Pierre de Sermoise, the second principal detractor of the traditionalist or classicist position (as it is sometimes called), adds considerable personal ammunition to the debate. He published a book on the subject in 1973, and he assisted David-Darnac during the research stage of his monograph. Claiming that he is the last in the line of the Armoises, he states that documents have been in the hands of his family for centuries that establish fairly conclusively that Joan escaped the burning, was released from imprisonment after several years, and went to live near Metz where she married Robert des Armoises, a relative some twenty-or-so generations removed from de Sermoise. These documents, which include deeds, bills of sale, and family records, also suggest that she was born of royal blood and was one of a select brood known as the "Enfants de France." Genealogists, he says, are almost certain that her mother was Queen Isabelle and her father was probably Louis of Orléans.

Even though his basic thesis is filled with conditional defenses such as "fairly," "suggest that," and "almost," he is emphatic in his insistence that the truth never surfaced mainly for political reasons and partly to protect the royal family who would have been put in an extremely awkward position. Joan's presence at Orléans, he postulates, served essentially as a morale booster. Medieval French literature and popular superstition that spanned centuries held firmly to the belief that, at France's most critical hour, a shepherdess would save the country. To de Sermoise, the entire episode was nothing but a big publicity stunt, perhaps the most successful one in European history, devised cleverly by the French government of Charles VII to turn the tide of battle after the debacle of Agincourt. In his defense, the French have always referred to this famous encounter as a disaster or, at least, a national disgrace. He sees the story used again for political purposes in 1870 when France claimed Lorraine as her legal territory on the premise that Joan came from Lorraine. In his defense again, this dispute dates back as far as 843 when the Treaty of Verdun divided the empire of Louis the Pious, the son of Charlemagne, among his three sons. Three kingdoms were created: France, Germany, and a Middle Kingdom which included the land eventually known as Alsace-Lorraine. For more than a thousand years it would be one of the major causes of dispute between France and Germany, would alternately be shared by both powers, and would be the cause of numerous wars. Finally, de Sermoise posits that the ultimate political applicability of the Joan of Arc legend occurred in 1920, when she was canonized in order to consolidate relations between France and the Vatican following World War I. To him, Joan of Arc has been used as a vehicle through the ages to advance French political interests.

Finally, other evidence that de Sermoise marshals to reinforce his case includes pictures from the Château de Jaulny, one of the family's many residences at that time in history, showing portraits of Joan and Robert. Deeds refer to Robert's wife as Jehanne, la Pucelle de France; a poem celebrates her military accomplishments; and a supposed coat of arms for Joan includes the fleur de lys, which was only given to children of royal blood. So ends the contribution of de Sermoise to this dimension of the Joan debate.

What can be said at this point in my examination of the most publicized detractors? The writings and public interviews of both de Sermoise and David-Darnac are part of the historical record and an integral segment of the continuing fascination with this intriguing subject. Putting aside all of the suppositions in their arguments, especially those of de Sermoise, their theses must be taken seriously until historical research in the next decade and beyond, following the proper methodological techniques of authenticity and verification, prove them to be misguided or incorrect. They may be correct, or they may be yet another attempt to gain fame and publicity from the exploits of the Maid of Orleans.

The last dimension on the debate of Joan's true identity dwells first in the realm of her presentation in other writings devoted to a myriad of diverse and oftentimes obtuse subjects; second, to her principal literary sources, since she is one of the greatest historical figures imaginable for such purposes; and, finally, to her current persona as exemplified on the World Wide Web Network, more commonly known as the Internet.

After more than thirty years of research on the life of Joan in connection with my own scholarly writings and for my preparations for up-to-date lectures on Medieval England, the Hundred Years' War, the Black Death, and many other medieval themes, I have found a Joan who can be classified in any category that any author has an inclination to pursue. For example, in the first area mentioned above, Joan is frequently made out to be the foremost medieval freedom fighter, leading the charge for women's liberation in a rigidly fundamentalist, male-dominated society. She is a medieval Betty Friedan encouraging her sisters to do their own thing. There is nothing whatsoever in the historical record, especially in the many trial records and among Joan's personal documents, to suggest that women's liberation was ever part of her agenda. Besides, most writers advancing this position never mention Joan's many predecessors, among whom, just one, Eleanor of Aquitaine, would make a much better candidate.

Joan is also a popular figure in the literature dealing with magic, sorcery, and witchcraft. Her voices are said to be magically summoned and her actions mirror those of someone who is frequently under a spell. Her prophesies are the result of incantations conjured up through the daily ingestion of strange and exotic mixtures. To some, she is a sorceress; to others, a world-class magician; to still others, a witch. Some writers point to her family's southern French origins as proof of their claims since this section of France produced more heretical cults and popular movements than virtually any other European region. They point to the Albigensians as the prime example. She is a heroine to those who like to delve into and write about the world of the supernatural, the world of apparitions and ghost-like appearances. She is even honored by those who spend their lives studying shamanism, hysterics, and ecstatic religions. Again, even though sorcery was one of the principal charges made against Joan at her trial, there was no evidence that surfaced then, nor has any come to light since, to prove that she was knowledgeable concerning such matters. Anyone given credit for the ability to make miracles and to hear the voices of angels and saints—of which their were thousands in the history of the Church—could fall victim to such malicious charges.

Lastly, and oddly enough the obverse of this last category, Joan is an extremely important subject in the world of religious studies. For obvious reasons, she is a major player in the cult of the saints. She has been portrayed in numerous sources as a mystic, and, in the minds of some, she possessed powers that transcend the normal cognitive and extrasensory abilities of ordinary humans. To others, she is the leading Free Spirit of the Middle Ages. The latter movement surfaced at various times from the thirteenth through the fifteenth centuries; its members espoused a love of nature, being one with the environment, staying in communion with the flora and fauna surrounding them, eschewing the hum-drum existence of work and obligations, and doing whatever seemed to be enjoyable at the moment—such as free love. To the admirers of these medieval and later movements, Joan is the ultimate hippie or flower-child of the premodern world. Still others see Joan as the original Puritan or proto-Protestant. To them she answered the call of her inner conscience. She stood firm when challenged by the religious establishment. She put her faith in her voices above that of dogma and ecclesiastical tradition. She believed, therefore, she was saved. The saints and angels used her as their vehicle for God's messages. God did not save France through the intercession of the pope or the Roman Curia. God chose Joan: She had a direct pipeline to Heaven's mandates. She was justification by faith and the spiritual priesthood of all believers rolled into one. What those advocating Joan-as-Protestant fail to take into consideration is that many of the basic positions taken by Martin Luther, John Calvin, and a host of other religious reformers of the sixteenth century, were already professed in one form or another by such individuals as Peter of Bruys, Henry of Lausanne, Peter Waldo, and Tancelm, and by such organizations as the Apostolics and the Humiliati, to name but a few. They all pre-dated Joan by at least two centuries. Their ideas and movements were declared heretical; they were persecuted and many died. No Protestant Reformation occurred then due to many reasons, among which two were critical: the level of literacy enabling a significant percentage of the population to read was still too low and the printing press had not yet become a reality. Joan did defy the established Church and did stand by her convictions, but her basic drive was to save France. She did not want to reform the Church. She adored it.

How has Joan fared in the realm of drama? Since many programs of this Joan of Arc celebration present plays and reenactments of various episodes of her life, it is necessary here only to touch upon the figure of Joan as she is treated by several well-known playwrights to give an added dimension to the historical discussions presented heretofore. It must be emphasized that playwrights operate on a playing ground significantly different from that of historians. Dramatists seek to ferret out the innermost recesses of their subjects' psyches, to probe beneath the surface in order to expose desires and intentions that are normally hidden from most people who have an interest in the leading figures of their productions. They are not constrained by the same rules that bind historians to their craft, the most important of which is historical veracity. They must entertain and, hopefully, enthrall their audiences. The mundane, the common, the ordinary does not sell at the box office. That which appeals most to playgoers is to escape from a part of their normal lives. The greater the dilemma, the more impossible the challenge, the deeper the depravity or, conversely, the sublime innocence of the hero or heroine produces a catharsis among the audience that leaves them in anger, tears, laughter, rapture, or a myriad of other emotions. I shall briefly present four dramatists who fit this mold when treating Joan of Arc in their plays.

William Shakespeare was one of the greatest English dramatists of all time. Unfortunately, however, he had an axe to grind in his various "historical" plays. He was a major sympathizer with the House of Tudor and utilized sources that favored the winning dynasty. After the demise of Henry VII and Yorkist aspirations at Bosworth Field in 1485, he cast many significant historical figures in a very negative light, the most noteworthy being Richard III, who lost to Henry Tudor, and whom Shakespeare characterized as a hunch-backed, mentally incapacitated monarch who was a blight on his nation. Richard has been reintroduced to modern history enthusiasts in a far more favorable fashion in the twentieth century due to continuing and intensive scholarship. True to his fervent English nationalism, writing in an era—the late 1500s and early 1600s—that was not far removed in time from the saga of Joan, and relishing the demise of the woman who had been responsible for the loss of England's continental possessions in France, it should not be surprising that his portrayal of Joan is less than complimentary. In Part 1 of his memorable play, *Henry VI*, Shakespeare presents Joan as nothing more than a witch. England lost the war because its forces were pitted against a demonic force. Stating this another way, France did not win the prolonged struggle of more than a century because Joan was guided by her angelic and saintly voices, but England was thrown asunder by the devil and his chosen vassal of insidious designs. Joan did England in.

Voltaire, the renowned French philosopher, novelist, and playwright—never noted for his adherence to established religion or the more traditional aspects of his society—cast Joan, in *La Pucelle d'Orléans*, as a stereotypical bawd who used men for her own political and social purposes. She had grand desires. These deep seated wishes, that would thrill modern psycho-historians, could only be realized as an aftermath of her battlefield successes. She was a modern siren. Perhaps she would now be typecast as a Hollywood vixen, one who captures unsuspecting males by her sexual innuendoes. Modern films provide many examples of such personae from Mae West to Madonna.

To the German Romanticist, Friedrich von Schiller, Joan had an entirely different personality. Her power came from her virginity, her total innocence, her abstinence from the usual joys of everyday life, her devotion to her God-centered mission, and her heavenly voices. This, however, did not prevent him, for theatrical purposes, from having the Maid lose both her virginity and her incredible spiritual powers when she falls in love with, of all people, an English soldier. Perhaps, to Schiller, she was a faithful member of the Free Spirits. Love, after all, conquers all.

Last there is the nineteenth-century American literary genius, Samuel Clemens, known more often by his pen name of Mark Twain. Twain's Joan is, perhaps, the most far-fetched heroine of any in history. Credulity is strained here to the excess, to say the least. Joan, in Twain's misguided musings, was a wonder child whose innate wisdom was greater than any other person in recorded history. Perhaps life on the Mississippi River, where Twain wrote his account of Joan, was so uncomfortable during the summers of those years that he needed a respite to his intolerable conditions. He achieved it, but it hardly coincides with the historical record. His Joan never existed.

The last major source of information on Joan is the Internet. It is well known that virtually anything can be found there and that materials can surface on web sites that could never appear in print anywhere else, due either to the content or to the shoddiness of preparation and execution. The Internet Joan is no exception. Ten search engines brought me to substantial coverage on various themes connected with Joan's life: Yahoo, Atrium, Alta Vista, Deja News, Hot-Bot, Excite, Infoseek, Magellan, Open Text, and Web Crawler. Although there is an occasional informative article or discussion which reveals some new idea or fact that is of value to serious scholarship, the overwhelming emphasis of the Internet Joan is the macabre, the mysterious, the erotic, the esoteric, and the shocking.

A quick perusal of some of the titles of articles and reports that I have found will prove my point: "Angels or Seizures? The Truth Behind Joan of Arc's Visions," "A Historical Case of Disseminated Tuberculosis," "Joan of Arc and Women's Medieval Military Tradition: A Lesson Plan," "Was Joan of Arc an Epileptic?," "Joan of Arc and DSMIII," "A Playwright Strives to Enter the Psyche of Joan of Arc," and "Jeanne la Pucelle and the Dying God." The last one links Joan with William Rufus and Thomas à Becket, all three of whom were supposedly killed partly as the result of a folk memory of ritualized murder and sacrifice.

Elsewhere on the Internet, Joan can be found on a calendar of lesbian, gay, bisexual, and transgender saints. A World War II savings stamp features a Joan who bears a striking resemblance to Rita Hayworth while a photograph, obviously touched up, has Joan walking arm in arm with Marilyn Monroe.

There are discussions of her paranoia and mental instability; some even see her as the reenactment of the Drummer of Niklashausen, a medieval child's legend. Fortunately, no one attempted to claim that she was the prototype of the Little Drummer Boy of modern Christmas lore. One contributor argues fervently that she was persecuted because she had the attributes of a man—courage, bravery, leadership, tactical awareness, and success, and that is why she wore men's clothes and acted like a man. It never occurs to those who pursue this argument that Joan wore male attire because her troops would be more likely to follow her orders if she resembled one of them. Finally, there are scores of sources purporting to prove her status as a witch and the similarity of her actions to those of the practitioners of the evil arts throughout the ages. These examples are sufficient to prove my initial reservations about using this dimension of the modern media as a source of pertinent information concerning Joan.

Conclusion

What can finally be said of Joan of Arc, based on this intensive examination of her admirers, her defenders, her detractors, her skeptics, her anything? She lived. She was a woman. She played a significant role in turning the tide of the Hundred Years' War against the English, which eventually resulted in a French victory. It does not matter whether she was peasant-born or royal. She did what she did. She was who she was. And she was sainted. Let future historical research provide the answers to the nuances.

Appendix 1
KINGS DURING THE HUNDRED YEARS' WAR
Prelude of war to war's end

ENGLAND

House of Plantagenet (Angevin)

Edward I (1272 - 1307)
Edward II (1307 - 1327)
Edward III (1327 -1377)
Richard II (1377 - 1399)

House of Lancaster

Henry IV (1399 - 1413)
Henry V (1413 - 1422)
Henry VI (1422 -1461)

FRANCE

Capetian Dynasty

Philip IV (1285 - 1314)
Louis X (1314 - 1316)
Philip V (1316 - 1322)
Charles IV (1322 - 1328)

Capetian-Valois House

Philip VI (1328 - 1350)
John the Good (1350 - 1364)
Charles V (1364 - 1380)
Charles VI (1380 - 1422)
Charles VII (1422 - 1461)

Appendix II
Major Events in The Hundred Years' War
Prelude of war to war's end

Prelude to war: 1294 to 1298

    1. Aquitaine debate

    2. Flanders debate

    3. Gascony debate

    4. Succession question

    5. Church and State confrontation begins

    6. Sporadic military action begins

Phase 1: 1337 to 1369 (English success)

1340 (June)	English defeat French at Sluys
1346 (August)	English defeat French at Crécy
1347 (August)	English defeat French at Calais
1347 ff.	Black Death ravages France and England
1356 (September)	English defeat French at Poitiers
1358 (summer)	Jacquerie Revolt in northern France
1360	Treaty of Bretigny ends military action
1363	John the Good returns to England
	Philip the Bold of Burgundy emerges
1364	John the Good dies

Phase 2: 1369 to 1380 (French turnaround)

1370 ff.	Charles V and Bertrand du Guesclin revamp French military forces, reverse French losses
1380	Charles V dies, ending French revitalization

Phase 3: 1380 to 1420 (English resurgence)

1382 ff.	Philip the Bold victorious
1384	Charles VI marries Isabelle of Bavaria
1392	Charles VI goes insane
1392 ff.	Burgundian and Armagnac civil war; temporary truce
1396	Richard II of England marries Isabelle, daughter of Charles VI; drops the title, "King of France"

1403	Dauphin Charles (later Charles VII) born
1404	Philip the Bold dies; son, John the Fearless, succeeds
1407 (November)	Louis of Orléans murdered at instigation of John the Fearless
1412 (January)	Joan of Arc born at Domremy
1415 (October)	English defeat French at Agincourt
1415 ff.	English and Burgundian dominance in France

Phase 4: 1420 to 1453 (French victory)

1419	John the Fearless murdered; son, Philip the Good, succeeds
1420	Treaty of Troyes
1422	Henry V of England dies
	Charles VI of France dies
1429 ff.	Emergence of Joan (see Appendix 3)
1435	Burgundians abandon English alliance
1436	French seize Paris and most of northern France
1448 ff.	French take Maine and Normandy
1453	French take Bordeaux; war ends

Appendix III
MAJOR EVENTS IN JOAN'S LIFE

1412 (?)	Joan of Arc born at Domremy, Castellany of Vaucouleurs
1422 ff.	Period of hearing voices of Saints Michael, Catherine, and Margaret
1428	
(May)	Joan's first approach to Baudricourt at Vaucouleurs
(October)	Siege of Orléans begins
1429	
(February)	Joan's departure from Vaucouleurs
	Joan's arrival at Chinon
	Joan's first interview with the dauphin
(March)	Joan's initial challenge to the English
(April)	Joan and royal army leave Blois for Orléans
	Joan's entry into Orléans

(May)	Joan wounded by an arrow
	Deliverance of Orléans
(June)	French capture Jargeau, Meung, Beaugency, and Patay
(July)	French capture Troyes; Anglo/Burgundian army retreats
	Joan and royal army enter Chalons and Rheims
	Charles VII crowned in the cathedral at Rheims
(September)	Joan attacks Paris unsuccessfully
(December)	Patent of nobility given to Joan by Charles VII
1430	
(April)	New English forces debark at Calais
	Joan resumes operations in Melun, Lagny, and Senlis
(May)	Joan at Compiègne and Soissons
	Burgundian army besieges Compiègne
	Joan captured
	First demand that Joan be tried for heresy
(July)	Burgundians asked to turn Joan over to English
(December)	Joan taken to Rouen under English escort
1431	
(January)	Joan's trial begins
(February)	First sitting of public hearings of the trial
(March)	Private inquisitorial interrogations begin
	Closing of inquiry trial period
	Completion of indictment against Joan
(April)	Consultations with ecclesiastical authorities begin
	Admonitions made to Joan as inducement to confess
(May)	Joan threatened with possible torture
	Final admonitions made to Joan
	Joan confesses; agrees to wear women's clothing
	Joan recants; reassumes male clothing
	Trial for relapse into heresy
	Joan burned at the stake in Rouen
1450	
(February)	Charles VII orders inquiry into Joan's trial
(March)	Royal inquiry conducted
1452 (May)	Ecclesiastical inquiry conducted
1455	
(June)	Papal inquiry begun
(November)	Retrial of Joan begins

1456 (July)	Joan rehabilitated; former verdict annulled
1903 (February)	Formal proposal of canonization
1904 (January)	Pope Pius X gives Joan the title "Venerable"
1909 (April)	Joan named "Blessed"
1920 (May)	Joan canonized by Pope Benedict XV

SELECT BIBLIOGRAPHY
Historical Documents

Barrett, W.P., ed. *The Trial of Jeanne d'Arc: A Complete Translation of the Text of the Original Documents*, trans. Coley Taylor and Ruth Kerr. London, 1931.

Beaune, Colette, ed. *Journal d'un Bourgeois de Paris*. Paris, 1990.

Champion, P., ed. *Procès de condemnation de Jeanne d'Arc*. Geneva, 1976.

Cousinot, Guillaume, ed. *Chronique de la Pucelle*. Caen, 1992.

Doncoeur, P. and Y. Lanhers, eds. *Minute français des interrogatoires de Jeanne la Pucelle*. Melun, 1956.

_____. *Rédaction Episcopale du Procès de 1455-56*. Paris, 1961.

_____. *Réhabilitation de Jeanne la Pucelle*. Paris, 1956.

Pernoud, Régine. *The Retrial of Joan of Arc: The Evidence at the Trial for Her Rehabilitation*, trans. J.M. Cohen. New York, 1955.

Quicherat, Jules, ed. *Procès de condemnation et de réhabilitation de Jeanne d'Arc, dite la Pucelle d'Orléans*. 5 vols. New York, rpr. 1965.

Quintal, Claire and Daniel Rankin, eds. *The First Biography of Joan of Arc, with the Chronicle Record of a Contemporary Account*. Pittsburgh, 1964.

_____. *Letters of Joan of Arc*. Pittsburgh, 1969.

Scott, W.S., trans. *The Trial of Joan of Arc, Being the Verbatim Report of the Proceedings from the Orleans Manuscript*. Westport, Conn., 1956.

Shirley, Janet, trans. *A Parisian Journal 1405-1499: Translated from the Anonymous 'Journal d'un Bourgeois de Paris.'* Oxford, rpr. 1968.

Tisset, Pierre and Yvonne Lanhers, eds. *Procès de condemnation de Jeanne d'Arc*. 3 vols. Paris, 1960, 1970-1971.

Biographies, Plays, and Poetry

Adams, W.H.D. *The Maid of Orleans*. London, 1889.

Anderson, Maxwell. *Joan of Lorraine*. Washington, D.C., 1947.

Anouilh, Jean. *The Lark*, trans. Lillian Hellman. New York, 1956.

Ayroles, Jean. *La vraie vie de Jeanne d Arc*. 5 vols. Paris, 1890-1902.

Bancal, Jean. *Jeanne d'Arc, Princesse Royale*. Paris, 1971.

Bangs, Mary R. *Jeanne d'Arc, the Maid of France*. Boston, 1910.

Beevers, John. *Saint Joan of Arc*. Garden City, N.Y., 1962.

Belloc, Hilaire. *Joan of Arc*. New York, 1949.

Boutet de Monvel, Louis M. *Joan of Arc*. Philadelphia, 1918.

Bromby, D. Mary. *Joan of Arc*. Exeter, 1935.

Buchan, Alice. *Joan of Arc and the Recovery of France*. London, 1948.

Calvert, George Henry. *Joan of Arc: A Narrative Poem in Four Books*. Boston, 1883.

Cook, Ernest H. *The Story of Joan of Arc*. Chester, 1916.

Fabre, Lucien. *Joan of Arc*, trans. Gerard Hopkins. New York, 1954.

Ferguson, A.B.O. *The Story of Saint Jeanne*. Dublin, 1923.

Fixel, Arthur E. *Joan of Arc: A Chronicle Play*. New York, 1959.

France, Anatole. *The Life of Joan of Arc*, trans. Winifred Stephens. New York, 1923.

Fumet, Stanislas. *Joan the Saint*, trans. F.J.Sheed. New York, 1937.

Funck Brentano, F. *Joan of Arc*, trans. Regis Michaud. New York, 1912.

Gower, Ronald. *Joan of Arc*. London, 1893.

Guillemin, Henri. *Jeanne dite Jeanne d'Arc*. Paris, 1970.

James, Grace. *Joan of Arc*. New York, 1910.

Lamartine, Alphonse de. *Jeanne d Arc*. London, 1893.

Lang, Andrew. *The Maid of France: Being the Story of the Life and Death of Jeanne d'Arc*. London, 1908.

Larkin, Sarah. *Joan of Arc*. New York, 1951.

Lowell, Francis C. *Joan of Arc*. Boston, 1896.

Lucie-Smith, Edward. *Joan of Arc*. New York, 1977.

MacKaye, Percy. *Jeanne d'Arc, a Drama*. New York, 1906.

Michelet, Jules. *Joan of Arc*, trans. Albert Guerard. Ann Arbor, 1967.

Murray, T. Douglas. *Jeanne d Arc, Maid of Orleans, Deliverer of France*. London, 1907.

Paine, Albert B. *Joan of Arc, Maid of France*. 2 vols. New York, 1925.

Péguy, Charles. *Jeanne d'Arc: Drame en Trois Pièces*. Paris, 1948.

Pernoud, Régine. *Jeanne d'Arc*. Paris, 1959.

Purcell, Mary. *The Halo on the Sword*. Westminster, Md., 1952.

Robo, Etienne. *Saint Joan: The Woman and the Saint*. London, 1959.

Sackville-West, Victoria. *Saint Joan of Arc*. Garden City, N.Y., 1936.

Saint Georges de Bouhelier. *Jeanne d'Arc*. Paris, 1934.

Schiller, Friedrich von. *The Maiden of Orleans*, trans. J.T. Krumpelmann in *Joan of Arc: Fact, Legend and Literature*, ed. Wilfrid T. Jewkes and Jerome B. Landfield. New York, 1964.

Shakespeare, William. *King Henry the Sixth: Part One*.

Shaw, Bernard. *Saint Joan: A Chronicle Play in Six Parts and an Epilogue*. New York, 1951.

Southey, Robert and Samuel T. Coleridge. *Joan of Arc*. Oxford, rpr. 1993.

Stolpe, S. *The Maid of Orleans*, trans. Eric Lewenhaupt. London, 1956.

Twain, Mark. *Personal Recollections of Joan of Arc by the Sieur Louis de Conte*. London, 1896.

Voltaire. *The Maid of Orleans*, trans. Ernest Dowson. London, 1899.

Wagenknecht, Edward. *Joan of Arc: An Anthology of History and Literature*. New York, 1948.

Warner, M. *Joan of Arc: The Image of Female Heroism*. New York, 1981.

Williams, Jay. *Joan of Arc*. New York, 1963.

Winwar, Frances. *The Saint and the Devil: Joan of Arc and Gilles de Rais, a Biographical Study in Good and Evil*. New York, 1948.

Critical Historical Studies

Barstow, A. *Joan of Arc: Heretic, Mystic, Shaman*. Lewiston, N.Y., 1986.

Bernanos, Georges. *Sanctity Will Out: An Essay on St. Joan*, trans. R. Batchelor. New York, 1947.

Bingham, Marjorie. "Joan of Arc & Women's Medieval Tradition: A Lesson Plan," *Social Education* 58 (1994): 71-73.

Boulanger, Charles. *Enterrement de l'affaire Jeanne d'Arc: Triomphe de l'Université de Paris*. Rouen, 1956.

David-Darnac, Maurice. *Histoire véridique et merveilleuse de la Pucelle d'Orléans*. Paris, 1965, London, 1969. (The English version of 1969 is entitled *The True Story of the Maid of Orléans*, trans. Peter de Polnay).

De la Martinière, Jules. "Frère Richard et Jeanne d'Arc à Orléans, mars-juillet 1430," *Le Moyen Age*, 3rd ser., vol. 1 (1934): 189-98.

Delaruelle, E. "La spiritualité de Jeanne d'Arc," *Bulletin de Littérature Ecclésiastique*, Toulouse, 1964, parts 1 and 2.

Denis, Léon. *The Mystery of Joan of Arc*, trans. Sir Arthur Conan Doyle. London, 1924.

Dunn, Susan. "Michelet and Lamartine: Making and Unmaking the Nationalist Myth of Jeanne d'Arc," *The Romantic Review*, 80 (1989): 404-19.

Endore, S. Guy. *The Sword of God: Jeanne d'Arc*. New York, 1931.

Evans, Joan. *Saint Joan of Orleans*, ed. Paul Studer. Oxford, 1926.

Fraioli, Deborah. "The Literary Image of Joan of Arc," *Speculum* 56 (1981): 811-30.

Gies, Frances. *Joan of Arc: The Legend and the Reality*. New York, 1981.

Guérin, André. *Operation Shepherdess*. London, 1961.

Guitton, Jean. *Problème et mystère de Jeanne d'Arc*. Paris, 1961.

Gutierrez, Nancy A. "Gender and Value in 1 Henry VI : The Role of Joan de Pucelle," *Theatre Journal* 42 (1990): 183-94.

Ince, R.B. *Joan of Arc*. London, 1921.

Jan, Eduard Feodor von. *Das Literarische Bild des Jeanne d'Arc 1429-1926*. Halle, 1928.

Jeanné, Egide. *L'Image de la Pucelle d'Orléans dans la littérature historique française depuis Voltaire*. Liège, 1935.

Johnston, Kenneth R. "Narcissus and Joan: Wordsworth's Feminist Recluse?," *Studies in Romanticism* 29 (1990): 197-222.

Kelly, H. Ansgar. "The Right to Remain Silent: Before and After Joan of Arc," *Speculum* 68 (1993): 992-1026.

Lenglet du Fresnoy, Abbé. *Memoirs of Joan d'Arc, or du Lys, The Maid of Orléans*, trans. George Ann Grave. London, 1812.

Lightbody, Charles W. *The Judgments of Joan: A Study in Cultural History*. London, 1961.

Maik, Thomas A. *A Reexamination of Mark Twain's Joan of Arc*. Lewiston, N.Y., 1992.

Margolis, Nadia. *Joan of Arc in History, Literature, and Film: A Select Annotated Bibliography*. New York, 1990.

Marot, Pierre. *Joan the Good Lorrainer at Domremy*. Colmar, 1981.

O'Reilly, Isabel M. "The Maid of Orleans and the New Womanhood," *American Catholic Quarterly Review*, 1975 (1894): 582-606.

Raknem, I. *Joan of Arc in History, Legend, and Literature*. Oslo, 1971.

Riggs, Thomas L. *Saving Angel: The Truth about Joan of Arc and the Church*. Milwaukee, 1944.

Schwertman, M. Rene. "The Character of Joan of Arc as She Appears in English Plays on the Subject, 1798-1924." Master's thesis, Marquette University, 1948.

Searle, William. *The Saint and the Skeptics: Joan of Arc in the Work of Mark Twain, Anatole France, and Bernard Shaw*. Detroit, 1976.

Sermoise, Pierre de. *Joan of Arc and Her Secret Missions*, trans. Jennifer Taylor. London, 1973.

Silver, Arnold J. *Saint Joan: Playing with Fire*. New York, 1993.

Tyson, Brian. *The Story of Shaw's Saint Joan*. Kingston, 1982.

Vale, Malcolm. *Jeanne d'Arc et ses adversaires: la victime d'une guerre civile?* Orléans, 1981.

Valois, Noel. "Jeanne d'Arc et la prophétie de Marie Robine," *Mélanges Paul Fabre*. Paris, 1902.

————. "Un nouveau témoinage sur Jeanne d Arc," *L'Annuaire Bulletin de la Société de l'Histoire de France*, 1906. Paris, 1907.

Vauchez, A. "Les Soeurs de Jeanne," *Le Monde*, January 6, 1980, p. 15.

Weintraub, Stanley, ed. *Saint Joan: Fifty Years After: 1923/24-1973/74*. Baton Rouge, 1973.

Wood, Charles. *Joan of Arc and Richard III: Sex, Saints, and Government in the Middle Ages*. New York, 1988.

Joan of Arc's Mystery, History, and Intelligibility

Phillip C. Naylor

Marie d'Orléans, Orléans

What a pleasure it was to read and reread Professor Ronald Zupko's paper. It is an honor to have been named commentator of the work of one of my own graduate professors. As you heard and as I anticipated, Dr. Zupko's paper was a *tour de force*. He started off by placing Joan in historical perspective. This was a daunting endeavor given the complexity of relations between the two antagonists, France and England. He proceeded by presenting the traditional historiographic interpretation followed by the detractive assessment. His conclusion affirming Joan's universal attraction is axiomatic. So where does this leave me? Simply in professional double jeopardy. First, as a modern historian, I had to muster some nerve to comment upon the work of an internationally renown medieval scholar, whose reputation grows as we speak given his recent book on fourteenth and fifteenth century Italian environmental politics. Furthermore, he was featured this month in the prestigious *Chronicle of Higher Education*. Dr. Zupko has been a mentor and is a friend and colleague. Second, the sheer comprehensive treatment left me repeatedly impressed with few questions. But here I am, about to reflect upon Dr. Zupko's paper but through my own optic of Joan.

Dr. Naylor teaches History at Marquette University.

Let me start by confessing how Joan entered and influenced my life. As a boy, I read the romanticized, colorful *Classics Illustrated* version of Joan of Arc, modeled after the movie with Ingrid Bergman. When I was eleven, I recall ordering *sandwiches jambon* with my mother at a café at the place des Pyramides in Paris and admiring the heroic, gilded equestrian Joan across from the Tuileries. Then as a punk graduate student investigating Algerian emigrant worker problems in France, I remember a wintry day in Rouen with snowflakes (that a relative of mine would have classified as the size of "kleenex") sailing about me. I had just completed an interview at the Algerian Consulate and had some time before my return train to Paris. I entered a café and ordered an immense *crème*. I was a lonely American so I plugged my Marquette University Smith Fellowship francs into a jukebox and selected, several times, Elvis's rendition of "America the Beautiful" and then the Rolling Stones's "It's only Rock n'Roll (and I Like It)." The latter song was played over and over to the probable chagrin of the regular clientele; but I needed to rock, and I did like it. So there I was enjoying myself when I felt a sudden rush of remorse. I was adjacent to the marketplace where Joan was immolated and here I was having a wonderful time. Guilt gutted me. As a Professor at Merrimack College, I returned six years later to Rouen in a kind of penitential personal pilgrimage (perhaps this is why I am participating in this celebration). So, beyond the role of a Western Civilization professor with the familiar, obligatory coverage of Joan and the late Hundred Years' War, I believe that I have a "relationship" with her. I am *branché*, connected, perhaps a bit wired, but hopefully from her perspective and yours not terribly *mal branché*.

This celebration and commemoration of Joan of Arc, her continuing attraction, is simply because we identify with Joan's modernity, her relevance, and her patriotism. In addition, the visage of Joan we discern (and I submit to you, this is her most recognizable profile) is a reflection and production of modern knowledge which has empowered her identity and radiated her appeal. As mentioned, she is impressively displayed on the Internet—the Zupko coined "cyber-Joan." We are able to admire her today, not only because of historical insight and hindsight, but also because she is so much like us or what we would like to be. She claimed an intangible power, from spiritual voices, but what really mattered in her time and certainly ours, was the secular political power she exercised and incarnated.

What about the voices? Questions of Joan being schizophrenic or epileptic are simply irrelevant concerning her political historical significance. Joan was different. She was unique. Her voices are unanswerable except to her, the inner Joan. This will remain and should remain a mystery. We are all moved in different personal ways. (Lou Reed, a prominent influence on punk/new wave/alternative rock n'roll, once composed that people who do not hear a voice within themselves simply have "bad luck.") What is important was how Joan's psychogenic dimension always linked her to a political mission. This distinguished her from women mystics such as Hildegaard of Bingen, St. Clare, and others. Voices and visions were not unusual in the medieval period or even today. What was extraordinary was *how* Joan fused religion with politics (and we know how combustible that compound can be given the recent histories of Iran, Ireland, Bosnia, Algeria, Israel, Palestine, and the United States). This remarkable synthesis catalyzed a country and still does.

Joan had an image of a French nation. She had, in Gaullist terms, a "certain idea of France." She was a Gaullist before de Gaulle. Professor Zupko has provided you with the historical substantiation. To Joan, her vocation was truly national. France must realize her natural greatness. To be great, to radiate France's naturally effulgent culture, or perhaps, in her mind, to practice and proselytize a more profound, purified, personal Christianity, France had to be independent—in her time, to be delivered from English ambitions and armies. France needed strong leadership. Her quest to have Charles VII crowned or legitimatized demonstrated her political passion. (Joan deserved at least consideration of beatification by seeing goodness and greatness in that dissolute monarch.) As Professor Zupko elucidated, she was a product of a tumultuous period in French history. This was when increasingly centralized monarchies assaulted feudalism. She contributed to that political process. She wanted to "restore France," to regenerate the monarchy as de Gaulle, five hundred years later, wanted France renovated. To Joan, that restoration was also intrinsically tied to a deep devotion for Christianity.

She engaged completely with France: "St. Michael told me that I must be a good child, and that God would help me....He said that I would have to go into France."[1] Notice the wording: not "to France" but "into France." She becomes one with France. She identifies her life, her destiny with France. Charles Péguy, the early twentieth century poet and mystic, envisioned her (like himself) as a religious nationalist. She became France. She idealized the French monarchy and especially the French people. In Péguy's play, *The Mystery of the Charity of Joan of Arc*, Joan asserts:

Never would the men of this country, never would the saints of this country, never would even simple Christians of our regions have forsaken [Christ]. Never would French knights; never would French peasants; never would simple parishioners of French parishes. Never would the men of the crusades have forsaken him. Never would those men have denied him. You would sooner have wrenched their heads off.

She continued soon afterward: "Never would the king of France have forsaken him. Never would Charlemagne and Roland..Never would Saint Denis and Saint Martin, Saint Genevieve and Saint Aignan, never would Saint Loup, never would Saint Ouen...They were saints who weren't afraid."[2] And neither was she. To Joan, the French were a"chosen people." Notice, too, how Péguy has Joan ascribe piety to French political and martial leaders. The linkage is an accurate reflection of Joan. Of course, what is ironic is that she would be abandoned by the French.

As you heard, the trial must be understood within the trilateral geopolitics of England, France, and Burgundy. But perhaps, Dr. Zupko could elaborate: why didn't Charles VII aid "The Maid" or rescue her? (Or did he actually pay the ransom?)[3] Had Joan become a political disability, given her unilateral, albeit divinely directed initiatives? Was this an example of the emerging modern age where the secular submerged the spiritual? This can relate to the entire litigation, i.e., the doubt about the nature of individual revelations and their relationship to politics. As Professor Zupko reminded you, the Church was under extreme protracted pressure from a variety of outspoken people: Peter Waldo, John Wyclif, John Hus, Thomas à Kempis. In addition, it was still reeling from the secular interference of the Conciliar Movement and the moral consequences of the Great Schism. This inquisition, like others, not only targeted individuals but also testified to the power and legitimacy of a political-besides-religious institution. The Church was under seige; Joan's personal Christian praxis, engaged to the secular idea of a powerful French state—that "France-to-be" (de Gaulle's term in reference to Joan)[4] —loomed as a even more fearful political rival.

We recognize that Joan's threat was also social. She challenged the conventions of gender relations. Polly Schroyer Brooks explains:

> The only way a female with strong convictions on public events could be heard, in that male-oriented society, was to claim some visionary experience of prophetic power...I doubt that Joan was conscious of this but, nonetheless, I think her revelations gave her the chance to be believed. Stating that she had come at God's command to rescue France gave her recognition, made her the leader for whom all loyal French were waiting. Her virginity, so prized in those days, not only gave her prestige, but also helped her in a practical way. Had she been married or pregnant or a mother, she never could have been allowed to go to war.[5]

Her haircut, her clothes, her martial activities, all posed challenges to the patriarchal social order and the traditional image of a woman. Notice the reiterated importance of her clothing during her trial, i.e., dressing like a man. Did this woman who dared to confront convention deserve punishment for her independent attitude? For her couture? Her taste in clothes? Was this diabolical? Keep in mind, by the late medieval-early modern period, women were being forced from guilds (including their own), deepening their economic subservience. In addition, they were repeatedly victims of vicious, violent assaults by unmarried men, especially in urban areas.[6] As Professor Zupko related, it took great courage for Joan to approach the army and its camp. It was only natural for modern feminists to embrace a courageous sister. Joan is Katherine Hepburn or Mary Tyler Moore in slacks—and much more.

I acknowledge that Joan's providentialism links her to the medieval age, but I find that her mission and her trial was particularly identifiable as political and modern. Indeed, her popularity emerges from the modern period rather than from her contemporary one. As Professor Zupko surveyed, it took decades to rehabilitate Joan in her own country, and, of course, complex political considerations were part of this enduring process, especially the ramifications concerning the French monarchy's image. Then, in an obtuse way, the Protestant Reformation dislocated Joan's historical significance. Her individualized Christianity smacked of Protestantism; her martyrdom before an inquisition was arguably undeniable proof of Catholic intolerance. The Enlightenment's humanism assailed her. Ironically, it was the French Revolution, with its anti-clericalism and republicanism, that produced a consequential romantic nationalism which regenerated Joan's heroic reputation. This was the time, too, when the ideal of "Liberty" was personified as a woman, e.g., Delacroix's famous "Liberty at the Barricades" as well as the Athena-like bas relief of "Marianne" leading the revolutionary armies on the Arc de Triomphe. Joan's mission was codified as a nationalist metaphor. Her life received the attention of prominent French literary figures such as Jules Michelet, Alphonse de Lamartine, and, just after the turn of the century, Anatole France, besides the aforementioned Charles Péguy. Of course, Mark Twain also publicized her life, a testament to her growing universal appeal.

As Professor Zupko related, Joan acquired even greater symbolic attention through the Treaty of Frankfurt in 1871, wherein Alsace and part of Lorraine was severed from the *mère patrie*. Louis Marin, the influential anthropologist-politician, kept on his desk a bust of Joan of Arc who had, by that time, become "the heroine of the new right cultic nationalism that had come out of his native Lorraine at the end of the century."[7] Not surprising, a popular song during World War I was "Joan of Arc, They are Calling You." Undoubtedly, the Great War hastened Joan's acquiring of sainthood.

During World War II, both Vichy and the Free French tried to appropriate Joan in their efforts to project a popular legitimacy. Vichy fostered folklore and propagated an idea of "true France."[8] One poster portrayed Joan as "the heroine of national unity" standing in front of Marshal Pétain and French youth. (To this day the French Right has attached itself to Joan.[9]) On the other hand, de Gaulle saw himself thrust forward by destiny in a Joan of Arc role as leader of the resistance (detractors also contend that he promoted or invented the similarity). The "Cross of Lorraine" was a symbolic reminder of Joan's effort to save France from an invader. Indeed, President Franklin Delano Roosevelt chided de Gaulle for having a "Joan of Arc complex," disclosing the American president's surprising underestimation of the historical and cultural power of an idea and symbol. By the way, though he had great difficulties with de Gaulle, Winston Churchill was more circumspect and sympathetic concerning de Gaulle's identity with Joan; fallen France needed to be reminded of its heroic "Maid" during the Second World War. De Gaulle thought of her as he paraded triumphantly down the Champs Elysées in August, 1944.[10] Later, de Gaulle's successes in 1958 and 1961, when confronting the convulsive and divisive adversities of the Algerian War, underscored the effectiveness of an inspired "Joan of Arc complex." As you can imagine, and as Professor Zupko related to me, the publication of the David-Darnac book in 1965 irritated if not infuriated de Gaulle.

The revisionist arguments of David-Darnac, de Sermoise, Etienne Weill-Raynal, Jean Bancal,[11] and others are parenthetical even if ever absolutely verified. (The reported sightings of Joan are "Elvis-like.") What should be understood was that Joan's reputation, while enhanced by a martyrdom rather than a post-"Pucelle" life in the country, was already achieved by events up to her capture and trial. From her day to ours, the paramount image of Joan we have received and perceived is that of a dauntless, determined woman, unassailable and unrelenting, fitted in armor, often astride a steed—this rather than a helpless victim at the stake.

Published concurrently with those of the revisionists was a book by Pierre Virion entitled *Le Mystère de Jeanne d'Arc et la politique des nations* (1972); indeed, the author seemed quite oblivious to the detractors. I found Virion more interesting, though he would probably reject me as a "secular historian." He offers a providential interpretation of history in a political context, with Joan serving as a divine instrument. Virion asserts that Joan should still be seen as means to save France and the Church from secularism and to effect a spiritual, social, and political renewal.[12] Though the book could be classified as a reformulation of Péguy, it underscores how Joan's life constantly transcends as a mystical coalescence of religion and politics.

Joan is intelligible from our modern perspective. She is a supreme individualist, side by side with Zarathrustra, climbing the mountains of truth with her own will to power, her own creativity, her own faith. A Nietzschean Christian.[13] She is committed to authentic political and social liberation like an engaged, Gaulois-smoking existentialist. Finally, she rebels against a post-modernist-conceived constellation of repressive institutions with their debilitating, depersonalizing discourses and practices. We see ourselves in her struggles and victories. As Professor Zupko suggested, her world, with its passions, prejudices, and politics, was actually not that different from ours.

We cannot conclusively understand her élan, her mystical motivations, but we relate to her and we marvel—perhaps as much as her contemporaries. We may even respect her more than they did. Professor Zupko concluded that Joan has joined her voices. Let me add that we also celebrate Joan because she remains visible and vital among us. Thank you.

Notes

1 Willard Trask, ed. and trans. *Joan of Arc: Self Portrait* (New York: Stacpole Sons, 1936), 29.

2 Charles Péguy, *The Mystery of the Charity of Joan of Arc*, trans. Julian Green (New York: Pantheon, 1950), 181-82.

3 See Etienne Weill-Raynal, *Le Double Secret de Jeanne La Pucelle: Révélé par des documents de l'époque* (Paris: Le Pavillon, 1972).

4 André Malraux, *Fallen Oaks: Conversation with De Gaulle*, trans. Irene Clephane, rev. Linda Asher (New York: Holt, Rinehart and Winston, 1971), 66.

5 Polly Schroyer Brooks, *The Story of Joan of Arc* (New York: J. B. Lippincott, 1990), 163.

6 George Huppert, *After the Black Death: A Social History of Early Modern Europe* (Bloomington: Indiana University Press, 1986), 37-38.

7 Herman Lebovics, *True France: The Wars over Cultural Identity, 1900-1945* (Ithaca, New York: Cornell University Press, 1992), 12.

8 See Lebovics, 171-83.

9 Jean-Marie Le Pen associated his Front National movement with Joan in a dramatic demonstration on 8 May 1987. See Jean-Noël Jeanneney, "Jeanne d'Arc à tous vents," *Le Monde*, 29 July 1987.

10 Charles de Gaulle, *The War Memoirs of Charles de Gaulle: Unity*, trans. Richard Howard (New York: Simon and Schuster, 1959), 352.

11 Jean Bancal, *Jeanne d'Arc: Princesse royale* (Paris: Robert Laffont, 1971).

12 Pierre Virion, *Le Mystère de Jeanne d'Arc et la politique des nations* (Paris: Téqui, 1972), 259.

13 I am extending to Joan those notions of Pierre Lance offered in *Charles de Gaulle: Ce Chrétien nietzschéen* (Paris: La Septième Aurore, 1965).

The Spirituality of Saint Joan

George H. Tavard,

Bois Chenu

The life of Jeanne d'Arc presents us with the image of a seventeen to nineteen-year old peasant girl who never went to school, who could neither read nor write, who had learned from her mother all she knew about the Catholic faith, who ran away from home when she was about seventeen in order to join the army (at a time when the only women who hung around soldiers were prostitutes), a transvestite who refused the advice of a bishop who ordered her to change her style of clothing. This is not the sort of person to whom pious Catholics are inclined to look for lessons of deep spirituality. Her way of life will not recommend her to the average well-meaning parish priest or to parents of teenage girls who are looking for a suitable model for their daughters.

Yet this is the person whom the poet Péguy declared to be *la sainte la plus grande après sainte Marie:* "the greatest of saints after St. Mary." And Thérèse of the Child Jesus, undoubtedly one of the great saints of our epoch, felt a close affinity with that ignorant girl, even before the beatification of Jeanne. "It seemed to me," Thérèse wrote in her autobiography as she looked back at her early teen years, "that I felt in me the same ardor...the same heavenly inspiration [as Jeanne d'Arc]."[1] When she

---

Fr. Tavard held the Presidential Chair in Catholic Systematic Theology at Marquette University.

was a novice at Carmel, Thérèse wrote a play about Jeanne. And Elizabeth of the Trinity, another Carmelite saint and a better poet than Thérèse, also celebrated Jeanne in two poems and took her as a model of her own consecration to the Lord.[2] Yes, Jeanne *la bonne Lorraine*, as she was called by a poet of her own century, François Villon, is a paradoxical saint. But where exactly does the paradox lie?

Littleness

It is significant that Jeanne was not sure of her name. She was baptized Jeanne, and called Jeannette, a frequent diminutive form of the name, in her village. But she did not know if she had a surname: d'Arc (or rather *Darc*, the last consonant being mute) was her father's family name and Romée her mother's. In her village, she said, it was the custom for girls to take their mother's surname. But Jeanne did not herself use it. When the dauphin was on the way to Reims to be crowned and formally become Charles VII, he signed a decree of ennoblement for her and her brothers and their descendants, and he gave them a new name, *du Lys*. Jeanne's brothers, Jean and Pierre, eagerly adopted the name and the accompanying coat of arms. Jeanne did not. These were things she was not interested in. Yet she recognized an identity for herself, and this was purely spiritual. "My name," she said to the dauphin when she met him for the first time at Chinon, "is Jeanne *la Pucelle*."

In acknowledging this as her name, Jeanne unwittingly pointed to a basic aspect of her spirituality. She drew her self-identity neither from her origin nor from man-made privileges that reflected the king's indebtedness to her, but only from her status as a young woman who, for spiritual reasons, had promised to herself and to God to remain a virgin: Jeanne *la Pucelle*. This was what the angel, she said, called her.[3] And, one may well ask, who should know one's true name better than angels? *La Pucelle* is the appellation by which she introduced herself to everyone, and that is how she signed the letters addressed to the English commander of the Les Tourelles Fort at Orléans and even to the Duke of Bedford, Regent of France for the child king Henry VI (1421-1471, king in 1422) and commander-in-chief of all English soldiers on French soil. On the dauphin's side, likewise, the captains of the king's army and presumably also the ordinary soldiers called her Jeanne *la Pucelle*. The word means a female child and, by implication, a virgin. With its masculine counterpart, *puceau*, the term is not likely to derive from the Latin word *puella* (feminine of archaic *puellus*, "little boy," that evolved into the more common term *puer*); *puella* is itself cognate with *pullus*, *pulla*, the offspring, male and female, of quadrupeds. *Puceau*, *pucelle* are more likely to be constructed from the French word *puce* (Latin, *pulex*), "flea." Used metaphorically, the term is applied to a wee thing, something or someone tiny, of no manifest importance. It is no wonder then that Thérèse of the Child Jesus found that her "little way" had been anticipated by Jeanne d'Arc.

Spiritually, the lesson of Jeanne's name is clear. It is not the customs and decisions of a creature that determine who she is. A person is not defined by what she has inherited or what she has obtained from society or even by concern for her own self. In remaining nameless, Jeanne spontaneously renounced the fundamental human need for self-assertion. In calling herself *la Pucelle*, she declared that she was of no importance, a wee person.

Virginity

There is nonetheless a content to Jeanne's littleness. In her wee person, littleness and virginity converged. Jeanne insisted that she was a virgin. The first time she heard the angel, Jeanne declared, "she took the vow of virginity for as long as it would please God."[4] If, on two occasions, at Poitiers and in Rouen, she did not object to being examined by women to determine if she was truly a virgin, this was not simply because the medieval psyche had a more liberated attitude toward nudity and sexuality than the modern mind, and still less because of superstitious assumptions as to the superiority of virginity. It was because the positive content of her littleness was precisely virginity. Jeanne would not offer her body to any taker. She protected her virginity by wearing men's clothing in the middle of the soldiery and later in the prison where she was kept under a twenty-four hour watch. In Domremy, she had refused to marry a young man to whom she had been promised by her parents, and when he sued her for breach of promise at the court of the bishop of Toul, she was found not guilty because she herself had not consented to the promise. The fact was, at the deepest level of her personality, that virginity was the form of her relationship to God.

This is all the more significant as Jeanne also admitted that the first time she heard the voice she was very much afraid, and she did not yet understand that an angel had spoken to her. At that moment, the vow of virginity that she took was not the outcome of a deliberative option. It was not a well-reasoned choice but a spontaneous action that Jeanne found herself taking. And she took it because, in the depths of her being, she was changed by the encounter. Despite her original fear, she suddenly acquired a whole new purpose in life, a purpose that could not be better pursued than through an exclusive commitment to God. In the context of her time and place, this self-giving to God was spontaneously put in the form of vowed virginity. What she had heard was what St. John of the Cross would later call a "substantial word," an inner word that transforms the hearer.

Jeanne never presumed on her strength. She did not take public vows. She did not resolve to join a convent. What she did was much more radical. Her promise of virginity had no witnesses other than angels; it was strictly between her and God. When she vowed to keep her virginity, not for ever but only "for as long as it would please God," she placed her future totally in the hands of God. Availability to God became the center of her spiritual way. Virginity, as she understood it, however, was not merely a matter of sexual abstinence. It was a spiritual attitude: "I must keep the vow and promise that I have made to Our Lord, to preserve well my virginity of body and of soul."[5]

What is virginity of the soul? Jeanne was quite clear about this: "One cannot clean one's conscience too much." She cleansed her conscience through the ordinary means that are available in the Church: the sacraments, and, primarily, the sacrament of penance. There were periods in her campaigns when, according to her chaplain, the Augustinian friar Jean Pasquerel, she sought absolution from sins nearly everyday.[6] This, of course, denotes an awareness of imperfection and a corresponding wish for perfection in Joan that were much more sensitive than the average among persons of piety, and that must have been quite astonishing to the courtiers, soldiers, and mercenaries around her. And this, in turn, reveals a heightened sense of the holiness of God and of her own lowliness as God's creature. But virginity of the soul implies more than a frequent recourse to the sacraments and a concern about purity of intention and action. It has its source in a vivid perception of the totality and the holiness of God's presence and gifts. During her trial, one of the judges asked Jeanne if it had been revealed to her that she would loose her luck and that the voices would no longer come if she married. To her this kind of question was irrelevant. First, she said, she had no revelation about that. Second, in her own words, "I do not know. I refer to Our Lord." This is precisely the point of virginity of the soul. It is not a calculated bargain in which a personal sacrifice is exchanged for God's help and gift. It consists in referring to God always and in every way, in placing oneself in the divine light and not in any human embrace—be it bodily, psychological, intellectual, or even spiritual.

It was in keeping with her virginity of soul that Jeanne practiced the sacraments fervently, yet functioned without them when she was impeded. In the fifteenth century, it was not unusual for pious people to assist at several masses in one day, and Jeanne followed the custom. But she went further, for she also received holy communion more often than was commonly done in her time. She was even accused of receiving communion twice in one day. But when she was a prisoner in English hands, Jeanne was, by bishop Cauchon's specific orders, deprived of the Eucharist until the morning of her death. She was not refused the sacrament of penance, however, but the priest who heard her confession several times in prison, Nicolas Loyseleur, was an impostor who reported to the bishop whatever she had said that could be used against her. During that dark period, Jeanne still communed with the Savior in the virginity of her soul. This was not dependent on practices of devotion. Union with God was the fruit of an utter reliance on God and on God's gracious will, not on human achievement, and not even on her own desires and thoughts.

The transformation of the self that Jeanne underwent the first time she heard the angel reorganized her life around virginity of soul. And this was possible because it first of all refocused her very self on her virgin soul. For this reason, she became *la Pucelle* while never ceasing to be Jeanne. Her choice of this appellation was not due to narcissistic self-absorption. Rather, she placed her soul and body at the service of God's purpose.

Daughter of God

So far we have seen Jeanne, the peasant girl from Domremy, abandoning all concerns about herself and putting this abandonment into the name by which she wished to be known. Yet there was nothing negative in her fundamental self-understanding. It was highly positive, not only because virginity of soul implied a continuing reliance on God, but also because there was a remarkable counterpart to Jeanne's littleness.

Jean de la Fontaine, one of her judges, asked if it was true that her voices called her *fille de Dieu, fille de l'Eglise, la fille au grand coeur* ("daughter of God, daughter of the Church, the big-hearted girl"). "Yes," Jeanne responded, "before the siege of Orléans and everyday since then, when they speak with me they have called me several times, Jeanne *la Pucelle*, daughter of God."[7] I would like to understand "daughter of God" as meaning *the* daughter of God rather than *a* daughter of God, for I find it attractive to think that God, who has only one Son, the divine Word made flesh, has also chosen to have only one daughter among the multitude of the saints. But I would not presume to affirm this, and so I will leave it to you to decide if "daughter of God" should be understood as "the" or "a" daughter of God. In any case, it means at least that Jeanne experienced a unique relationship of filiation to God the Father.

"Since you call yourself daughter of God," the judge continued, "why do you not willingly say the Lord's Prayer?" The allusion was to Jeanne's previous request, when bishop Cauchon had told her to recite the *Pater noster*, and she had refused to recite the prayer except in the sacrament of penance. Precisely, *Pater noster*, "Our Father," expressed a filial relation to God, and this was too precious in the eyes of God's daughter to be said except precisely as prayer. In the context of her trial, reciting the prayer would satisfy the curiosity of the judges who wanted to test if Jeanne really knew it, as she had testified, in Latin. But this very use would ruin it as prayer. Prayer is addressed to God. It is said in one's heart. In the public life of the Church, the liturgy and the sacraments are proper contexts for it. Jeanne, daughter of God, would make the words of the Lord's Prayer her own prayer to her Father in heaven, but she would not use them to justify herself in front of a tribunal. If she was daughter of God, divine daughterhood must have been the very substance of the *Pater noster* that she said prayerfully. It was not something to be flaunted in public.

Jean de la Fontaine happened to be the most benevolent of her judges, so benevolent that at a crucial point in the trial he disagreed with the president of the tribunal, Bishop Cauchon; as a result, he disappeared from the bench and presumably from the city of Rouen. He was no party to her condemnation. Yet even if Jeanne was able to detect Jean de la Fontaine's fairness beneath the veneer of his officially hostile function, this could hardly affect her response. She paid no attention to the consequences for herself of what she did as a matter of conscience. She knew herself to be daughter of God since her voices said so, but the nature of this daughterhood was a secret between God and herself. Yet she was never shy about affirming what she knew to be true. Irritated by repeated requests to swear the same oath to tell the truth at the beginning of each session of the tribunal, she once retorted: "I have come by the will of God; I have nothing to do here. Send me back to God from whom I have come." The daughter of God belongs with God because she belongs to God.

Meanwhile, if Jeanne affirmed the angelic appellations, "*Jeanne la Pucelle, fille de Dieu*," she did not confirm that her voices also called her, "daughter of the Church," or "the big-hearted girl." It may be that she did not wish to stress these expressions. "Big-hearted girl" would draw attention to her own self rather than to God. "Daughter of the Church" became quite ambiguous in the course of the trial, when the judges tried to embroil Jeanne in confusing statements about the differences between the Church militant and the Church triumphant. More probably, however, the voices never used these titles. They could be hagiographic embellishments that Jeanne did not endorse. We know that popular exaggerations about her grew rapidly in the wake of her victory at Orléans. But she was never taken in by them. She never confused the authentic following of God and the search for extraordinary happenings or the ambition of personal glory.

"Light, plenty of light"

Jeanne was not a mystic of darkness. What she perceived of God was light. Light nearly always accompanied her voices, as she testified. To make sure this was well understood she did not hesitate to tell Jean Beau, who was questioning her on February 27: "Of course there was plenty of light. Not all the light is for you."[8] Jeanne liked the sound of bells, especially when they rang a call to prayer. As a child, she insisted with the sexton that he must ring the bells at the right times, and, as witnesses of her childhood reported, she stopped what she was doing and prayed when she heard the bells. Now, in medieval theology, light is commonly used in analogy with the divine nature. The divine Word is *Lumen de Lumine*. In relation to creation, the Creator said, *Fiat lux*, and there was light. In relation to humanity, the Word of God is the Light of the mind, the Enlightener. Jeanne perceived plenty of light as she heard the voices, and the light, at least the first time, came from the right, from the side of the Church (that is, when, standing in the front yard, she faced her parents' house).

Julian Jaynes has theorized that what Jeanne experienced was a way of knowing that was operative before the opening of consciousness, when knowledge came through flashes of enlightenment due to interaction between the right and the left sides of the brain.[9] There is, however, a simpler explanation. The right side was for her, as generally in the Middle Ages, a symbol of the rising sun, the East, the originating point of the "light" that "shines in the darkness" (John 1:5); it is the side of *Christus oriens*, the direction where one should look for the second coming of Christ. This was why churches were oriented looking East and why the central front portal of Gothic cathedrals often featured the eschatological return of Christ in judgment. Jeanne, of course, was neither a theologian nor a student of symbolism. She was not familiar with the analogy of being or the semiotic dimension of language. She had not read the Scriptures. She had never seen a major cathedral in her childhood; the only cathedral she had entered was the still unfinished cathedral of Toul. But she had absorbed the religious feelings of her times through the liturgy, by listening to preaching (and she had heard some of the Franciscans of Neufchâteau), and by looking at paintings and statues in churches and chapels.

At a deeper level, however, the way Jeanne described her perception of the light that accompanied her voices suggests a familiarity with what Origen had called "spiritual senses." The light and the voices were not outside; they were within. For the awakened soul has senses that can perceive spiritual sights, words, tastes, smells, and contacts. Jeanne assured the canon lawyers who sat in judgment over her in Rouen that she had seen the angels and the saints who came to her as well as she could see the judges, that she had seen them with her own eyes, that she had heard them, hugged and touched them, and that, naturally, they smelled good. In this she underlined the reality of her experience. But the spiritual senses so work together that seeing and hearing are not two operations but one, and one may then speak, as Jean Beau himself did in his questions, of "seeing the voice."[10] In this there is no attempt to reverse systematically the functioning of the senses—as there would be in the symbolic quest of the poet Arthur Rimbaud. There is simply an experience of totality in the perception of the divine. Jeanne's descriptions were, of course, inadequate formulas, translations in everyday language of perceptions that were purely spiritual. Like the light that came with the voice, they were marks and echoes in our world of what Jeanne *la Pucelle*, daughter of God, liked to call "the Kingdom of Paradise."

The Kingdom of Paradise

One of the major points in the charges against Jeanne was that she was rebellious against the Church militant. This marked what I see as the second phase of her trial. In the first and longest phase, from February 21 to March 15, 1431, the judges attempted to uncover witchcraft and devil-worship in her actions. This was the main line during most of the "official trial." Having failed to find anything substantial, they next tried to establish that Jeanne was in rebellion against the Church. Putting themselves forward as competent representatives of the Church militant, pretending to act in the name of the University of Paris, of the council that had met in Constance and was about to continue in Basle,[11] and of the pope in Rome, they enjoined Jeanne to obey whatever they would order. This was the guiding rule of their actions from March 15 on, especially when the "ordinary trial" opened on March 26. In the end, they found her guilty of heretical rebellion against the Church through the miserable subterfuge of deciding that a woman who, for whatever reasons, insisted on dressing like a man was in contempt of the Church's ordinary teaching.

Jeanne protested generally against the form of the trial, specifically against taking an unqualified oath at the beginning of each session, and against being kept in a secular prison rather than in a church prison where she would have been guarded by women. Several times she warned the bishop: "Be careful, you who call yourself my judge. Be careful what you do. For it is true that I have received my mission from God, and you put yourself in great danger."[12] Jeanne and the bishop were at odds in their understanding of the Church. For the bishop and his assistants, there was a clear distinction between the Church triumphant and the Church militant. The first they described as "God, the saints, the angels, and the souls that have been saved." The second they identified as "Our Holy Father the Pope, vicar of God on earth, the cardinals, the church prelates, the clergy, and all good Christians and Catholics; and this Church, when gathered, cannot err; it is governed by the Holy Spirit."

For Jeanne, however, such a distinction was meaningless. In the first place, she saw "no difference between the St. Catherine who is in heaven and the one who reveals herself to me…"[13] In the second place, she did not understand the distinction between the Church triumphant and the Church militant. She knew that the true Church could not be where a bishop is trying to condemn the innocent to death. So she answered: "I came to the king of France by the order of God, the Virgin Mary, all the blessed saints of Paradise, the victorious Church on high, and by their command. To this Church I submit all my past and future actions. As to submitting to the Church militant I will not answer any more for the time being."[14] This was taken by the judges as an instance of revolt. But it was the direct consequence of her spiritual experience: living on earth in nearness to angels and saints of heaven, she cut through the distinctions made by theologians and canon lawyers in regard to the nature of the Church: "I refer to Our Lord who sent me, to Our Lady, and to all the blessed saints of Paradise. It seems to me that it is all one, Our Lord and the Church; there is no difficulty. Why do you make difficulties of it?"

What emerges is that Jeanne experienced no difference between the Church on earth and the Church in heaven. The Kingdom of Paradise, where Our Lord is King, extends to this earth. Obviously, Jeanne ran against the fact that churchmen wanted to condemn her as a witch and a heretic. But this did not affect her fundamental faith about the Church: "I believe that our Holy Father the Pope of Rome, the bishops and other men of the Church are there to keep the Christian faith and to punish delinquents. But as to me and my actions I will submit only to the Church of heaven, that is, to God, to the Virgin Mary, to the saints of Paradise. I firmly believe that I have not failed in our Christian faith and I would not want to fail."[15] It is possible, Jeanne is showing us, that by the grace of God, there are Christians who live on earth as though they already were in the Kingdom of Paradise. Whatever distinction should be made between earth and Paradise does not mean that there are two Churches, triumphant and militant. There is only one Church, that is on earth as well as in heaven. But the inhabitants of heaven are not normally visible to all Christians on earth. And yet Jeanne reported, "angels often come among Christians and are not seen, but I have seen them many times among Christians."

The kingdoms of this earth

In the eyes of Jeanne, Jesus Christ is the only King of heaven and earth. As such, he is not only Lord of the Church but also Lord of all the kingdoms of earth. The model for these kingdoms is no other than the Kingdom of Paradise. This is the key to Jeanne's understanding of her mission. Naturally, she looked at secular realities with a premodern mind. In fact, she did not even fit into the latest political views of her times. Her own views were, in the first half of the fifteenth century, antiquated if not entirely obsolete. Jeanne opposed the claims of the king of England to be the lawful king of France. Henry VI was only a child, but his uncles—the duke of Gloucester in England and the duke of Bedford in France—acted in his name in pursuance of the policies of his father, Henry V. Jeanne denied the legitimacy of the treaty of Troyes (1420), negotiated between the duke of Bedford and the queen of France, Isabeau de Bavière, by which Henry V's son, who was Charles VI's grandson through his mother, would become king of France at the death of his grandfather, Charles VI. Jeanne supported the opposite claim of the dauphin of France, Charles VII, who had been officially disinherited by his father, Charles VI, because of his alleged participation in the assassination of the duke of Burgundy, Jean *Sans-peur*, in 1419.

When Jeanne insisted, however, that Charles VII was not truly the king until he went to the cathedral of Reims and was crowned and anointed with the oil of the *Sainte Ampule*, she took her stand by the old-fashioned theory of the quasi-priesthood of the King. The oil was that of the baptism of Clovis, King of the Franks, which took place in 497; it was believed to have been brought from heaven by a dove. The fleur-de-lys of the French monarchy was a stylized image of the dove, its three white petals representing the theological virtues of faith, hope, and charity. Jeanne understood from this that it is Christ himself who is the king of France, the earthly king being his image and his representative. In this feudal view of the social order, justice consisted in keeping true to the heavenly hierarchy manifested in the earthly. The oath of knighthood grew out of this view: the knight vowed to put his sword at the service of the weak. The French army was still built around the con-

cept of knighthood; the basic unit was the "lance," made of a mounted knight assisted by five or six foot soldiers and archers. Since the battle of Crécy, however, the
English army was based on the technical superiority of several hundred archers
armed with long bows and protected by sharp stakes against which, at Crécy,
Azincourt, and other battles, the French knights and their horses had been im-
paled and consequently slaughtered. Jeanne seemed to care little about the tech-
nique of war. In battle, she took her chance on individual courage and the grace of
God. This was not, for armies, the wave of the future.

In these conditions, Jeanne's overwhelming personal experience of the Kingdom
of Paradise did not shield her from the sinfulness and the hardships of the present
world. She had been moved to compassion in her childhood toward "the great misery of the kingdom of France." In her military career, she was moved to tears by the
spilling of blood. On the battlefield, she did her best to comfort the wounded and
dying, both French and English. She wished for peace though she was ready for
war. On March 22, 1429, before the sortie on the English who were besieging the
city of Orléans, Jeanne sent a letter to the Duke of Bedford in which she stated her
basic view of kingship:

> King of England, and you, duke of Bedford, who call yourself Regent of the king-
> dom of France...go back, in God's name, to your countries.... Do not entertain
> the thought that you will ever hold the kingdom of France from God, the King of
> Heaven, the son of St. Mary; but it is King Charles, the true heir, who will hold it,
> for God, the King of Heaven, wants it so, and has revealed it to him through *la
> Pucelle*.[16]

Regarding Burgundy and its powerful duke, who for the time being favored the
English claim, Jeanne was clear-sighted. She did not believe that peace would come
with Burgundy except, as she stated, "at the tip of the lance." Yet she wrote to the
duke of Burgundy, inviting him to attend the coronation of Charles in the cathedral of Reims and urging him to acknowledge the authority of his lawful sovereign,
Charles VII. The king preferred diplomacy to war, and he thwarted Jeanne's desire
to take Paris by force. Yet there was a point on which he was in deep agreement
with her: the recovery of the kingdom had to be done without hatred or revenge.
When, after Jeanne's death, he made a deal with Burgundy and his armies recon-
quered Normandy city by city, King Charles promulgated "edicts of abolition." We
might call them general pardons or general amnesties. The king announced before-
hand that the crimes committed against him and his partisans during the English
occupation were entirely forgiven and there would be no retaliation of any kind

against their perpetrators. Among those, there certainly were what we would call today war crimes or crimes against humanity. What we could not do after the Second World War and what we cannot do now in the former Yugoslavia was done at the end of the Hundred Years' War. It was entirely in keeping with the spirituality of Jeanne *la Pucelle* that social justice could not do away with the primacy of charity. Victory must not be tainted by revenge.

Indeed, Jeanne did not condone crimes. When it was found that her prisoner, Franquet d'Arras, could not be exchanged for a prisoner of the Burgundians (as this person had just died), she abandoned Franquet d'Arras to his fate as an ordinary criminal, and the bailiff of Senlis had him hanged. But the surviving judges who had unjustly condemned Jeanne were left undisturbed when the investigation of the trial of Rouen ended, on July 7 1456, with the declaration that the proceedings and sentences of 1430-31 "contained injustice, calumny, iniquity, contradiction, manifest error of law and of fact, and therefore that...they had been, were, and would be null, invalid, and void: *fuisse, fore et esse nullos et nullas, invalidos et invalidas, irritas et inanes.*"[17] Jeanne was officially vindicated by the Church. This done, the king took no measures against any one of Jeanne's opponents, not even against Thomas de Courcelles. This theologian had written to Henry VI in the name of the University of Paris to claim the right of judging Jeanne for heresy. At the Nullity Investigation, he lied when he affirmed that he had never said she was a heretic and that he had never voted in favor of any punishment of Jeanne. He had, in fact, voted that she be tortured, that she was a relapsed heretic, and that she be abandoned to the secular arm for death by burning. In spite of this, the king's forgiveness was total. Justice and charity must go hand in hand. This is, I would think, the central lesson of Jeanne's view of the social order.

"Go, go, go..."

The repeated message of Jeanne's voices in Domremy, was "*Jeanne, fille de Dieu, va, va, va...*" "Jeanne, daughter of God, go, go, go..." Later, when she was imprisoned, the chief message became that she should *faire hardiment face*, that is, that she should face her judges fearlessly and answer them boldly. There was nothing static in what Jeanne learned from her voices. "To go" meant in the first place to travel to the kingdom of France and speak to the king, to go to the city of Orléans and force the English to lift the siege, to go from there to the cathedral of Reims to have the king crowned and anointed. In fact, whenever Jeanne had to stay for more than a few days at the court, waiting for the king to make up his mind, she grew restless. She wanted to move and go. Her tactic in battle was the same: on horseback and carrying her standard rather than a sword, she led the soldiers across the ditches, against the walls of a city, or into the ranks of the enemy. This was her principle: "The soldiers will battle, and God will give the victory."

An intriguing comparison can be made between this impelling sense of forward movement and the implication of pilgrimage in her mother's name, Isabelle Romée. This surname, Romée, may have two origins. The one that is mentioned by most authors is that it was the title of any person who had made the pilgrimage to Rome. As Isabelle's surname, it would suggest that either she or one of her ancestors had made that pilgrimage. It is known from testimonies at the Nullity Investigation that Jeanne's mother made the pilgrimage to the Black Virgin of Notre-Dame du Puy as soon as her daughter left for Chinon on her mission to king. One may infer from this that Jeanne's mother's piety inclined her to go on pilgrimage to famous shrines. This was, of course, a well-known form of medieval piety. The other possible origin of Isabelle Romée's name is that Romée is a form of *roumi*, a term that designates gypsies. In this case, Isabelle would have had some degree of gypsy blood. The gypsies roamed freely, as they still do to some extent, through the countries of Europe.

In either case, Jeanne would have inherited an urge to go, a desire to look ahead, an expectation of the grace to come. Jeanne herself, as a child, had frequently walked two or three kilometers to a small chapel in the woods, Notre-Dame de Bermont. One may describe her subsequent life as a pilgrimage to Orléans and to Reims. From the moment, on Easter Sunday, 1430, when Jeanne's voices told her that she would be captured by the enemy before the feast of St. John, her life became a pilgrimage into darkness, the darkness of the totally unknown and yet totally accepted will of God. She could have taken as motto these words of St. Bernard of Clairvaux: *"Semper ad ea quae ante sunt,"* "always turned to the things ahead."

Jeanne's prayer

Only one prayer used by Jeanne la Pucelle has come to us. She willingly formulated it on Wednesday, March 28, when the promoter Jean d'Estivet asked what words she uses when she asks Our Lord to send her help and comfort:

> Most sweet God, in honor of your holy passion, I beg you, if you love me, to reveal to me what I must answer these churchmen. As to my dress I well know by what command I took it; but I do not know how I should abandon it. On this may it please you to teach me.[18]

Several points emerge from this prayer. Jeanne asks for what she is in urgent need of. She wants to give the right answer to this bishop who calls himself her judge. But she makes her request in a very special way. In the first place, she addresses God and Christ, the Father and the incarnate Son, at the same time and together. In the second place, she speaks familiarly, basing her request on what she knows of God's love for her. "If you love me" does not imply that she doubts God's love for her. Rather, she is so certain of it that she puts it forth as the ground of her request. If, with the theology of the Trinity that was standard since St. Augustine, one sees the Holy Spirit as the love between the Father and the Son, then Jeanne's prayer is profoundly Trinitarian. The love by which we are loved of God is the Holy Spirit. This Jeanne may have heard in numberless sermons. It is therefore in the name of the Holy Spirit that Jeanne, the ignorant little creature who considers herself to be of no importance before God, presents her request to God. The background for her simple request of enlightenment on a difficult practical point that has become vital to her is a profound familiarity with the three divine Persons. She is the daughter of a loving God.

All the witnesses of her burning on the 30th of May, 1431, reported that Jeanne invoked Jesus from the midst of the flames before she choked on the smoke and was unable to speak. Jesus was the king in whose name she had left her village and the one whom she served to the end. In much of the friars' preaching in the fifteenth century, as with Jeanne's contemporaries, the Dominican St. Vincent Ferrer (1350-1419) and the Franciscan St. Bernardine of Siena (1380-1444), the name of Jesus is said to contain all the mysteries of God.

Conclusion

It is not easy to place Jeanne *la Pucelle* in one of the classical schools of spirituality. The influence of the friars is certain, and some aspects of her relation to God and Jesus evoke the *devotio moderna* that spread through the valley of the Rhine precisely in the fifteenth century. I asked at the beginning of this paper where the paradox of Jeanne's life and sainthood lies. It does not lie in her. She was simplicity itself and there is no paradox without at least the appearance of duplicity. The paradox lies in us, in our inability or reluctance to learn the lessons of her life. It lies in the contrary assessments that have been given of her.

Jean Gerson, one of the better theologians of her time, wrote in 1429, when Jeanne was still alive, that "by the grace of God... [*la Pucelle*] labored in kindness and prayer with thanksgiving...so that peace may spread at last in our homes and that, freed from the hand of our enemies we may with God's help serve him in holiness and justice all the days of our life. *Amen. A Domino factum est istud!*"[19] Yet Bishop Pierre Cauchon, who was paid for that purpose by the duke of Bedford, declared her a relapsed heretic and had her burnt.

Twenty-five years later, however, on July 7, 1456, the archbishop of Rouen promulgated the decree of the Inquisition that annulled her condemnation. Yet the humanist, Aeneas Sylvius Piccolomini, who was to become Pope Pius II (1458-1464), wrote in his commentary on the memorable events of the period: "Thus Jeanne died, an admirable and astonishing virgin who restored the collapsed and nearly wiped out kingdom of the Franks…. Whether this was a divine or a human event I would settle with difficulty."[20] Aeneas Sylvius could not make up his mind on the question.

Jeanne's final recognition as a saint was due to the efforts of Félix Dupanloup, the Gallican bishop of Orléans, to promote her beatification. She was beatified by Pius X in 1909 and canonized by Benedict XV in 1920. The first steps toward the nullification of Bishop Cauchon's sentence had been taken in 1450 when the victorious Charles VII was reconquering Normandy. Dupanloup pushed for the beatification of Jeanne on the eve of the Franco-Prussian war of 1870. And the dates of 1909 and 1920 framed the First World War. Because of this, the Church has been accused of bowing to pressure from France to honor *la sainte de la patrie*, the saint of the fatherland.

Whatever influences may be discovered in the recognition of holiness and of the spirituality that has nurtured it, the task of the saints has always been to challenge the lukewarm. Jeanne *la Pucelle*, daughter of God, continues to do so.

Notes

1. Sainte Thérèse de l'Enfant-Jésus, *Manuscrits autobiographiques* (Lisieu: Carmel, 1957), 75.
2. Elisabeth de la Trinité, *Oeuvres complètes*, ed. Conrad de Meester (Paris: Editions du Cerf, 1991), 936 and 943-944.
3. Oursel, Raymond, *Le Procès de condamnation et le procès de réhabilitation de Jeanne d'Arc* (Paris: Editions Denoël, 1959), 66.
4. Oursel, 65.
5. Oursel, 74.
6. Oursel, 292.
7. Oursel, 66.

[8] Oursel, 41.

[9] Julian Jaynes, *The Origin of Consciousness in the Breakdown of the Bicameral Mind* (New York: Houghton Mifflin, 1990), 73-74 and 180.

[10] Oursel, 41.

[11] The council of Constance met from 1414 to 1418; the council of Basle would start on July 14, 1431, and be dissolved by Eugene IV on December 18, 1431. But while the pope's partisans moved to Ferrara and later to Florence, a group of conciliarist cardinals and bishops continued to meet in Basle.

[12] Oursel, 34.

[13] Oursel, 79.

[14] Oursel, 82.

[15] Oursel, 93.

[16] Oursel, 47.

[17] Oursel, 366.

[18] Oursel, 95.

[19] "...*in mansuetudine et orationibus, cum gratiarum actione, cum liberali praeterea temporalium subventione, qui...laboret in inipsum quatenus veniat pax in dubili suo, ut de manu inimicorum nostrorum liberati, Deo propitio, serviamus illi in sanctitate justitia coram ipso omnibus diebus nostris. Amen. A Deo factum est istud*" Jean Gerson, "De Mirabili Victoria Cujusdam Puellae," in Jules Quicherat, ed., *Procès de condemnation et de réhabilitation de Jeanne d'Arc, dite la Pucelle d'Orléans* (Paris: J. Renouard et cils, 1841-1849; New York: Johnson Reprint Corp., 1965), 664.

[20] Adrianus Van Heck, *Pii II Commentarii rerum mirabilium que temporibus suis contingerint*, 2 vol. (Città del Vaticano: Biblioteca apostolica vaticana, 1984).

Joan, l'Agent Provocateur

Thomas D. Hughson, S.J.

Charpentier, Ste Catherine de Fierbois

We have listened to a brief masterpiece of spiritual theology. When have hearers or readers been led into the life of a saint by a more intriguing first paragraph? Fr. George Tavard's "The Spirituality of Saint Joan" conveys the unconventional, luminous quality in this saint whose life was anything but banal. With the sure, deft strokes of an artist, Fr. Tavard has sketched Joan of Arc's vibrant heroism and most human commitment to God.

From her birth in Domremy to her death outside Rouen, from exultant victory at Orléans to the coronation of Charles VII at Rheims, Fr. Tavard omits no facet of her existence. Not her family, not her prayer, not her love for France, not her suffering, not her vindication. Spirituality was not an element, a part, a single feature of her life. Spirituality was the whole particularity of her life seen from its center— communion with God, Christ, the saints and angels. Spirituality was the core which irradiated, illuminated, and guided her spectacular deeds. It sent her on behalf of a French people beleaguered by the Hundred Years' War yet divided in reaction to the English incursion.

Fr. Hughson teaches Theology at Marquette University.

"Go, go!" the voices urged Joan. And hasten she did, to raise the siege at Orléans, to rally dispirited troops around the cause of liberating their land, to see the dauphin crowned at Rheims. Her canonization in 1920 put the Church's official seal on the link between her spirituality and the specifics of her mission. Was it a religious mission? God did not send Joan to nurse the sick or to teach children their catechism. God formed her into a sacred militant, dedicated to a political goal, which was the just sovereignty of Charles VII as successor to the line of Clovis, first Christian king of France. Joan saw Christ, Fr. Tavard mentioned, as Lord of all kings. Charles VII became his agent and representative in service of the people of France. It is worth noting that Joan's mission was not committed to the exaggerated position that popes succeeded Peter as repositories of all temporal and spiritual power. She did not exceed her people or the Church, however, in clarity on the difference between the purposes of church and state. She accepted without known regret— as the new king's solemn acceptance of a duty in service of the Church's mission— to use the sword of temporal power to repress heresy. Nonetheless, the ultimate beneficiaries of a just sovereignty within that defective understanding would be people like Joan's family and neighbors in Domremy. Her divinely appointed mission was military in order to be political. The effect of securing legitimate rule was justice in the land, riddance of invaders, and eventual but not permanent peace.

The indissolubility of spirituality and mission means, of course, that we can attribute to God her intervention to promote French liberty under a rightful sovereign. The scope of her task lay in the temporal order of society. Are we to think because her effect was not within the ambit of Word and Sacrament that she thereby departed from the Church's own mission? Did she not exemplify, rather, the active concern for social reality latterly at the heart of Catholic social teaching? Did she not have a spirituality and mission directed to building up the kingdom of God in temporal dimensions of liberty and justice? Has excessive secularization removed from our minds what Joan and Thomas Jefferson alike knew—that justice and liberty in this world is also a divine purpose?

"The Kingdom of Paradise" was Joan's phrase for the provenance of the light and voices she experienced. Yet, 565 years ago, an ecclesiastical court at Rouen indicted her for, Fr. Tavard recounts, "heretical rebellion against the Church." The unhappy bishop of Beauvais, Pierre Cauchon, handed her over for burning. She was nineteen and died calling on the name of Jesus. Sometime later, Cauchon, while a barber was trimming his beard, tipped back in his chair and died. The court split the Church into a heavenly Church triumphant and an earthly Church militant. God ruled the former; his vicar, the Pope, aided by the Holy Spirit, apparently had the latter as domain. Joan responded, and Vatican II teaches, that Christ's Church was not so divided. Her fidelity to God and to conscience in this belief met, though, with the severest judgment. The subsequent voiding of the court's procedures and nullification of the verdict do not remove the original scandal. Authority not only was abused but was exercised within arrangements permitting easy abuse, and on behalf of Catholic truth about the Church! Raymond E. Brown remarks that Matthew's Gospel counteracted a tendency for the Church to "become a self-sufficient entity, ruling (in the name of Christ, to be sure) by its own authority, its own teaching, and its own commandments."[1] The court at Rouen seems to have surpassed itself in just that tendency. Joan expressed indignation at the injustice visited upon her under ecclesiastical authority. But her charity had been universal, reaching to the English through demands for their peaceful exit before armed combat commenced. Also, in response to the court, her charity took the more strenuous path of not hating her ecclesiastical tormentors. Joan practiced the gospel God had formed her in and did not curse the Churchmen for their manifest treachery, deceit, and use of authority to vilify a holy woman. Her forgiving charity was a weighty precedent when Charles VII, Fr. Tavard notes, decreed an amnesty for her guilty judges and for other crimes performed by Burgundians during the years of war. This charity of Joan's toward the Church may be one of her most provocative challenges to us.

Fr. Tavard concludes with a proposal that the paradox of Joan lies in the eyes of beholders unable to grasp the unique simplicity of her fidelity to God. He remarks, too, that she does not sit comfortably in any of the well-known schools of spirituality. Reversing matters, we can ask about her influence on others, whether she might be the origin of a current of spirituality. I do not know the details of the history of her influence, though the tradition of French reverence for her is clear. Might she become an influence upon us in the way she has been upon poets François Villon and Charles Péguy, Saints Thérèse of the Child Jesus and Elizabeth of the Trinity? How might she be an *agent provocateur* of God's reign in our midst?

So many aspects of her spirituality remain inimitable and incommunicable; her singular mission cannot be duplicated or shared. Still, she gave heroic witness to communion with God. To what about God or the gospel does Joan *la Pucelle* continue to witness? Whatever the answer, it is first of all important to acknowledge the value of the question. The lives of saints have not yet become the theological topic Karl Rahner thought they deserved to be. George Tavard's work on Joan of Arc brings her into the realm of theology, if that might be considered a happy fate. He extends to Joan's words and deeds the kind of respect Rahner had for writings by the saints and mystics. Their writings, said Rahner, are "wiser and more experienced than the wisdom of the learned." In them we find, he continued, "an original assimilation of God's revelation...a creative prototype in accord with historical circumstances, and by way of example...a new gift by God's Spirit of the ancient Christianity to a new age."[2] Might not Joan's personal dedication as a member of the laity and her witness to God's activity on behalf of temporal justice and a free society speak to postconciliar Catholic laity? Might she be paired with a later English witness to liberty under the just sovereignty of law, St. Thomas More, as singular yet exemplary lay witnesses to God's care for justice in society?

Notes

[1] Raymond Edward Brown, *The Churches the Apostles Left Behind* (New York: Paulist Press, 1984),138.

[2] Karl Rahner, *The Dynamic Element in the Church* (New York: Herder and Herder, 1964), 85-86.

Changing Images of Joan of Arc

Linda Seidel

Foyatier, Orléans

In the aftermath of the Revolution, France came to celebrate the memory of its cherished, political patriot with three different images, each of which glorified a distinct aspect of the maiden's short life: Joan the victorious soldier, Joan the virtuous martyr, and Joan the humble peasant. Each of these images partook of a venerable tradition of visual forms and associations, none of which had anything to do with Joan, and each should be understood in relation to enduring ideological positions regarding issues of national identity, heroic sacrifice, and gender—issues that transcend facts about specific events in the French girl's life.

Because so much of the imagery associated with Joan is site specific, congregating in and around the city she successfully regained from the occupying English army in May of 1429, I begin my review of depictions of Joan in art there, with the sculptor Foyatier's imposing, bronze equestrian statue of Joan which was erected at the geographical and historical center of Orléans in 1855.

The statue is located on the Place du Martroi, the site of an ancient burial ground at the end of the Rue Royale, a grand arcaded shopping street that had been con-

Dr. Seidel teaches Art History at the University of Chicago.

structed under the patronage of Louis XVI a century before. Horse and rider face south in the direction of the bridge over the River Loire, where the fortification

known as les Tourelles stood on the far bank. There the English invaders were defeated by the Maid's armies. Ritual celebration of her triumphant procession into the city the next day, May 8th of 1429, began almost immediately and continued until 1793. The festival of Orléans was re-installed by Napoleon in the year X (1801-1802) and was declared a national *fête* in 1894.

The statue shows an armor-clad Joan, holding a sword in her extended right hand (figure 1). Her triumphant pose is reminiscent of that struck by ancient Roman military heroes such as Marcus Aurelius, whose well known, ancient bronze statue was brought to the Campidoglio in Rome towards the middle of the sixteenth century by Michelangelo and positioned at the center of the piazza he designed there for it. It remained there until relatively recently, when it was removed for preservation to the inside of an adjacent museum.

1. *"Joan as warrior," Foyatier, Orléans*

Running east from the north-south axis over which Joan's statue looms is a street bearing her name; it leads to the colossal Cathedral of the Holy Cross, begun in the thirteenth century on the site of earlier structures and completed only in the nineteenth. The square in front of the façade is framed on either side by two massive, free-standing stone blocks, the western or front faces of which present the alternate images of Joan as identified above, while the sides are inscribed with texts quoting words from the record of her life; the most frequently used sources here are the documents of her trial.

The depiction on the stone block on the left, or north side of the square shows Joan, the country maid, listening to an angelic voice (figure 2); the inscription defines her as a shepherdess and refers to the voices she claimed to have heard in her garden and which she said told her to save France from the invading English armies and restore King Charles VII to the throne.

Across the square, we see Joan the martyr, engulfed by flames (figure 3). She is accompanied by the words that emboldened her during her last moments, her voices' promise that true life awaited her after the fire had burned out. Because of this last visit from her voices, Joan recanted the "confession" of heresy she had made in a moment of weakness, a confession which would have saved her from the stake.

Two decades later, towards the middle of the century, Joan would be absolved of the accusation of heresy; nearly five hundred years after her death, she would be canonized. But her martyrdom stands, along with her military prowess and her youthful, pastoral innocence, as one of the defining aspects of her short life. These moments—her early days in the field and with the flocks, her successes as a military leader, and her death by fire—are the moments in which Joan is most often depicted in the extant monuments to her.

2. *"Joan as country maid," Orléans*

Each of these phases of her life did not receive comparable artistic attention, and all of them were not equally appreciated at the same time. Indeed, in the decades and centuries following her death, Joan was not the subject of visual imagery at all. Lacking a portrait as well as a

3. *"Joan as martyr," Orléans*

tomb, she went without a palpable shrine. Absent tangible traces for inspiration or a material locus for commemoration, there was no urge to evoke the memory of Joan's presence with illustrations of her life or images of her form; her ashes had been cast into the Seine at Rouen. We learn from this that visual representations are tied to larger interests than the simple fact of an individual's existence; these have to do with the changing needs of posterity.

Joan as soldier

The oldest of the characterizations of Joan, that of victorious soldier, was verbally constructed during her own lifetime by her contemporary, the writer Christine de Pizan, who, immediately after the siege of Orléans and before the turn in French fortunes, portrayed Joan in prose as a holy warrior, the savior of France.[1]

The later appearance of painted and sculpted images of Joan as warrior, in the early decades of the nineteenth century, is closely connected to political events. After the failures and embarrassments of the Napoleonic Wars came to an end and the short-lived Empire had collapsed, Christian monarchy, with its celebration of the divine right of kings, was reasserted as the central feature of French national identity. (The visit of the Pope John Paul II to Reims in 1996, on the occasion of the 1500th anniversary of Clovis's baptism, reminded the world of the intimate association of French nationhood with Christianity.) Restoration of the monarchy in 1830 heightened interest in the great themes of medieval Christianity, and these came to enjoy increased popularity in art and literature. In this atmosphere, Joan's part in the preservation of the line of Valois Kings centuries before received heightened attention. She had, we recall, succeeded in having the young Charles VII crowned at Reims against English and Burgundian desires.

Toward the middle of the century, Joan began to be depicted as the military leader of a nation, sitting astride a noble steed in the way in which successful commanders had been represented since Roman times in an especially celebratory, well-known image, paying tribute to their victorious troops. The conception of a mounted ruler had become particularly significant to the French more than a thousand years before, during the reign of Charles the Great, King of the Franks. His introduction of horses into local warfare late in the eighth century swiftly converted his armies from pedestrians into cavaliers.[2] From the moment of his coronation as Emperor by Pope Leo III in the year 800, the image of the mounted warrior in sculptures and on coins evoked the notion of invincible defense of both the state and the church.

A second tradition of mounted warrior imagery is commemorative rather than celebratory. In it, a fallen warrior is fitted out with weaponry as he was in life in a representation of his final ride; death, not any worldly rival, is the vanquished enemy. This image appeared on Gallo-Roman and Viking slabs in the early Middle Ages, projecting the notion of an individual's entry into immortality. It merged in later centuries with the image of the victorious soldier in the creation of a new type, the Holy Warrior, an armed Christian who falls in the fight for his faith and achieves, thereby, instant salvation.[3] These depictions celebrate worldly courage as well as the spiritual victory that is its reward.

In the Loire River valley, the area of France in which Joan achieved her glory, images of "holy" rider figures enjoyed particular prominence in the late eleventh and twelfth centuries. The façades of numerous Romanesque churches, especially around Poitiers, where Joan had been taken for special questioning at the time she first set out on her mission to save France, are adorned with images of mounted figures. In this public, architectural context, the riders are explicitly understood as protectors of the Church and thus as defenders of the faith. The figures carry different objects, are seen in varied poses, and may well enjoy diverse specific identities; as a group, however, they represent the knights who participated in the Crusades to recapture Jerusalem and the sites sacred to Christianity from the Muslims. Those campaigns, beginning with the first Crusade in 1095, were regarded as Holy Wars; they lasted well into Joan's own time, as the Burgundian Duke's plan for a Crusade in the third decade of the fifteenth century attests.

In the nineteenth century, with national attention focussed on the glorification of this splendid medieval moment in French history, artists like Delacroix painted such subjects as the Crusaders entering Constantinople. This heightened historical interest in Christian kingship and conquest, combined with the contemporary renewal of appreciation for related imagery on medieval churches throughout the region of Joan's triumphs, suggests an important motivation for the depictions of Joan on horseback that began to appear at this time. As part of the effort to present France as a strong Christian monarchy, the image of the mounted, military hero— a throw-back to Roman, Romanesque, and Renaissance times—was re-invented in the figure of Joan of Arc.

There were other traditions at play as well in the development and appreciation of this type. Tours, the city in which Joan's armor had been procured, was the site of the tomb of St. Martin, the Apostle of Gaul and patron saint of France, who died in 496. Martin's legend identifies him as a Roman foot soldier in occupied Gaul, a pagan who shared his cloak with a beggar he encountered while walking along the road. In a dream later that night, Christ appeared to Martin and revealed that He had been the recipient of his charity. Immediately thereafter, Martin converted to Christianity; his torn cape became a critical relic in the construction and design of the church over his tomb. The moment is central to Martin's *vita* and was, from earliest times, depicted in art whenever Martin's life was recounted.[4] Sometime after the year 1000, a remarkable change took place in the representation of Martin's charity; instead of being described as a foot soldier (which is what lesser Romans were), he was now conceived of as an aristocratic soldier and depicted riding a horse in the style of knightly warriors. The image on a capital from the late eleventh-century in the cloister at the abbey church of Moissac in the south of France counts among the first of such representations; a sixteenth-century painting by El Greco, two versions of which are in the National Gallery, Washington, shows the action of an elegantly garbed Martin splitting his cloak while seated on horseback.

Thus the tradition of the *saint*-soldier on horseback had special and longstanding significance in the territories in which Joan enjoyed her brief moments of triumph. It was an image of importance in other countries as well; Spain, for example, cherished the figure of St. James, patron of Compostela, as a *matamoro* on horseback, and England coveted, as something of a national logo, the depiction of a mounted St. George, lance extended, killing the dragon. I want to suggest that national politics in the second quarter of the nineteenth century, as well as local history and imagery in the area of France from which Joan came, coalesced in the formation and popularity of the most familiar representation of Joan that we know, the image of her astride her horse and clothed in armor; it is a triumphant, powerful, but not necessarily aggressive image.

The issue of gender addresses the occasional passivity of Joan's pose as well as the decision to show her in ordinary, specifically female dress. She was, after all, still a girl at the time of her trial, even though her actions had been those of a vigorous man. In 1824, Hippolyte Delaroche painted a boldly conceived canvas of a

4. *"Joan as woman/soldier," Foyatier, Orléans*

very young Joan being interrogated by Cardinal Winchester. The painting, now in the museum in Rouen, signalled the awakening of interest in her as a pre-sexual adolescent through its contrast of her with a dramatically positioned, over-bearing ecclesiastical authority. To establish and emphasize a lofty tone for the painting and to associate its large figure with the Roman Church, the artist took as his model for the Cardinal nothing less than Michelangelo's Prophet Ezekiel on the ceiling of the Sistine Chapel: the pathetic, luminous shape of the young girl in a simple shift was all the more striking as it cowered in his clerically garbed shadow. Thirty years later, Joan was still being represented as a sexually ambiguous figure. In a painting by Ingres, she was shown armored and with sword but androgynous in form and restrained in pose; Foyatier dresses her in a billowing skirt but makes it visible only in side views of the statue (figure 4).

Women were not supposed to be soldiers, and Joan's crossdressing, her wearing of men's clothing and armor, was one of the heretical acts for which she had been put on trial in the fifteenth century. One of the ways in which artists got around the problem posed by such a figure in the nineteenth century was by referencing images that either showed female personifications in armor, for example, virtues engaged in combat against vices, or scantily clad goddesses leading armies in triumph. Augustus Saint-Gaudens's equestrian statue of the Civil War General, William Tecumseh Sherman, on Grand Army Plaza in New York City, shows him following a diaphanously dressed, striding, winged figure of victory; she wears a laurel wreath crown on her head and holds a palm branch in one hand while the other arm is raised in salutation. Delacroix's *Liberty at the Barricades*, a painting of a bare-breasted, mythic female figure at the head of armed rabble-rousers, had monumentalized a similar theme in France more than half a century before. Familiarity with such public depictions of women *with* soldiers helped naturalize, and thus make acceptable, Joan's otherwise unnatural and unacceptable behavior as active head of an army. Her heroic image on horseback must be appreciated then as a conflation of the traditions of militant rider and virtuous personification which, together, had flourished in medieval sculpture in the Loire Valley and in Poitou. Such visual models alert us to the associations that accrued to Joan's imagery when and whether she was shown in dress instead of armor, or in a combination of both.

Recent discovery of an unusually small suit of armor, which appears to have been made in the early fifteenth century, has brought new attention to the issue of Joan's dress.[5] Metallurgic testing indicates that at least parts of the armor were made between the fourteenth and sixteenth centuries; moreover, three repairs to the suit—on top of the headpiece and in the area of the waist—correspond to physical injuries Joan is known to have suffered. A scar on her lower abdomen, probably from a fall from a horse, was observed during one of the several physical examinations Joan had to endure, in part in connection with efforts to determine whether or not she was virginal. We know that Charles VII had armor made for Joan in 1429, before the battle of Orléans, at a cost equivalent to that of a hundred horses; it was fashioned by a craftsman who lived on rue Colbert in Tours. A modern sign with the words "to the armed maid," "*à la Pucelle armée*," hangs outside the house in which he lived and worked, identifying the building—which serves as a shoe store—to this day.

The recently identified thirty-five pound armored suit that might have been his work has its own fascinating and fairy-tale like associations. It was purchased by an antique dealer from a Parisian collector whose family had owned it for more than two centuries and who acquired it "in an English port." The English, we remember, had bought Joan from the Burgundians who captured her, and it is not impossible that Joan's armor remained in English hands. One day, the new owner of the suit asked his five foot tall, fourteen year old daughter to try it on; it fit her like a glove, or perhaps a glass-slipper, provoking her mother to exclaim, as her daughter admired herself in a glass mirror, "You'd think she was Joan of Arc."

Joan as martyr

We return from here to the equestrian statue on the Place du Martroi. On the base of the sculpture are a series of bas-reliefs which narrate the main events in Joan's life. These begin with a rendering of Joan hearing her voices in the vicinity of a huge tree (see figure 2); this plaque is located at the far (north) end of the left side of the base. We then proceed through her story sequentially, moving in a counter-clockwise fashion past the scene of Joan before Charles and around to the front where the battle of Orléans is depicted. The scenes continue along the right side of the base with a depiction of Joan in prison; a cast of this scene is in the Centre Jeanne D'Arc a few blocks away. On the rear face of the base, Joan is shown on the stake as she succumbs to the fire (see figure 3).

What is interesting is the movement of the narrative, from left to right around the base so that the pictures serve as a substitute textual narration, proceeding in the same direction as words would. If we imagine that the base of the statue traces the shape of a church nave, however, then we see another pattern in the directionality of the narrative: the scenes follow in their movement the Stations of the Cross, a point that comes into view more clearly when we turn our attention to the ten stained glass windows, with scenes of the main events in Joan's life, in the side aisles of the Cathedral of Orléans, a few streets away from the statue. Made by Galland and Gibelin between 1895 and 1897, the giant, colorful panels accompany the Stations in their movement from the northern arm of the crossing, down the left aisle, past the western entry and into the south aisle. Joan's life is presented in concordance with and as imitation of Christ's.

The Stations begin with Jesus being condemned to death and proceed forward to His crucifixion and His placement in the tomb. The story is known; the movement toward death inexorable. So with the windows depicting Joan's brief passage through life: although they begin with a gloriously golden, winged Saint Michael appearing to Joan, who is being tenderly embraced by Saints Catherine and Margaret, and continue through her victory at Orléans and the splendidly costumed coronation of Charles VII, we know what awaits Joan—the movement forward is equally relentless.

The final window instructs the viewer: "Thus was she burned by the cunning English" (figure 5). Although Joan had requested beheading—a kinder, quicker, and more noble death—this was denied her. In the Middle Ages, execution by fire was the painful end to which those who had erred against the Church were routinely condemned; fire, with its total destruction of the body, meant degradation not simply death. The image of burning fills the imagination with a horror similar to that evoked by the idea of crucifixion: the painful, ultimate punishment which, in Roman times, was reserved for criminals and outlaws.

The most important of the comparisons the viewer is encouraged to make, given the parallel placement of Stations and windows, lies in what is not depicted. The resurrection of Jesus, or what occurred after the last Station, is the central celebration of Christianity; that Jesus was triumphant over death guaranteed the possibility of salvation to all Christians. The final window, that of Joan's death, also says: "Her voices told her 'through your martyrdom you will arrive in heaven.'" Joan is victorious in her martyrdom; she has earned salvation. Many depictions of Joan's burning, such as that of J. P. Gaudin in the Joan of Arc Basilica near Domremy, show a dove flying out of the flames or the words "Jesu, Jesu" imprinted on the clouds above her, suggesting that a glorious outcome—her resurrection—was foreseen at the time of her bodily death.

5. "Joan as martyred saint," Galland/Gibelin, Orléans

Images of Joan as martyred saint, with sword, and either tormented in prison, at prayer, or engulfed in flames, became more popular in the course of the nineteenth century. The depictions suggest fascination with her ability to withstand the degradations of imprisonment and to hold fast to her belief in her voices; they served as well as a stimulus for the growing interest in her holiness. In 1909, her blessedness was established by the church; she was canonized a saint in 1920.

Joan as peasant

The third tradition in Joan of Arc imagery emerged in the second half of the nineteenth century when the country girl took her place in the pastoral landscapes that had recently been validated by painters such as Millet. Bastien-Lepage's *Shepherdess* of 1862, a large painting in the Metropolitan Museum in New York, shows a grown but still girlish Joan in the garden of her house in Domremy listening to the voices of her saints; Michael, in golden armor, appears caught in the branches above and behind her (figure 6). The painting brings to mind a carefully detailed, smaller panel by Giovanni Bellini in the Frick Museum in New York in which St. Francis is seen before his hut communicating with nature. The painting is often called *St. Francis in Ecstasy* and has been thought to represent the moment at which Francis received the stigmata; the bent tree at the upper left is believed by some to be the active source of the power from which his wounds resulted. While the notion of the spiritualization of the landscape is firmly imbedded in Franciscan thought, other traditions, more indigenous French ones in fact, focus on the primal power of nature and its particular connection to women. These are likely to have played a role in the invention of depictions of Joan.

6. *"Shepherdess," Bastien-Lepage, New York*
The Metropolitan Museum of Art, Gift of Erwin Davis, 1889. (89.21.1)
© 1988 By the Metropolitan Museum of Art

I am thinking here of Celtic and Gallo-Roman lore, the subjects of French fairy tales, in which female deities play a significant role as earth and river goddesses and as tree spirits.[6] Women's connection with the land, as herbalists and healers especially, perpetuated problematic identities for them; from the end of the Middle Ages on, these skills have associated them with witchcraft. Since the second quarter of the fifteenth century, the use of potions and poltices for curative purposes has threatened mainstream medical practice; in the 1430s, midwives, who had long ministered to women in matters relating to the well-being of their bodies, began to have their work regulated by male authorities. From this point on, they were identified as witches more and more frequently whenever they were thought to have transgressed authorized norms in their efforts to practice the healing arts.

Part of the appeal of Bastien-Lepage's painting of Joan resides in its lush brushwork and richly textured surface, which bonds the woman's body in a material way to nature. Here, the peasant Joan is shown as belonging to the land before she receives her Christian calling. Joan said that her voices came to her when she was out in the fields, and, in the film of her life which stars Ingrid Bergman, a tree is featured prominently as music announces the voices' arrival. The maid is in touch with the power of the flowers and the fields as were the druid priests of Celtic tribes who were said to live in forests: they are invoked in venerable anecdotes in St. Martin's *Vita* where their magical cures are supplanted by the holy man's miraculous healings.[7] These representations of Joan as shepherdess or country maid, in addition to invoking older cultural traditions, provide a requisite prelude to the heroic activities and poignant finale of a saint's life.

The three types of images in which we find Joan represented—the country girl, the brave soldier, and the martyr—serve as visual condensations of stages in her biography and provide us with a pictorial *vita* that paves the way for our acceptance and celebration of her as a saint. The images I have discussed secure her legend to great, earlier moments of French Catholicism and to such Christian heroes as Charlemagne and Martin—either by echoing their actions or by engaging aspects of their lives. In this respect, the development of Joan's visual *vita* resembles the way in which the stories of celebrated saints' lives had been fashioned in earlier times. The creators of older legends drew on Biblical history for inspiration, borrowing the plot for events from the pages of both the Old Testament and Christ's life in an effort to ground their accounts of the lives of holy figures in immediately recognizable spiritual sources. Using a similar strategy, the crafting of Joan's illustrated "life" based itself on significant themes and images in French history in order to construct a pictorial narrative for the Maid of Lorraine that was at once a patriotic as well as religious tale.

Notes

[1] Kevin Brownlee, "Structures of Authority in Christine de Pizan's *Ditié de Jehanne d'Arc*," in *Discourses of Authority in Medieval and Renaissance Literature*, ed. Kevin Brownlee and Walter Stephens (Hanover, N.H.: University Press of New England, 1989), 131-50.

[2] See Linda Seidel, "Holy Warriors: The Romanesque Rider and the Fight Against Islam," in *The Holy War*, ed. Thomas P. Murphy (Columbus, Ohio: Ohio University Press, 1976), 33-77.

[3] For more on this, see Linda Seidel, *Songs of Glory: the Romanesque Façades of Aquitaine* (Chicago: University of Chicago Press, 1981), 55-66.

[4] For Martin's life, see Clare Stancliffe, *St. Martin and His Hagiographer. History and Miracle in Sulpicius Severus* (Oxford: Clarendon Press, 1983); for a discussion of illustrations of Martin's life in Gaul, see Herbert L. Kessler, *Studies in Pictorial Narrative* (London: Pindar Press, 1994).

[5] Craig R. Whitney, "This Suit (a well-worn petite) May Have Been Joan of Arc's," *The New York Times*, June 28, 1996, A6.

[6] See *Roman and European Mythologies*, compiled by Yves Bonnefoy and translated under the direction of Wendy Doniger (Chicago: University of Chicago Press, 1992), 244-56; also Pamela Berger, *The Goddess Obscured: Transformation of the Grain Protectress from Goddess to Saint* (Boston: Beacon Press, 1985).

[7] See Aline Rousselle, "From Sanctuary to Miracle-Worker: Healing in Fourth Century Gaul," in *Ritual, Religion and the Sacred*, ed. Robert Forster and Orest Ranum, trans. Elborg Forster and Patricia M. Ranum (Baltimore: Johns Hopkins Press, 1982), 95-127; also Valerie I. J. Flint, *The Rise of Magic in Early Medieval Europe* (Princeton, N.J.: Princeton University Press, 1991).

Joan of Arc: Saint or Terrorist?

State of the Question — Howard Eisenberg
Representing Joan — Michael Gillick
Representing the Church — Joseph Perry

Frémiet, Paris

Mr. EISENBERG: Some months ago, when the initial planning was being made for the Joan of Arc Celebration, someone thought it would be appropriate that the Law School do something as part of the overall observance. So they came to me and I must tell you, as many people who are not of the Catholic tradition, I knew very little about Joan of Arc. In fact, I'm giving myself credit by saying I knew very little; I knew virtually nothing about Joan of Arc. So I started reading about Joan and how law related to her life and death and subsequent events.

As I was reading the biography of Joan of Arc, it occurred to me that her situation raised a couple of obvious issues, one of which was this: what would happen if Joan arrived today and told somebody that she had been told by God to raise an army and do something? How would the organized Church, how would organized government react to someone like that? Would it have been much different than it

Atty Eisenberg is dean of Law at Marquette University.
Atty Gillick is a partner at Murphy, Gillick, Wicht and Prachthauser.
Fr. Perry, a canon lawyer, is Auxiliary Bishop for the Archdiocese of Chicago.

was in the fifteenth century? The second thing that occurred to me is the parallels—and I hope I'm not offending anybody by what I'm about to say—between Joan of Arc's experience and that of David Koresh and the Branch Davidians in Texas a few years ago. Why have we canonized Joan of Arc as a saint on the one hand, but view David Koresh—who also said that God was speaking to him and raised sort of an army (at least he raised an arsenal in Texas)—as someone very different from a saint? It occurred to me that both of those issues speak to us in a contemporaneous way: how do organized religion and organized government relate to someone like Joan? Where do we distinguish and how do we distinguish between someone who really does talk to God and someone who says that in order to get money or power? So it seemed to us appropriate that, rather than restaging the trial of Joan, we discuss and debate how the Church should deal today with people who are like Joan of Arc. And I think we want to make clear that, while Father Perry is more or less going to represent the Church's position and Mr. Gillick is more or less going to represent Joan's position, they are not relitigating the trial of Joan. We decided early on that was not entirely a fair match, particularly after five hundred years of anti-Inquisition opinion, so we will discuss the issues of the trial in a contemporaneous way.

Let us begin with Mr. Gillick.

Mr. GILLICK: Thank you, Dean Eisenberg. This has been a great opportunity for me to work with people of extraordinary quality. It was Dean Eisenberg, whose creativity led to our topic tonight, and Father Perry has given me many insights over the course of preparing for this discussion. In fact, it is one of Father Perry's insights that serves as a springboard for what I have to say. First of all, Father Perry pointed out to me that if this debate was about whether Joan of Arc was a really a saint—and if I were arguing that she was—this would be a very short debate. Rather, we are here, as the Dean suggested, to discuss the place of rebellion, dissent, mysticism, and prophecy within the institutional Church. Father Perry made another interesting observation: Joan of Arc, a thirteen year old, uneducated shepherdess from the fringes of France started having conversations with some saints, and those conversations led her, at the age of sixteen, to contact a French nobleman who took her to the presumptive heir to the throne of France—a man affectionately known in history as Charles the Bastard, primarily because his mother called him that. Joan convinced Charles and most of France that God wanted her to expel the English from the native soil of France and to help Charles to become the king of France. The interesting point here is that this is probably the first and only time in history that a recognized saint was given an assignment to fight a secular battle. "Why," Father Perry asked, "why would God do that?" How could that be of value as a prophecy or as a message from God to his people? And that caused me to think.

So I come here tonight to tell you the results of my thought. I suggest that Joan's effort to help France and Charles was not the reason God sent her. Does any of us remember what battles she fought? Can any of us name her particular deeds of daring? Not many can, but what we all do remember—what is forever contemplated by Eliot, Shaw, Anouilh, Twain and so many others—is the trial. What deeds Joan did in battle have faded, but her confrontation with the bishop of Beauvais, the nefarious character who had her tried and executed, lives and burns in our memory. I suggest that this was the purpose of her mission. *I suggest that God sent Joan to do battle, not with the English, but with the institutional Church of her time.* And in that battle, in the transcript which has astoundingly come down to us intact, the voice of God fairly leaps from the page. This illiterate, nineteen year old shepherdess, pitted against scores of diabolically clever wits, academics, and politicians, makes a mockery of them all. Clearly, here the voice is not that of an ignorant child, but the voice of God itself. And what is that voice saying? It is saying that the institutional Church should never forget that it is a tool, a servant of the people of God—that, in and by itself, it is nothing. If you prefer not to think of Joan of Arc in mystical terms, if you are uncomfortable with the idea of her voices, then let me ask this in a different way: what is the significance of the historical event of Joan of Arc? The answer that I am giving here tonight is that she is one of those signal events of history which objects to a derivative thing—the institutional Church— holding itself out as a primordial thing, as the root of meaning for Christianity. The fundamental position of the Church in the face of mysticism and prophecy, of all the little people hearing voices, has to be humility. And far too frequently it is not. Why does the Church leap so quickly and curtly to silence the likes of Copernicus and Galileo, and, in our own time, Teilhard and Rahner, Courtney Murray and Curran? Why does the Church need to prohibit debate, to prohibit even thinking? I believe this to be the reason: as a human institution, the Church has an inevitable tendency to lose sight of its own life, its own inspiriting core. It constantly forgets that it is derivative, that it exists as the result of and for the sake of a primordial reality, the journey of creation toward God. So what should be the Church's response to its Joans? To the dissenters and rebels, the mystics and prophets in its midst? Openness and encouragement. Courage rather than fear, daring rather than caution. Christianity, like all religions, is life itself; its institution should act as adrenaline rather than opiate. Its hands should be opened to embrace rather than closed to strike or worse, to grasp tightly.

Here is my point, my single thesis: To be true to its primordial ground, to the reason for its existence, the institutional Church needs to be so open as to be constantly reexamining its meaning in order to avoid disappearing. Every challenge to the teachings of the institutional Church should be met first, not by silencing and condemnation, but by self reflection and examination. Does this mean that the institutional Church must enter into debate and dialogue with every nut case who announces that Jesus just sent him an e-mail? Yes. Absolutely. For the following three reasons: first, because if you don't do that, if your first thought is to exclude, you end up so often being so absolutely wrong, as in the case of Joan and Galileo, Copernicus and Father Rahner. Second, because every human experience is significant, an expression of the historical meaning of the being which is the Church. I have on the wall in my den a sign, a saying of the Roman thinker Terence: "*Homo sum et nihil humani alienum.*" "I am a human being, and nothing human is foreign to me." Every human action is a call for me to examine what I am and where I am. That is the meaning of the historical event of me. Third, the very purpose of the Church is to develop and grow and it cannot do that by looking to itself as an institution, but can only do it by listening to the humans—all the humans—who constitute the mystical body of which the institutional church is merely a sign and a servant. The message of Christianity and in a way the very meaning of Christianity is that existence is linear, historical, and that participation in and encouragement of that history is the root of the significance of the institutional Church. Whenever the Church silences debate, it betrays its mission to work out historically the meaning of Christ. Whenever the Church refuses to listen to one claiming the status of prophet, it stunts the growth of the people of God. I'm not calling here for a noncritical acceptance of every human action and utterance, for mindless adoption of every hair-brained proposal. I am saying that the Church must be open; in fact, she must be characterized by openness to constant renewal, examination, and reflection of every aspect of Christian life.

Let me take an example: the question of whether women should be allowed to be ordained priests. I am not a theologian and so, frankly, I have no idea whether or why one needs a male sexual organ to be a priest. However, when that subject was addressed by Rome, a certain cardinal brought the message to the United States that the issue had been decided and that, therefore, there was to be no more discussion or debate about it. It is that attempt to silence, to blind, to numb that is wrong, that is contrary to the mission and the intrinsic purpose of the institutional Church.

It is what the trial and execution of Joan of Arc stand in such stark witness against. The life of the Church lies in openness, in vulnerability; every time it closes up, bars, bans, and silences, it defeats the very essence of its mission. Thank you.

Fr. PERRY: Too bad you weren't there for the trial! Your points are well taken, Mike, and certainly they are informed by an enlightened consciousness of rights in our society today—human rights, civil rights, procedural rights—those kinds of things. For whatever reason, the fifteenth century did not evidence those kinds of understandings, those kinds of insights. One wonders why not. It is easy to see that they were human, like we are human beings. One wonders what we are lacking in terms of insight today, in terms of future generations who will critique the twentieth century—what we are doing, what we are not doing, the mistakes we're making today.

The statement that was given to us to consider—whether Joan is a saint or a terrorist—had me thinking a long time about the terms "terrorist," "terrorism," "terrorizing." These terms carry a certain nuance in these times, obviously, given the high profile of foreign and domestic individuals and groups who would use violence and intimidation for political or personal purposes while holding citizens in the grip of fear or submission. Terrorism carries apocalyptic imagery of the antichrist coming over the horizon with roots in the barbarian invasions of the Dark Ages. That's one sense. But in another sense, any one who disturbs my peace of mind is a terrorist. And that onslaught can be of cyclonic proportions, depending upon the issue at stake. Now whether the onslaught is seen to be evil or good depends on the community's evaluation or the assessment of history's commentators. Yes, Joan of Arc is a terrorist, and her campaign to restore dignity to the monarchy and the people of France disturbed English political interest. History, as well as popular sentiment, titles her a saint, which means that her brand of terrorism is seen as prophetic—the work of God akin to the mission of the prophets and the martyrs to turn peoples thought's toward God and the things of God.

Now saints are persons of exceptional holiness. A great number are formally recognized by the Christian Church or are declared such in canonization rites. A saint, in other words, is a person of great virtue or benevolence, one who has taken the gospel and lived it with heroic seriousness and at great cost to self in most instances. Joan has been situated among these heroes and heroines of faith, at least since 1920. It takes us a while to realize the impact of certain people in our lives. In the case of some of the saints, there is a thin line between terrorism and sanctity.

Prophets and saints use a type of terrorism to quicken people's spirits and their institutions to belief and virtue.

In this sense, terrorism can be perceived in a variety of contexts. Anyone who troubles me or pushes me against my will is terrorizing me, even if the terrorists believes this to be for my good end. Given the fire and brimstone and sometimes destruction that's commonly associated with terrorist acts, it is easily seen how terrorists are often framed as crazed fanatics or the mentally ill who carry a skewed view of reality. Anyone who disturbs the status quo or provokes political and governmental representatives of power will often be accused of terrorism of some degree.

'Now Mike, in terms of institutional dealings with terrorists, it seems that civilization evidences some common strands from a philosophical point of view. For example, human beings are naturally prone to live in groups which results in the formation of institutions that sustain common life. Laws result from the emergence of institutions for the sake of order, to enforce a code of justice and for the harboring, meditation, reflection, protection, and implementation of values. Leaders lead these institutions either by self-appointment or the choice of the people. History shows that these groups or communities can structure injustice into the common life by discriminating against classes or races, by favoring one group over another group, by allowing the many to suffer for the sake of a few, or by letting hunger and ignorance poison the safety and the security of the whole. Communities and their institutions need saving from their inherent sinfulness as surely as individuals need saving—thus enters the figure of a Joan of Arc. Institutions, religious or secular, being harbingers of the highest aspirations and values of the community, tend of their nature to take on the cloak of conservatism. They are the mainstay of civic and spiritual values, while certain of their members move forward in knowledge and insight and progress. Made up of human beings, institutions are not always farsighted enough; they believe themselves better able to improve the human community. If there is reform, it often comes from within, and not without social upset. Institutions are therefore the guardians of convention in most instances—the guardians of orthodoxy for the sake of order and the reaching of common goals.

Amidst this effort, there are always found dissenters, those who reach for the frontiers of thought and action. Dissenters are thereby perceived as offenders against public order; their behavior often results in outright violation of the laws. The institution's condemnation of seers, pioneers, and dissenters can turn out counterproductive. I agree with you on that note. Generally, the reaction reaches the level of overkill. The passion of the moment, the vested interests of individuals and groups, and fear that the floor underneath is quaking, that the institution is crumbling, provokes the leaders of institutions to react. In this drama will always be found a mixture of saints and sinners, scoundrels and patriots, saviors and executioners. Thank you.

Mr. EISENBERG [to Mr. Gillick]: Does your open Church recognize heresy or blasphemy? And how do you know it when you see it?

Mr. GILLICK: It recognizes heresy and blasphemy as a limit. You know it by its historical development. It recognizes violations of itself; certainly, there are things against this open Church. But, my open Church lives on that border where its core exists and is constantly challenged.

Mr. EISENBERG: And who decides that, where the core and the border are?

Mr. GILLICK: St. Augustine, a bishop as well as one of the great thinkers of the Church, once made this statement: "All ought to allow themselves to be corrected even by those who are expected to follow them lest perchance the guides should depart from the right path." The significance of the development of truth within the Church indicates the difference between the Church as an institutional body and any other body. Comparison between the Church and governments is unfair because the Church is, in fact, a representative of a higher Church, if you will, and Rahner himself used to refer to two churches. So, the Church has constantly to be subservient to that other church, the Church of God. When does a final decision come or from where does a final decision come? I think the final decision on doctrines in the Church comes from history; it develops historically.

Mr. EISENBERG: Well, how would you have had the Church deal with Joan specifically?

Mr. GILLICK: Well, in the first place, I would have told the Church to stay out of politics. If you boil down the trial of Joan of Arc, she was charged with seventy-some charges that were finally reduced to twelve. Within these, the real charge leveled against her by the institutional Church was that she said her voices came from God and the prosecutors said her voices came from the devil. So long as they are voices, I say it is not for us to decide. So, I would have told them not to try her in the first place.

Mr. EISENBERG: Father Perry, how would the Church deal with Joan today?

Fr. PERRY: Probably similar to the way the Church is dealing with seers and people who admit to mystical intuitions and special gifts, and the way in which we deal with theologians who travel the boundaries of orthodoxy.

Mr. EISENBERG: Which is how?

Fr. PERRY: We probably would subject the individual to various commissions of study and, if we find the person is somehow outside of the norm, there probably would be assignments to some degree depending upon the issue at hand.

Mr. EISENBERG: And how does that differ from how Joan was dealt with five hundred years ago?

Fr. PERRY: Probably the only difference is that we don't use fire anymore! The fifteenth century was bereft of a lot of things. This is a very delicate enterprise, trying to evaluate the fifteenth century from the vantage point of the twentieth century, because we like to think we are far more informed and more knowledgeable. If institutions are going to exist, they are, in a large sense, compelled to act in response to public violations of their tenets. If the institution is to survive, some boundaries of thought and opinion and behavior are not only reasonable but are of the essence of being an institution. I think that a healthy feature of the institutional Church is that we have a group of people who can live on the edge of openness, another group of people who are in the middle, and maybe a large group of people who could care less. And then you have those champions and patriots, who are people psychologically oriented to living within boundaries.

It's these two groups on the extreme right and left that we end up refereeing in most respects. We can ask ourselves which camp can we live in, not only in Church community but in the realm of politics. Even within our own families, our own households, how do we prefer to live? Are we open to challenge, as Mike suggests? Take for example the adolescent who offends the family mores. That adolescent is put out of the family by the offended parent. That's a delicate situation because that family needs that child. But, for whatever reason, harmony, negotiation, and communication do not come together to the extent that this excommunication could be prevented. But someone made the decision, mom or dad, that this kid had to get out of the house because there's nothing but chaos and havoc created by this child.

This kid is such an individualist that it is harming the rest of the family. Now, if excommunication is going to do its healing job, somebody has to put into motion some healing remedy to bring that kid back into the family. It would be a shame if that kid was put out forever, but reconciliation doesn't always happen in the human situation. The challenge to resolve conflicts arising from breaches of an institution's tenets or breeches of order is going to be common to the Church as well as the state. It is a chore that seems to demand more objectivity than fallible human beings can muster.

Mr. EISENBERG: Can you have an organized Church that's as open as Mr. Gillick apparently wants?

Fr. PERRY: It's hard. It's hard, because you need a referee with due respect for individual rights—speech, thought, and so forth—that we understand in western society. You need an arbiter. Otherwise, the foundations of the institution can become unraveled. Someone has to state what we stand for. We have a creed on Sunday that we stand up and we recite. This is what Christians believe, catholic Christians with a small c. This is what we stand for but as soon as you list a creed, that means some other things are left out. What is the code of the Boy Scouts? The Girl Scouts? The 4-H Club or whatever?

Mr. EISENBERG [To Mr. Gillick]: Let me ask you the same question, can you have a Church that's as open as the model you suggest?

Mr. GILLICK: It would be hard.

Mr. EISENBERG: And can you point to any historical model—political or religious—that has that kind of openness?

Mr. GILLICK: Yes, I can point to the early Church, which had specifically that kind of openness. And I can point to local instances of operations and functions within the Church that have taken on a lot of that viewpoint. But, when I say that it's hard, I want to stress that. I'm serious, The last person I'd want to be in that kind of set up is the guy who ran the place. It is enormously difficult. I am a child of the sixties; I was in the Jesuits in the mid-sixties; I was in religious life in the mid-sixties. The last guy I wanted to be was my superior because that guy had headaches every night. That's his job. His job is to be on the fringe at all times.

What I wonder about is this: what you do with the groups that Father Perry listed? What do you do with those people who seek the Church as a sanctuary, who seek it as a place of peace and calm rather than the chaos and violence that what I propose would invite? That is a problem. How do you put people like the Berrigans and Father Rahner—who have done some pretty exciting things—how do you put them together with the Sodality? I'm not sure that you can, but what you can't do is kick out the Berrigans.

Fr. PERRY: It seems to me that we seldom have the tools to balance orthodoxy in any institution, be it military, government, politics, family, church. Communities and institutions have the toughest time attributing dignity to dissenters the same way they do to loyalists. It's the human drama of the thing. Dissidents, visionaries, and pioneers are subject to be designated the enemy by those so offended by their words and their actions. We burn them at the stake only for subsequent generations to declare some of them prophets, saints, and martyrs. Maybe there's no other way of doing it in the broken human situation. It's sad, we learn from our mistakes, we are not farsighted enough to see that some of the stuff that we do and say is genuinely overkill. Thomas More, Jesus, Socrates, Joan of Arc—all of them are present to history lesson trials, as it were, as the way not to do things. There is always someone down the line, similar to these personages; there are all kind of Jesuses around, whom we have crucified for many different reasons.

Mr. GILLICK: It is a remarkable thing in the history of humankind that we kill our heroes; I've never been able to understand it. Gandhi had to die. Martin Luther King had to die. Jesus had to die. Why is that? What are we doing? Well, first of all they are an embarrassment to us. We have to get them out of town. One of the fascinating things about the Joan of Arc trial was that they didn't want to just put her in jail; they needed to discredit and kill her. It was important to embarrass her, to show that she was evil—not just that she did something wrong, but that she was evil. So maybe those are wild examples of the fact that institutions necessarily have to drag behind the development of the human and the Christian community, which hopefully are the same thing. But the church, of all institutions, should not have that as one of its features.

Mr. EISENBERG: Now we would be glad to entertain questions from the audience.

Question: Is it fair to characterize the condemnation of Joan as an act of the institutional Church or is it only a small branch of the institutional Church? Didn't politics have more to do with her death than any problem that the institutional Church had with her voices?

Mr. GILLICK: Yes, that's an important point. In those days, when you caught somebody in a war, you could sell them. And so they sold Joan. The bishop of Beauvais, Pierre Cauchon, purchased her and arranged to have her tried in his diocese, although the jurisdictional problems here were endless. He did that for three reasons. One was that he represented the institutional Church and supposedly he was defending the institutional Church. The second was that he was supported by the English through a French party called the Burgundians. The third one was that, as Joan went rollicking through France knocking off towns for the dauphin, the supposed heir to the throne, she knocked off Beauvais. And whether the bishop of Beauvais had ever been in Beauvais didn't matter; his income was in Beauvais and, when Joan captured Beauvais for the dauphin, the citizens stopped paying the tithe to the bishop. The fact is that, whether or not the motivation was institutional, the event happened institutionally. It had the blessing of the Inquisitor General and so it was a recognized inquisitional trial. It also came at a bad time because there were at least two popes in existence at that time, some say three, so it came at a bad time for her request, for her appeal to Rome. "Which Rome?" they asked her.

Fr. PERRY: It was a situation that's totally unfamiliar to us, with the Church intertwined with politics and politics intertwined with the Church.

Mr. EISENBERG: Are you saying that seriously or sarcastically? I'm asking that seriously. Do you think that the nature of the entanglement may have been different? Certainly that's not something we are unfamiliar with.

Fr. PERRY: No, we're not unfamiliar with it; I think that the degree of the entanglement is something that we are unfamiliar with, at least to this extent—that the way the Church enacted discipline often meant that she went to the secular arm to do it. It was the English that put Joan to death, not the Church. Sometimes the Church meted out secular kinds of penal discipline. Cauchon and the gang lost a great deal because of Joan and they had every reason to take revenge on her. But in order to do it, they could not try her simply for warring against the English and being victorious. By the terms of the time, they had to make sure that she represented to the populace the very embodiment of everything that the Middle Ages feared, and that was the encroachment of evil in the name of the devil. That's why she was a witch, a heretic, a blasphemer—the whole litany. They had to trump up a case against her. That's what made the whole thing so fallacious.

Question: If Joan were alive today, what would she think of the Church's attitude toward women in the priesthood?

Mr. GILLICK: She'd be very angry. She *is* alive today and she *is* asking that question and she *is* angry about that. And she shows up in every dissenter.

Fr. PERRY: I like Mike's response, but then I look at Joan and I see she was a daughter of the Church. Her supplication and her docility toward the Church is probably not well understood today, especially by those who would see Joan as a challenger to the male dominated corridors of government, church, and military. I think it's hard to say with Joan—what contemporary issues she would champion if she were with us today. Joan's interest in France was stirred up by her voices; before that, she was doing everything expected of her by her family—taking care of the livestock, ordinary household chores and so on.

Mr. GILLICK: I think it should also be pointed out that there is a difference between rebellion and revolution. And that goes back to a question that you asked before, Dean Eisenberg. There are those who say, "I want change and I will effect change, contrary to the status quo." There are also those who say, "I want destruction, I want elimination of the entire institution." I don't think any institution can invite its own demise. The difference is that the Church, the institutional Church, this Church, the Church of God on earth, what we used to call the Church Militant (I don't know if they still use that term, but they used it in the trial) is destined to end. It is an institution that is programmed to end. We're looking forward to the day when there is no Church Militant. And that is unlike any other institution that I know of because I don't see anybody, for instance in the United States (as happy as we are with things here) suggesting that we're programmed to end all this two hundred years from now, that we'll want some other government. So that's an interesting feature about the Church that points out that it is a unique body as an institution.

Fr. PERRY: Institutions being institutions, I think we need our camps. We need the rebels and we need the revolutionaries. For some reason or another, things happen positively out of conflict for us. I think of the black civil rights struggle in this country; we have the Martin Luther Kings and then we have the H. Rap Browns and the Stokley Carmichaels. They warred against each other during the sixties. Each camp of opinions had different statements to make. In every struggle, you're going to have zealots—those who take up armed struggle because the institution is slow to move or the status quo is not hearing the voices of revolution, let alone rebellion.

Mr. EISENBERG: What I'm hearing you say is that the Church hasn't changed very much and is almost institutionally unable to change except that now the penalties may be different—perhaps to be silenced rather than being burnt at the stake.

Fr. PERRY: Where human beings gather, I don't think that part of it has changed our response to revolution from within.

Mr. EISENBERG: Is that a good thing or a bad thing?

Fr. PERRY: I think subsequent generations will be charged with carrying the baton (i.e. revolution) and making needed changes. Because the Church has to change if it's going to be a vital institution, if it's going to be of service to subsequent centuries. The insights we don't have today, the next generation and the generation after that will have. And we're going to be the objects of their critique. No doubt about that. We don't have all the answers. I'm willing to trust the future—that life, that newness, that vitality can be there as much as we can say that the twentieth century is in some way an improvement over the fifteenth—in the way we do things, the way we handle people, and so forth.

Question: If Joan's voices came from God, does that mean that God takes sides in nationalistic disputes?

Mr. GILLICK: Does Our Lady pull for Notre Dame? That's obvious.

Fr. PERRY: A parallel might be the Old Testament battles that Israel fought. Which side was God on, especially when Israel lost? Or when Israel won? It would seem, throughout the Hebrew scriptures, that God was involved in many of the political interests of Israel. Salvation was woven within all of that because it was all human, even the bloodshed. God worked himself through that in order to bring a people to Himself. That's the only parallel I can think of, at least within the dramas of faith.

But who are we to question what God is interested in—why was God interested in the French kingdom, or the likes of a Charles VII?

Question: Even in an Inquisition, doesn't the defendant have the right to advocacy? Did Joan get any such help?

Mr. GILLICK: She was offered one from among her sixty-six judges—the fox watching the hen house again—and that was the fact. She asked for counsel and Cauchon proffered counsel, which she could select from among any one of the men that he had called to sit in judgement of her. She also appealed to Rome and my understanding was that it was very much like the *jus civilis*—if you appealed to Rome all bets were off and you went to Rome. She did this twice and Cauchon said (I supposed he said), "I can't hear you."

Question: Nobody in that sixty-six was good enough for her?

Mr. GILLICK: Good enough? They were on Cauchon's side. Here she was, confronted by these sixty-six educated men who were judging her. It's amazing that this nineteen year old shepherdess would not be utterly intimidated, that she could come up with the astounding observations that she did. Her cunning judges asked this very devilish question: "Are you in the state of grace?" There is no correct answer to that, because if you say you are, you are presuming to know the mind of God. If you say you aren't, then you're a sinner. And she said, "If I am, I thank God for it and if I am not, I pray God to put me there." And the guy who was taking down this transcript wrote in the margin, "great answer!" I mean, that's not exactly what he wrote, it was in another language, but I say it was "great answer."

Fr. PERRY: For all her lack of education, her spiritual astuteness was astounding. But I don't know that Joan knew her procedural rights in this trial. I don't think she had a grasp of that, at least in my reading.

Question: But if she appealed to Rome, she must have had some savvy.

Mr. GILLICK: No, not the way she did it. She didn't say, I have the right to appeal to Rome and I appeal to Rome. She said, "ask the Pope, he'll tell you. I want to talk to the Pope. The Pope'll tell you that this is right."

Question: As lawyers; do you think that's the way to settle disputes in the Church? Why wouldn't the academic approach be better? You keep suggesting that history is a sort of court, but academics don't usually call counsels to settle questions of truth. They write their articles, their books, and they dialogue in this fashion. Why couldn't the Church, your vision of the Church, be more academic than juridical? Do you think it should be? In the Church, all the big issues are settled by vote of bishops, some ecumenical council, who perhaps have advice of theologians, but perhaps don't. Look at the two millennia we've had and the way some things have been defined and settled. Father Perry referred to the way that people like Rahner and others are summoned to Rome to defend themselves or sometimes they're not even summoned to Rome, they're just condemned without a hearing. But in academe, you're judged more likely on credibility and the defensibility of your argument.

Fr. PERRY: The procedure in the estimation of many probably could be more collegial, like having a panel of peer theologians to examine another peer. Right now, we haven't gotten to that point except insofar as the panel of interviewers right now is a commission that is made up of clergy and lay theologians, but it is still perhaps closeted to a degree rather than broadly open. These kinds of hearings are, in fact, academic rather than judicial. It's rare that a theologian is given a judicial trial today. Extremely rare.

Mr. GILLICK: I remember Courtney Murray, who was advised that he had to defend himself against a panel of bishops, and I remember his response to it: "Tell Montini, I am ready at any moment." Montini was the family name of the pope at the time. Maybe Courtney Murray should have been more gentle, more respectful. But I think that, ultimately, academics do get their day. For instance, in Vatican II. There was a great deal of lobbying by some of the great minds, Rahner included. Rahner shows up all over Vatican II as do many others who were writing and thinking at that time. Ultimately, it seems to me that the issues are decided or are certainly developed by academics. They're not developed by politicians.

Fr. PERRY: Courtney Murray was rehabilitated by the Second Vatican Council and Rahner was too. Ecumenical Councils only take place every hundred years or so. This historically vast Church of ours seems to need a few hundred years to germinate wisdom on some issues, whereas we tend to be impatient, we want it to happen now. Some of the questions now, we probably won't have answers to in our lifetime. But a generation or two later, certain issues will be decided.

Mr. GILLICK: And all I'm espousing is that you allow the debate.

Mr. EISENBERG: Do you oppose the debate?

Fr. PERRY: No, certainly not.

Question: Father Perry, if we wait for hundreds of years for the church to evolve and consider the changes which are necessary, what about the church members whose consciences are burnt at the stake in the meantime?

Fr. PERRY: That's true in every generation. It's part of the human drama—not only in the Church but even in civil society as well. What about people who are waiting for justice to happen in American society? It doesn't happen all at once. It didn't happen for my great grandparents; it's not happening for my parents—maybe it will for their great grandchildren. It's a human thing, sadly, but it's a human thing.

Question: Father Perry, Attorney Gillick stated at the beginning of his speech that the purpose of Joan's vision was to do battle with the institutional Church at the time. I just wanted to know what you're response to that assertion was? Do you agree with that?

Fr. PERRY: I'm inclined to believe Joan was a prophet for her time. There is a providence behind innocence and prayer; God uses them frequently to confound the proud.

Question: Joan of Arc was considered a saint; she was also connected with French royalty. When she was on trial, why didn't someone come to help her out?

Fr. PERRY: Well, she was taken, sequestered; they had to guarantee her demise, so all of her procedural rights were summarily violated; anything that she asked for, she was denied. Her appeal should have been honored and it wasn't. We didn't have e-mail in those days; we didn't have telephones to call up the pope and tell him "we've got an innocent girl here who's being held illegally. Why don't you send some of the Vatican troops here to save her." Joan suffered through the many human and historical limitations of the 15th century.

Mr. GILLICK: The royalty that you're referring to, I assume, is the royalty that she supported in the battles. The house of Valois, Charles VII. They didn't call him Charles the Bastard for just one reason. He was the most reluctant savior of France that one might ever see. He was having a good time when she came along and dragged him into battle. He kept her off in a corner for six months just to cool her heels and when finally she was captured, he did not support her. Unfortunately, France was not there to rescue her. They owed her a great debt.

Question: Father Perry, did Joan of Arc have a spiritual life?

Fr. PERRY: She had a spiritual director, a cousin who was a Cistercian monk in one of the monasteries not far away. And most of her biographers say that she was a student of her confessors and the priests who guided her. I think that gives some logic to her spiritual astuteness. Spiritual direction was a popular thing in her time, even for someone uneducated or someone considered to be of the peasant class. And she took to it quite well. All during her imprisonment, she asked to go to Mass; she asked for a confessor. She wanted that consistent spiritual input, but again, that was denied her. Yes she had a spiritual life. She was spiritually focussed.

Question: Did the bishop want her go to hell?

Fr. PERRY: Well that is the implication when you call someone a heretic and then you excommunicate them and then you burn them at the stake. That means that's where they're going!

Mr. EISENBERG: Any closing words of wisdom?

Mr. GILLICK: I would just like to say that being a Christian, or being committed to an historical linear event, being from a Judeo-Christian background, is not a matter of comfort, it is a matter of adventure and risk. However the Church may work that out, the fact of the matter is that all of that history has to be characterized by that risk.

Mr. EISENBERG: Father Perry? Last word.

Fr. PERRY: Prophets, visionaries, and missionaries are often treated with suspicion; no matter how good the human situation might be, these kinds of people are held suspect. They upset the status quo and they make a rather disturbing penetration into the strongholds of power that keep our institutions together. But in it all, God frequently has something to say to us that we don't want to hear. At best, we give these messengers a hard time; I suppose at worst, we murder them. Whether they come out of the halls of society or whether they come from the halls of the Church, they demand that we perk up our ears and learn from what we've done in the past, learn from history in order to create institutions that serve, institutions that are inclusive, institutions that enhance all that is human and dignified.

Mr. EISENBERG: We appreciate very much your attendance tonight and your participation and your good humor in talking about a fairly serious subject. We hope that you will look at the program for the other events relating to the Joan of Arc Celebration and attend as many as you can. Thank you and good night.

Joan of Arc Demythologized

Daniel C. Maguire

Echevins, Orléans

Pope Pius XII was, in his private life (inasmuch as he had one) a history buff. He once commented to his friend Count Galeazzi that "history at its best is 60% accurate." It is an interesting observation, but I think the pope was too generous. I don't think history is anywhere near that accurate. And I think it's particularly inaccurate when it comes to heroes, heroic figures, and certainly saints. In the Divine Office of the Catholic Church, the story of the life of the saint of the day is given at what is called the "second nocturne" of matins. Given the notorious inaccuracies of this genre, the Germans developed a saying that so and so "lies like a second nocturne." This is our plight when we sally forth into history looking for heroes. We are unprofitable servants when it comes to reaching the heroic target of our quest.

Walter Brueggemann, the biblical scholar, talks about King David as "the dominant figure in Israel's narrative." And yet, he says, the historical David is not available to us, we can't get to him. And even if he were, he said, he wouldn't be as interesting as the constructed David left to us by the literary crafters of the tradition. Brueggemann's words: "What is important is that David is the engine for Israel's

Dr. Maguire teaches Theology at Marquette University.

imagination. This David is no doubt a literary imaginative construction made by many hands. So we must settle for that. We cannot get behind the literary construction even as we cannot get behind the construction of any significant person."[1] And what Brueggemann says of David is relevant also to a figure like Jesus. Citing my own words in my The Moral Core of Judaism and Christianity:"We can substitute 'Jesus' for 'David' in those statements. We cannot, with surety, get beyond the 'constructed' Jesus," that semi-historical figure who was constructed for us by the many crafters of the Jesus traditions.[2] We can't get all the way back to the original.

Now enter someone as flamboyantly interesting as Joan of Arc, and the question presses itself:"what hope have we of really getting to her reality?" Well, what I was surprised to find out when I was pressed into this study was that there is an extraordinary amount of documentation on this fifteenth century teenager, because of the fact that she was subjected, in the course of her lifetime and after her death, to six ecclesiastical trials.[3] That was something of a record. And those trials were very well documented. On first reading those records, I was stunned to see the care with which events were recorded. Even taking into account the exuberance and controversy that swirled around the creation of this written record, it is still affords a remarkable view of the events; there is nothing comparable to its detail in this period of history.

One of the first places I looked for Joan material is one of the least helpful. It is Butler's Lives of the Saints, edited by Herbert Thurston and Donald Attwater. There we find the authors writing with all the apparatus of scholarship but failing to quite transcend the second nocturne genre. The section on Joan says:

> "there has been, almost inevitably, a tendency for various 'Joan-legends' to grow up. There is the 'Joan the Protestant' legend, popularized by George Bernard Shaw. Granted an inadequate understanding of Catholicism, this mistake is understandable: it is nevertheless a mistake.... There is 'Joan the feminist,' in some ways the most foolish of these legends, both historically and in sentiment."[4]

Thurston, Attwater, and Butler's Lives are completely wrong, patriarchically wrong, I submit, and simply miss the real Joan.

My approach will be this: first of all, I will discuss the mental state of Joan. If a modern Joan approached you and said she had messages from God delivered to her by supernatural emissaries, you would commend her swiftly to the care of a psychiatrist. Maybe Joan was psychotic; we ought to look into that. Secondly, we must look at Joan's stubbornly ideological commitment to transvestitism, to cross-dressing. We will see that it was not merely a practical commitment, not a mere matter of the most convenient clothes for battle or efforts at sexual modesty, since she insisted on these clothes elsewhere and for other reasons and was willing to sacrifice the sacraments to keep them on. Thirdly, I'll look at the incredible amount of physical data that we have on Joan's body, on the state and even shape of her body. There's no comparable data on the bodies of men of that period or any period, be they saints or whatever. Next, I will look to Joan as witch, bitch, and feminist. All those titles in some way apply to her. And finally, we will look to Joan as the proto-Protestant. George Bernard Shaw appropriately commends the Roman church for having canonized a Protestant saint.[5] I applaud Shaw for the accuracy of his statement.

Psychosis or Inspiration

First of all, to the mental state of Joan: she heard voices that no one else heard. Was she psychotic? I would definitely say she was not. There's just too much evidence, especially from the records of the trials, that this is not a psychotic person but an incredibly self-possessed, bright person. "A genius and a saint," Shaw called her, though he also called her "the queerest fish among the eccentric worthies of the Middle Ages."[6] To understand Joan and her auditory illuminations and visions, you have to recognize that in that period of time everybody thought they were hearing divine voices. Mohammed, who was the Holy Prophet of Islam, claimed, like Joan, inspiration, visions, and voices and no one blots him out of history as a psychotic. There was a long tradition in Christianity of feeling that God was speaking directly to you. The mantra of bishops like Clement of Rome when they spoke was that they were doing so "*spiritu sancto dictante*" with the "holy spirit dictating" to them. Well, Joan claimed nothing less or nothing more. In fact, her very judges and inquisitors were people who thought that God had told them, and not Joan, what the truth of things was. It was a battle of competing alleged revelations. They were all in their fashion hearing voices. It was simply the vernacular of the day, their idiom to express conviction.

At times, Joan even lets this slip out. Shortly before her death, she mentioned that she had said earlier that an angel came with a crown for Charles but now conceded that she was that angel, giving us a blunt hermeneutical hint of her literary form.[7] Also, you can see she didn't always take her voices very seriously. She did what she wanted to do and then dialogued with her voices. When she jumped from the tower at Beaurevoir, a fall of some sixty feet, and did manage to survive, she said that the voices had counseled her against that and afterward forgave her for her disobedience. So I would say that we would have to say that Joan was using an idiom which usually worked in her day. It got people to listen, if not to be ultimately convinced, but I don't see any signs of mental illness. To accuse her of that is simply to misunderstand her context. It would also be necessary to accuse most of her contemporaries of the same.

Joan as Cross-Dresser

Next comes the subject of her ideological commitment to transvestitism. This salient fact of her life has been systematically distorted and fudged. After all, they had to get Joan canonized and declared imitable but it took five hundred years of refashioning to do that. Joan, however, was fervently committed to cross-dressing. To distort this commitment, it was said that she had to use armor and since there was no female armor so she had to wear men's clothes to be in battle. But that was not the whole story. She wore it at other times also. A second argument is that she just did it for modesty, since she was with men so much and this was a way of protecting her chastity. But that also does not hold up, and here are the reasons why I think it does not hold up. Dressing like a man was for Joan an act of obedience to "the will and command of God."[8] The very first thing that she demanded when she left home, against the wishes of her authoritarian father, was that she was going to move out and dress as a man. She quickly did so, and did so consistently to the outrage of the patriarchy of the day. She even at times received the sacraments in this dress, though she said "she would die and go without holy communion rather than give up man's dress."[9] Cross-dressing was an essential symbol of her mission.

The charge of her wearing men's clothes was brought up no fewer than thirty times at the trial. It was indeed the most frequent charge brought against her and was often listed first even before the heresy. It was said by her indignant accusers that this cross-dressing was contrary to divine law, abominable to God, and condemned and prohibited by every law. (Notice that the accusers claimed to know what God thought of clothing and style! So, again, Joan was not exceptional in her claims to divine inspiration.) In fact, she said she had direct orders from St. Catherine and St. Margaret to wear men's clothes, and she wore them consistently. St. Margaret was someone who had practiced what she was preaching to Joan, because she herself had cross-dressed to get out of a marriage. She disguised herself as a man, went off and joined an order, and became known as Brother Pelagius. Her disguise was so convincing that she was later accused of having gotten some nun pregnant! Obviously, she had the evidence to establish her innocence.

Clearly, then, there was much more involved here than practicality in war or the preservation of modesty. She presented herself so regularly as a man that when she was burned, halfway through the process, they ripped the semi-burned clothes off her to point out that she really was a woman.[10] Some people apparently had questions about that.

Now to the theological issue in all of this. Among the charges brought against Joan was idolatry. She had mimicked sacrality. How? She had belittled the sacred by pretending to male status in a society that divinized that status. She was fussing with and she was a pretender to the divine rights of men.[11] These clothes were a radical symbol; the patriarchy knew it and reacted violently. Her crime was her refusal to accept "the estate proper to womankind" as defined by the patriarchal conspiracy of church and state.[12] As Shaw puts it: "She refused to accept the specific woman's lot."[13] Small wonder Joan's canonization came slowly. It took five hundred years to change not only her clothing but her persona. She was given the stereotypical feminine image; indeed, in many portrayals she was even eroticized. She is a perfect example of men defining gender and female identity.

Joan was carefully recast by subsequent art forms and ecclesiastical and popular mythology. Why? There must have been a lot at stake. As Susan Schibanoff says: "What was at stake was not merely God, king and nation but the traditional constituent of all three, manhood."[14] Even glamour was added in the service of male heterosexual desire itself. So there was a studied rewriting of Joan in art for over five hundred years until she seemed quite safely feminine, even rather cute, with the shock of cross-dressing and other rebellions carefully expunged. Only then did Pope Benedict XV declare her worthy of veneration and imitation.

Joan's Body

It is amazing what we know about the body of Joan of Arc. We have data on the shape of her breasts, the condition of her vagina, and even on the calFOUses on her buttocks. Why? Why was this information exacted and passed on to posterity? There is no male saint on whom we have comparable data as to the size of his penis or the contours of his pectoral muscles. Whence this extraordinary preoccupation?

One of our body-witnesses was the duke of Alençon, who claimed that he saw her breasts bare three times and he added the detail that they were beautiful.[15] Joan's page, Jean d'Aulon, thought it worth mentioning that he saw Joan's nipples and bare legs.[16] Now, these peeks at Joan's breasts by the duke of Alençon *et al.* were peeks that were heard around the world and over the centuries. They were still being discussed five hundred years later when the process of her canonization came up. Few have had their breasts discussed five hundred years after their death. George Bernard Shaw wrote that no men around Joan "ever claimed that she was pretty."[17] Shaw was wrong. The duke of Alençon was impressed. The peeping Duke claimed he did not have any unchaste thoughts about her even after seeing them, but of course he was still talking about them and all we have is his word for his chastity of mind. Also, he did think it a miracle of grace that he had no sexual desires after what he had seen. Aside from the duke's interest in Joan's breasts, we also know that she was sexually attractive enough to be sexually harassed. And pawed. And her reaction to her harassers was quite fit. According to the record, she slugged them.[18] Even the trial record makes indirect allusion to the curves of Joan's body, saying that, in spite of wearing doublet and breeches and cutting her hair short, she could not conceal "nature's own distinctive marks."[19]

This absorption with the body is in many ways the soul of sexism because it reduces woman to her genital definition, and I see Joan as simply another example of that. It is one more example of the extraordinary preoccupation with the female biology which characterizes men even to this day. It is depersonalizing in the extreme.

Witch, Bitch, and Feminist

But what of these other titles that seem to apply to Joan? The record shows that she was accused of being a witch. Joan arrived on the European scene when the hatred of women who were called witches was just commencing. She lived fifty years before the publication by two Dominicans of the *Malleus Maleficarum (The Hammer of Witches)*. By that time, women were accused of everything—from causing plagues and bad weather to inflicting disease and male impotence. Any and every kind of evil was attributed to women. Of course, the image of woman as source of evil had been around for a long time. Augustine believed in it. Tertullian believed in it. Eve and Pandora are classical examples of woman as source of evil. Some of the gentler Church fathers disagreed that a woman could be so wed to the devil that she could cause all these evils, but the myth had enduring popularity. And the myth was acted on.

The Islamic Taliban in Afghanistan today, who are persecuting women, are a pale reflection of what the Christian witch-hunters did. When the witch-killing fever really caught on some fifty years after Joan, certain historians claim that the female population in certain areas of France and Germany was literally decimated, threatening the future of the particular regions.[20] So Joan was hated and killed as a woman, and she was the precursor of many to follow.

I used the term bitch because it is, however impolite, a strategic and technical word in our culture. It involves two qualities, uppityness and anger. It refers to women who do not know their assigned place and, sure enough, Joan was accused precisely of that. She lacked humility. She was not at all deferential. On trial, the male authorities asked her to take an oath and she wouldn't take it.[21] They asked her for information, and she replied that she might tell them on Saturday, or, then again, she might not. She was tried by the patriarchy, civil and ecclesiastical, and she did not bow. She was accused of "lifting herself above all ecclesiastical power."[22] When asked about her obedience to the pope, she always qualified her answer with "Our Lord being first served."[23] The trial was all about authority. "When she says she will not submit her acts and sayings to the decision and judgment of the Church Militant she utterly destroys the power and authority of the Church."[24]

And then there was the anger. She had it and she showed it.[25] Bitch is a word used today to subdue women and their righteous indignation. Joan was a bitch worthy of the name. Even in our day, anger is tolerated in a man. If Mike Wallace gives a tough interview, we say he's highly professional. If Barbara Walters does it, she's a bitch because of the totally different criteria for what is allowed to women. Anger in victims threatens oppressors, and so we develop language to discourage it.

In defense of her noble anger, I would quote Saint Thomas Aquinas who in turn was quoting St. John Chrysostom: "Whoever is not angry when there is cause for anger, sins."[26] Just anger is the virtuous response to injustice, says Thomas. So she expressed her anger and the Church patriarchs deemed it unbefitting a candidate for sainthood—especially, I would say, for female sainthood.

Was she a feminist? Indeed she was, a thoroughgoing feminist. I think that was her whole mission. I do not see Joan wearing men's attire to say that she would buy all their values. By doing what men did, and dressing like them, she was saying that she invaded their caste in order to end its hostile divisiveness. She died to protest the passivity imposed on women by patriarchal society to ensure their subjugation.

Joan was also a woman-instructed woman. She said she got her religious education from her mother and not from her authoritarian father. And I think the switching of clothes was a symbol of her feminist mentality. It is principally for this that she was a threatening person to the ecclesiastical and civil authorities. Her goal was the subverting of male dominance in church and state. Again, her message is quite contemporaneous. If a woman is uppity and moves into male-dominated places today, we burn her. Hillary Clinton is an obvious example. When she tried to do something with our disgraceful health care system, which leaves some forty million persons uninsured—fully a third of them children—she was burned at the stake. A recent issue of *Fortune* magazine did a cover story on extremely able, successful women CEO's.[27] These women are running major corporations, but the cover headline read: "Women, Sex, and Power." Even when women make it to the top in a harsh male world, we focus on their sexuality. "How has your sexual attractiveness contributed to your success?" The masculine inability to see women as subjects, not as sexual objects, seems ineradicable. Joan is extremely contemporaneous.

Joan, The Protestant Saint

Finally, Joan as proto-Protestant. I see Joan as another example of what someone once said: conservatives are the worshipers of dead liberals. History distorts prophets into something less discomfiting. But the real charges against Joan—the trial did not have much on her military career, which has dominated many of the plays and Hollywood representations of Joan—"she was assuming the authority of God and his angels, lifting above herself above all ecclesiastical power to lead people into error."[28] Recall her important proviso when she was asked if she would obey Church authority: "Our Lord being first served". An important precondition, recognizing as it does that Church laws may not represent her Lord. She claimed direct access to Our Lord. As G.B. Shaw correctly said: Joan's "notion of a Catholic Church was one in which the Pope was Pope Joan."[29] She was, in effect, establishing her conscience as superior to the pope's authority. She would consider what church authorities ordered or taught but assess it before the supreme court of her own conscience. And very boldly, when the Inquisitor asked her what sort of light she was claiming, she said to him: "not all the light comes to you alone."[30] Spoken like a good Baptist. She also told the bishop, the man who had the power to put her to death, "you take too much upon yourself."[31] And when asked one time whether she would indeed ultimately obey the Church, she asked this critical ecclesiological question: "What is the Church?"

That is a radical theological question. She was accused of lifting herself above all ecclesiastical power. And that is true as charged. "She said it was for God, without an intermediary, to judge her...."[32] Even her military colleagues did not stir themselves to rescue her when she was captured; they too resented her idolatry. She was accused of never consulting with a male expert on her visions, as Teresa of Avila and other female visionaries did. She said she would even disobey the pope if he opposed her private visions. Joan repeatedly said, before Luther could, "here I stand." She was not only a Protestant but a splendid one.

Now to some further theological analysis of Joan's protest against hierarchical idolatry and its excessive certitude. Joan represented an assault on the kind of total confidence of the Abrahamic religions, Judaism, Christianity, and Islam. These are the most intolerant of world religions. They are imbued with the confidence that they can capture the mystery of the sacred in structures and in doctrines. *Si quis aliter dixerit, anathema sit*: if anyone even *says* anything contrary to what we have said, let them be accursed. After all, Paul said in Galatians 1:8: if anyone tells us anything other than what he has said, even if it be an angel from heaven, let that angel be cast out. Not even messengers from heaven can shake Abrahamic confidence. Joan was threatening a system of excessive confidence in the face of life's undefeatable mysteries. In this, she was even more Protestant than the Protestants.

When you look at other religions, at Hinduism for example, you find a profound sense of divinity and sacrality in their theology. But they are not at all threatened by other experiences of the sacred. It was very frustrating to Christian missionaries who presented Jesus to the Hindus saying that Jesus is God. The Hindus replied: "we're not surprised; we have incarnations of divinity going on all the time here." They would welcome Jesus as one more God, but that would not satisfy their Christian visitors. Catholics called such an attitude "religious indifferentism" in the old days and it was totally repudiated. Joan intuited that religious structures and dogmas, whatever faith you have in them, are not adequate to the mystery of the sacred. When we have formulated our best Credo in any faith, we remain stumbling servants. The reductionist rationalism of the Abrahamic religions rejects epistemological humility.

Joan felt that everyone had access to the truth. With the Christian scriptures, she believed that the Spirit could breathe wherever it wished—without going through hierarchical channels. The spirit-filled person, as Paul wrote, need be taught by no one. That's almost a description of Joan's life—she felt she was spirit-filled.

Secondly, Joan was challenging the five modes of male authority that existed in her day: *church* authority, *parental* authority, *civil* authority, *intellectual* and *military* authority. All of her judges were male; she attacked them all. Obviously, she threatened the Church and its hierarchical conception of Christianity. That is why they took her so seriously. It is interesting to observe that they did afford her, in their crude fashion, a form of due process. There was some procedural effort at fairness. It did not matter since the conclusion was foregone, given the threat this teenager posed, but they did bring in a tremendous number of people and consultants from all areas of expertise. A lot of work and money went into these trials and documentation was piled high. They had to convince themselves that they were on solid theological ground.

The intellectuals were also threatened by this teenage illiterate. Joan was a threat to all the regnant pretensions. The University of Paris called for her prosecution.[33] Civil and canon lawyers rose against her, and the temporal arm imprisoned her. She resisted her father, who was totally opposed to what she was up to. And finally, she even threatened military authority, trivializing it in a certain sense by saying she could move in and change it.

In all of this, I would say Joan was basically a good Thomist. Thomas Aquinas in his *Summa theologiae Prima Secundae*, Question 106, has a principle which I have referred to as "the Protestant principle plus one." The Protestant principle is that you cannot give ecclesiastical officers ultimate say on matters of faith because the scriptures may give you better advice. Thomas goes further. The prime law for Christians, says Thomas, is the illumining spirit of God entering into the hearts of the faithful. All other law, even the words of scripture themselves—and here is where he goes beyond much of Protestantism—is secondary and to be tested by one's exposure to the illumining Spirit of God. The primary contact with truth is the spirit of God which is poured into the hearts of the faithful. And everything else he says—written in scripture, spoken by patriarchs in the Church and by theologians—everything else is *lex secondaria*, secondary law, to be tested by the primary experience of the truth. In different language, that was Joan's theology at the trial. You can test church edicts; they are not the last word.

In many ways I also see Joan as a kind of Adupa. In Colin Turnbull's book, *The Mountain People*, he writes of the tragic Ik people.[34] They were driven from the land where they had been happy hunters, confined in an arid little space, and told to be farmers, though farming was impossible. They began to starve to death and were transmuted into a horrible kind of people. They were filled with hatred. They cheated one another and would kill one another just for a little bit of food. Everything about them was mean-spirited. They dumped their children out at age three and sent them out to scavenge for themselves. In the midst of this social horror there was a little girl named Adupa. She simply did not buy the *mores* of the group. When she was dismissed at three and sent out on her own, she would not accept the rejection. When she found food, she brought it back to her parents and shared it with them. And she was a total embarrassment to her parents. Eventually she came back to the hut, terribly weak, begging for some help; the parents were so embarrassed, they closed her in the hut, went away for two weeks, and came back later to shovel up her remains. Their embarrassment was ended.

Joan, like Adupa, was a miracle of grace appearing in a hostile land. Joan entered that authoritarian, male-dominated Church and society and witnessed to a higher truth. Like Adupa, she died a martyr to that truth. I am unlettered, she was saying to them, but I can see a gentler truth. "Can you not see?" she asked them almost desperately.

I also see Joan as Mary of the Mary and Martha story in Luke 10. Martha was working and fulfilling the assigned female role of service. Mary instead joined the men in studying scripture and looking for the meaning of life. Some exegetes see in this a kind of a Yentl story. Mary was claiming she had the right, in effect, to do theology and think and express herself about the sacred. And about life's great challenges. And remarkably, Jesus, the feminist rabbi, came down on Mary's side. Mary, he said, has chosen the better part and it will not be taken from her.

Joan was a Mary. There still is today a prodigious amount of pressure on women; their lives are male dominated, even male-defined. Men tell women how to dress, how to live, and what to aspire to. Martha bought the men-defined role; Mary did not. Neither did Joan.

I end my words with a vision. Joan would not mind. In that vision I see Joan, in pants and a jacket, standing defiantly, with strength and grace, before the claims of patriarchy. And I hear a voice. Again Joan would not mind. It is the voice of Jesus, once again standing with a woman against the patriarchy and saying to us all: "Joan has chosen the better part and the glory of that shall never be taken from her."

Notes

[1] Walter Brueggemann, *David's Truth* (Minneapolis: Fortress Press, 1985), 13-14.

[2] Daniel C. Maguire, *The Moral Core of Judaism and Christianity* (Minneapolis: Fortress Press, 1993), 99.

[3] Bonnie Wheeler and Charles T. Wood, *Fresh Verdicts on Joan of Arc* (New York: Garland Publishing, Inc., 1996), 205.

[4] Alban Butler, *Lives of the Saints*, ed. and rev. by Herbert Thurston and Donald Attwater (New York: Kennedy, 1956), 430.

[5] Bernard Shaw, *The Complete Prefaces*: Vol. 2: 1914-1929, ed. Dan H. Laurence and Daniel J. Leary (London: Allen Lane: The Penguin Press, 1995), 531.

[6] Shaw, 504.

[7] Wheeler and Wood, 212.

[8] W. P. Barrett, *The Trial of Jeanne d'Arc* (London: Routledge and Sons, 1931), 230.

[9] Barrett, 239, 254.

[10] Wheeler and Wood, 114.

[11] See Susan Schibanoff, "True Lies: Transvestism and Idolatry in the Trial of Joan of Arc," in Wheeler and Wood, 31-60.

[12] Barrett, 33.

[13] Bernard Shaw, 500.

[14] Susan Schibanoff, 53.

[15] Wheeler and Wood, 210, 218.

[16] Shaw, 505.

[17] Wheeler and Wood, 54, 218.

[18] Barrett, 230.

[19] See Rosemary Radford Ruether, *Sexism and God-Talk* (Boston: Beacon Press, 1983), 82, 170-72.

[20] Barrett, 211.

[21] Barrett, 220.

[22] Barrett, 219.

[23] Barrett, 257.

[24] For Joan's impatience with her interrogators, see Barrett, 221.

[25] Thomas Aquinas, *Summa theologiae* II II, q. 158, a. 8, c. The citation is from John Chrysostom, Super Mt. 1c, n. 7.

[26] *Fortune*, Vol. 134, No. 3, August 5, 1996.

[27] Barrett, 220.

[28] Shaw, 524.

[29] Shaw, 70.

[30] Shaw, 14.

[31] Shaw, 217.

[32] Shaw, 30-31.

[33] (New York: Simon & Schuster, 1972), 261-62.

Right or Left, Who Owns Joan of Arc?

Brigitte Coste

Halbout, Vaucouleurs

When I was a teenager, I had a haircut that made me look like Joan of Arc —a short bob, as I have now, but with bangs. I remember a construction worker yelling at me one day, "hey, Joan, when are you burning?" I have not forgotten that; forty years later I still remember "when are you burning" and the feeling I had, proud to share a sense of destiny with Joan of Arc. As they haven't burned me yet, I am here to talk with you about Joan and who it is that "owns" her.

I would like to tell you another small anecdote which may help explain my special attachment to Joan of Arc. There is a statue of her on the place St. Augustin which is just in front of my former parish church and I get to see that statue periodically when I go back to France. I have memories of singing there in full regalia on the feast of Joan of Arc. We're talking about pre-Vatican II—stiffly starched and perfectly ironed organdy, veils of ornate lace, the boys in their white suits; this was our First Communion garb. All the children of the parish would gather in the church and line up in perfect rows with our baskets of flowers. Then we would process solemnly around the statue and sing a hymn: "Saint Joan…save, save France in the name of the Sacred Heart." I haven't pursued the theological implications of the

---

Dr. Coste teaches French at Marquette University.

connection between Joan of Arc and devotion to the Sacred Heart, but the historical and political ones are quite clear. But let me come back to that.

Joan of Arc appears in French thought and literature before the nineteenth century, of course, but it is at the end of that century that she emerges as a cult figure,
so to speak, and this is related to the rise of nationalism in Europe and particularly
in France. As you know, nationalism (with the help of the Romantic movement)
glorified the idea of unity among peoples of common heritage, culture, and, more
pragmatically, lands. On the good side, this meant the rights of the individual, won
by revolution, extended to sovereign states. On the other hand, this meant a long-
ing for ancient glory—and real estate—and so to wars of expansion. During the
nineteenth century then, you have the growth of parallel nationalist sentiments,
especially for our purposes in France and Germany.

By 1870, both France and Germany had galvanized for war. The tensions were
apparently over the question of the Spanish succession, but really both countries
wanted to go to war for the glory of their respective lands and in order to regain
some terrotories they considered hereditarily theirs. What happened was a great
shock to the French. Their forces were routed, Napoleon III captured, and, worst
of all, Paris was besieged. In January of 1871, faced with starvation, Paris had no
choice but to surrender. France had to pay a large indemnity and—this is very
significant, this terrible blow to French pride—France had to cede the eastern border provinces of Alsace and Lorraine to Germany. While Joan of Arc was not yet a
saint, not even beatified, she was a military heroine who came from Lorraine and
that is very important here.

Then in the spring of 1871, more problems arose for France—this time domestic
ones. Many Parisians (they called themselves the Paris Commune) rose up against
the armistice with Germany. Their movement, a patriotic refusal to accept defeat,
was fueled by bitterness—against Napoleon III, against the provisional government which had signed the armistice, and by anger about the loss of French soil. So
the provisional government outside of Paris attacked them. The Communards re-
volted and, in the brutal conflict that followed, much French blood was shed and
large sections of Paris were destroyed. The Communards were defeated, 20,000 of
them executed without a trial.

France was demoralized. They had lost to Germany, and to one another in a
dreadful civil war. You can understand then, when it was proposed that France
build a great basilica to the Sacred Heart—to the wounded heart of Jesus—in
expiation for all the war dead and as an attempt to restore the dignity of France,
that there was a great cry of "Yes!" Remember Sacré Coeur, that big Byzantine

church that you like or don't like which really dominates Paris? Well, that's how it began; it was in 1873. Now, at the same time, another monument was begun in an atelier in another part of Paris. Smaller, but no less popular as it turned out, this statue was erected in the Place des Pyramides in 1874. It was of Joan of Arc—in armor, astride a proud stallion, her victorious banner unfurled to a new political wind.

The Franco Prussian war, the Commune, and the rancor of defeat brought Joan, "the good Lorrainer," to the fore and linked her to the Sacred Heart—both as saviors of France. And that's actually where it started, the modern sense of ownership of Joan of Arc, by all of France and, as we will see, by any group—left or right, secular or religious—that chose to appropriate her image to fit their cause.

In 1884, ten years after that statue was erected, Joseph Fabre, a senator from the conservative camp, proposed a national feast day in honor of Joan of Arc. His plan, which had the support of many liberals as well, explicitly foresaw the uniting of "both believers and liberal thinkers" in common respect for Joan. His phrase gives a hint of what was to come—its opposite, rather. Fabre's idea did not in fact become law for another ten years. In the barrage of words that followed the proposal, the conservatives insisted more and more on Joan's stance as an anti-revolutionary (Joan of Arc an anti-revolutionary?) and a xenophobe. The Catholics added that the new feast day would be a good opportunity to get rid of the "feast of the assassins" (in other words, Bastille Day). Provocative words, less than a hundred years after the Revolution! The liberals were divided in their response. While the moderates pointed out that Joan was a daughter of the people and that's all that counted, the radicals retorted that it was the Church that had betrayed Joan in the first place; they warned that the Joan of the ultra right would lead France to Mass, rather than to liberty. There was a manifestation by hundreds of students (students are always the most liberal, of course); they carried a crown of flowers which said, "To Joan of Arc: abandoned by the royalty, by the priests, a victim of the clergy," which they placed at the foot of the statue of Joan on the Place des Pyramides—now popularly known as the Place Jeanne d'Arc. It was not until 1894—ten years later—that May 8th became a national feast day dedicated to Joan of Arc.

It was also in 1894 that the famous Dreyfus affair exploded in France. Alfred Dreyfus, an Alsatian Jewish officer in the French army, was accused of espionage. The question engaged and divided public feeling: the right, ardent enemies of Dreyfus, were defending, they said, the honor of France. On the left, the liberals stood for the rights of man. Really, the issues of nationalism, both healthy and not, came to the surface again. Ultimately, there was a retrial and Dreyfus was cleared in

1906. The radicals, however, the "winners" of the argument if you will, launched a virulent attack on the conservatives and the Church and forced the separation of church and state. France, for so long a religious state, was officially secularized; taxes no longer supported parishes and their schools. Then the battles began between the public education system, which was set up at the time as a free secular and mandatory type of education and the Catholic school system, which was still very, very important. Because Catholic schools were no longer supported by the state, they had to charge tuition; the public schools were, as I said, free. So many Catholic students had no choice but to attend public school. Well, a league was formed to protect the rights of the parochial schools and Catholic school children, and this league had eight thousand little pins made with the image of Joan of Arc on them; these were given as rewards to the young pupils who agreed to defend religion and Catholic values in the secular schools.

There is a more sinister—I don't mean leftist—association of Joan of Arc with the Dreyfus incident. A pivotal aspect of the case was the fact that Dreyfus was Jewish. As the battle of ideals raged in the twelve years between accusation and acquittal, a man named Drumont decided to invoke Joan of Arc to serve the cause of anti-semitism. He pointed out that Joan, a country girl, was pure French, simple and healthy; on the contrary, the Jews were foreigners, city merchants, and given to the maladies generated by bad blood. Also, whereas Joan was a virgin, all of the women of the Old Testament (Jewish) had known men, and it was "common knowledge" that Jewish men were the principal customers of prostitutes in the big cities. As their ultimate argument, the anti-semites—dragging Joan to their side—pointed out that, after all, Cauchon (the French bishop who had condemned Joan) "was nothing more than a Jew."[1]

By the time of the First World War, two decades later, Joan had been formally beatified by the Church—it was in 1909—and her image inspired a unified France in the face of World War I. My mother tells me that French school children at that time learned to recite this phrase: "All the French must love with their whole heart the admirable Joan, who died for her king, for France, for us." In fact, I saw a poster which says "women of America, save your country, buy war savings bonds." And guess what woman is depicted on the poster? It's Joan of Arc! So Joan was also an international figure.

Joan was canonized in 1920. Part of the canonization process—ratified by the French parliament—was to make Joan officially the patron saint of France (the second one, rather; France has one patron saint which is Mary, the mother of Jesus, but the other one is Joan of Arc). As a saint and France's patron, Joan's stature as an icon gained in value. And when, during World War II, there were two French governments, Joan was again split in half to serve opposing causes. De Gaulle in London celebrated Joan of Arc. She was a great resistante. But on the other side of the Channel, Pétain (we are talking about the Pétain of occupied France) was celebrating the fact that Joan had fought the English and won! De Gaulle, naturally, being in London, did not stress this. Even the Germans claimed Joan during the war, at least as a propaganda device. Another poster shows Joan at the stake; she is rising out of the flames of the burning city of Rouen, which had been bombed by the English during World War II and was also the site of Joan's burning by the English in 1431. The poster says: "Assassins always return to the scene of their crime!"

Now here is a final story, one that brings us up to the present time. On May 8, 1987, Jean-Marie Le Pen, head of the Front National, which is an ultra rightist political party in France, decided to make a statement at the Place des Pyramides—the Place Jean d'Arc. (I have to be honest with you, I will try to be as objective as I can and should be talking about LePen, but I have a hard time.) Anyway, he had a high platform built right next to Joan; it was the same height as the statue so that he could speak to her—eye to eye as it were—and name her as the inspiration of his movement. What is the association? Why did LePen latch on to Joan of Arc? Well, Joan had said once that while she loved the English, she loved them "chez eux"—in England. She had a mission; she engaged in a holy war against a foreign enemy. The slogan LePen uses is "France for the French;" he has a mission also, a holy war against those foreign immigrants, all three million of them (it is a number he is likely to refer to over and over again), who are polluting the purity of French society, not to mention taking over too many jobs. His ultra nationalist party has found their heroine in one who fought a foreign enemy in the name of France. Le Pen is very much in the news these days because he has now garnered about fifteen percent of the vote of the French people, which is a very large figure considering his extreme views.

Now if we mention the importance of Joan of Arc in the public mind, maybe we should remember that Orléans has been celebrating for 567 years Joan's having liberated the city from the English (May 8, 1429). There is a tradition that after a new French president is inaugurated, he is invited specially to the celebration. Mitterrand came and, of course, mentioned Joan of Arc as a heroine of the French resistance. Chirac, in May of 1995, was very careful to emphasize the fact that Joan of Arc was exactly the opposite of the image that *some* people (he did not mention Jean-Marie le Pen) wanted to make of her: that she did not promote exclusion and intolerance. Again he reaffirmed the symbolic value of Joan of Arc as a heroine for *all* the French.

His speech was well received as an important counterpoint to the speech that Jean-Marie Le Pen did on the same occasion.

Who owns Joan of Arc, then? Everyone. Anyone with a cause. You might say that the reason so many disparate ideologies can find a model in her is because they see her only superficially. Perhaps. But she has qualities that are at the same time profoundly universal and truly polar: she is both simple and wise, vulnerable and courageous, human and saintly, humble and arrogant, womanly and manly, worldly and contemplative. She *can* be a heroine for all the French and all the world. So it is to her credit that Joan of Arc belongs to us all.

Notes

[1] Michael Winock, "Jeanne d'Arc et les juifs," in *Edouard Drumont et compagnie. Antisemitisme et fascisme en France* (Paris: Le Seuil, 1982), 67-79.

Institutions and Individuals: Joan of Arc in the Balance

Joseph Perry

Legendre-Héral, Domremy

Institutions, religious or secular, shelter the best aspirations of a community; they are the mainstay of civic and spiritual values, the guardians of convention and orthodoxy for the sake of order and the reaching of common goals. If the institution is to survive, boundaries of thought, opinion, and behavior are not only reasonable but essential and must be maintained. Of their nature, then, institutions take on the cloak of conservatism; they are the preservers of the status quo.

Any institution, religious or secular, that stands for long is bound to experience questioning of its abiding beliefs, both from within and without. There are those who reach for the frontiers of thought and action, who test the vitality of groups; they may be named seers or dissenters, depending on one's institutional politics. We might even say that the guarantee of an institution's viability lies as much in its ability to progress as in its maintenance of the status quo. Communities and their institutions need saving as surely as do individuals—from their inherent subjectivity, from their tendency to become rigid or trivial.

Fr. Perry, a canon lawyer, is Auxiliary Bishop for the Archdiocese of Chicago.

When challenged, the institution's valid representatives are compelled to act in response to violations of its tenets. Typically, dissenters are perceived as offenders against public order and their behavior as outright violation of the law. But given that these seers or dissenters often bear a kernel of truth which only time authenticates, institutions stand to be embarrassed by actions taken to squelch disagreement. To give some examples: Governor George Wallace's mid-fifties championing of segregation in Alabama schools; the Kent State "massacre" or any of the related, legitimate protests against governmental and military policy; the Church's condemnation of Galileo Galilei; its twentieth century crushing of theologians who travel the boundaries of orthodoxy; and on and on.

The challenge to resolve conflicts arising from breaches of institutional order, common both to church and state, is a nervous task that is subject to judgment by subsequent generations; momentous cases throughout history carry reverberations far beyond the historical moment.

The Catholic Church had the distinction, unique in human history, of having already existed as an institution for fourteen centuries by the time of Joan of Arc's trial. In 1231, faced with an epidemic of challenges to its ecclesiastical hegemony—the Cathars, the Waldensians, the Beguines and Beghards, John Wyclif and Jan Hus and their followers to name only some—the Church had established the Inquisition to quash them. The term "heretic" and its synonyms had long been generously applied to label anyone the Church could not, for whatever reason, tolerate. And by the time of Joan's trial, in 1431, the Inquisition had become quick, if not wise, to name dissenters "heretics" and hound them into schism.

The church did have a case against Joan, however; at least they had good reason to investigate her. From the beginning of her campaign, she had sidestepped the Church; she revealed her mission to the governor of Vaucouleurs and the king at Chinon rather than to her bishop or parish priest. She named her voices in the persons of Saints Michael, Margaret, and Catherine and claimed that they brought her messages from God. She insisted on the reality of their presence (she said they smelled good, for example), thus challenging the church's belief that true spiritual messengers could never be concretely sensed. If her voices were not heavenly, then they were from hell, which made Joan a servant of the devil. Moreover, Joan dressed as a man, which, according to her judges, was "...contrary to divine law, abominable to God, condemned and prohibited by every law..."[1]

A final thorn in the side of Bishop Pierre Cauchon's court (it was he who presided over Joan's trial): why had God sided with the French? Joan insisted that her voices spoke French and that God wanted to her to "boot" the English back across the channel. Her judges, although French born, belonged to a powerful political group, the Burgundians, which had sided with the English. We know from history, as well as from Shakespeare's *Henry V*, that the English king, pitifully outnumbered at the pivotal battle of Agincourt, prayed for divine assistance and got it: he beat the French—after which he sang a stirring *Te Deum* right on the battlefield. If only a few years before, God had been on the side of the English, why had He switched allegiances, as Joan implied?

If the Church had points to make, Joan had answers. She had already been thoroughly examined by priests and theologians at Poitiers in the spring of 1429; they declared her an intact virgin and worthy of the dauphin's trust. She had also twice passed the "litmus test" for witches. At Vaucouleurs and at Reims she had been sprinkled with holy water under the assumption that, were she a witch, she would fly. She did not. Joan reasonably defended her wearing of military dress, which she had donned for the sake of her mission and to hide her gender from the soldiers. The intelligence of Joan's answers failed only under the calculated trickery of her questioners, who took advantage of her lack of education and theological sophistication. Nevertheless, her insights were everywhere exceptional.

Joan was also different from typical heretics in this way: it was only by default that she had become a gadfly to the Church. She loved the Church; she said it over and over. Her purpose was not, at least not obviously, to reform the Church; her mission was to save France. But if in the process, the Church expected her to belie her voices, she drew the line there—rightfully challenging an institution that bade her go against her conscience.

Joan was ahead of her time; she was "too much" for fifteenth century Europe. This extraordinary girl, a king-maker whose military genius had made her the wonder of Europe, had come from the people. She was a woman-soldier, a woman-patriot, a cannily wise woman. She seems to belong to a later era, perhaps closer to our own. But she was dropped into medieval France, a Savior-type that every epoch seems to need to sort out the misdeeds of folk, although usually at great personal cost.

The Church, seeking to protect itself from a heretic, and Joan, trusting that she would be protected by the Church, entered into the juridical process.

She was tried by an extraordinary confrerie of experts. Most of her judges were graduates and members of the faculty of the University of Paris which, at that time, governed the Church through a kind of overseership of the General Council. Joan stood in a pit, observed by these men (more than fifty in number) who were trained in all the complexities of legal questioning and sophistry—all of them well versed in academic hair-splitting.

At the beginning, Joan fielded their questions with a skill based on the strength of truth. Gradually, she grew weary (having to fight off the advances of English soldiers at night) and confused. Joan's right to appeal to higher Church authority was denied; her appeal for a more balanced roster of inquisitors was denied. Essentially, all of her procedural rights were denied. The outline of prejudgement began to show through the thinning legal veneer. Was Joan a heretic, a true enemy of the institutional Church? We believe she was not; many guessed that she was not even then. Was she a dissenter who had "a kernel of truth" to offer the institutional Church? We say yes to that; her judges would not have admitted it. We have come to learn, then, that Joan did not truly threaten the ecclesiastical institution which had called her to task; the charges against her were rather motivated by the concerns of a foreign state.

Most of her judges were avowedly her enemies. Joan's victories for Charles VII had driven many of them, including Bishop Cauchon, away from their seats of authority and revenue. Many, including Bishop Cauchon, served the king of England or his regent, the Duke of Bedford, as ambassadors or councillors. Nearly all of them were, at one time or another, on the English payroll, directly or indirectly (through ecclesiastical appointments that were in the hands of the English king). The political taint of her trial was never clearer than in the days preceding her death. Joan had been pressured to concede her guilt. Ignorant of the content of the "confession" she was given to sign (she could not read), Joan signed it. But in the days that followed, she understood Cauchon's betrayal, and she recanted the confession. This was, in fact, what the English wanted: the Church's punishment for a relapsed heretic—one who had confessed and then recanted—was death.

As the Church was not permitted to take life, they handed Joan over to the conveniently attendant English to burn. Such close church-state collaboration, which was common in fifteenth century France, is seen in these modern times at variance with the theological and pastoral aims of the Church and, therefore, is a thing of the past. Yet, even by the standards of the medieval Church, Cauchon and his fellow judges mishandled episcopal, canonical, and civil power in this trial. That men of this stature and learning would have squeezed out of Joan's evidence an assessment of witch, heretic, blasphemer, apostate and "...many other dangerous dogmatizations most prejudicial and scandalous to our holy faith"[2] is remarkable; it says much about the caliber of her accusers. The Maid of Orleans ranks among those most famous victims of miscarriage of justice: Jesus, Socrates, and Thomas More.

This is my main point then: while the Church was within their institutional rights to try Joan, the charges and penalties needed to be—*de facto* as well as *de jure*—within their jurisdiction. If I burn my flag, the county auditor won't arrest me; neither will my bishop give me a ticket for speeding. And if the Church charges me as a heretic, they must not condemn me as a traitor.

One last thought: To understand the mission of the Maid of Orléans, one has to admit the existence of the spiritual world and to accept its potential goodness. Indeed, as Lucien Fabre points out, any other explanation of her mission "...runs head on into insurmountable difficulties which only the assumption of a divine origin can successfully resolve."[3] Although fifteenth century Europeans did not have sophisticated categories to deal with visions, dreams, ecstasies, and inspirations, they accepted the reality of the spiritual. They were open to the mystical, even if they were disturbed by the prospect of encountering bad spirits: fairies or goblins or the witches that called them forth. Joan's sentence—despite the political motivation of her trial and condemnation—was cast in the terminology of the spiritual.

Now it was the business of the Church to recognize and honor authentic (good) spirituality and to ferret out the bad and the false. Had Cauchon been more objective, less driven by personal concerns, we assume he would have seen the truth and quality of Joan's spirituality. But it served him, and the English, to prove that she had trafficked with dark spirits and tried to pass them off as ministers of light. Cauchon could not condemn her for simply warring against his friends and winning. He had to titillate the culture's greatest fear, that of evil spirits, to prove that the English reversals were the result of witchcraft, of Joan's conjuring of the dark prince.

To an age like ours, of heightened consciousness with respect to civil and ecclesiastical rights, the "case" of Joan of Arc is an affront to all that is humane and forthright. A witch, indeed! But how sophisticated really is the twentieth century approach to spiritual phenomena? We are rational and sensible; we have the behavioral sciences to teach us about voices and prophecies; we "know" they are not the work of the devil, but merely of diseased minds. But whether they are pathological or diabolical, isn't the larger issue this: that our out-of-hand dismissal of the spiritual is just as skewed or even violent as "crying witch" was in the Middle Ages? We treat prophets and visionaries, especially dissenters who are motivated by dreams, with suspicion. They upset the status-quo and make a disturbing penetration into the strongholds of rational power. At best, we give them a hard time; at worst, we murder them.

God frequently has something to say to us that we don't want to hear, so we throw up a shield of legal interpretation to keep us from listening. When the crumbs of our behavior will have been picked over by the historians of the future, how will we be judged?

Notes

[1] *The Trial of Jeanne d'Arc*, trans. W.P. Barrett (New York: Gotham House, 1932), 16.
[2] *Barrett*, 38.
[3] Lucien Fabre, *Joan of Arc*, trans. Gerard M. Hopkins (New York: McGraw-Hill, 1954), 45.

Charles de Gaulle and Joan of Arc: A Comparison of Person and Praxis

Phillip C. Naylor

Leroux, Compiègne

Charles de Gaulle began his *War Memoirs* with the reflection that he had "conceived a certain idea of France." What was this "certain idea?" As events proved, it was a notion that France had an essence of political, cultural, and moral greatness, a cherished independence, enabling it to fulfill a global destiny. His perspective was essentialist, that of an eternal, gifted France, blessed with a cultural élan that was universal, a France whose mission was to extend itself to liberate others. If Joan of Arc had a "certain idea" of France, it would have been similar. The Maid's mission was divine and patriotic and, arguably from our secular perspective, even nationalist. She incarnated France as de Gaulle would. Indeed, they were both deeply engaged in redeeming and refashioning France.

Joan's historical emergence was much more improbable than de Gaulle's who had groomed or, less charitably, invented himself or promoted his historic role. A close reading of his *The Edge of the Sword*,[1] a compilation of his lectures at the *Ecole militaire* (published in 1932), serves as a matrix for his political life and pursuits.

Like Joan he lived in an age of "uncertainty" (7) a period where he recognized "a decline in the moral standards, both in society and in politics" (55). He called for

Dr. Naylor teaches History at Marquette University.

leaders characterized by "prestige," a quality which he defined as "largely a matter of feeling, suggestion, and impression [depending] primarily on the possession of an elementary gift, a natural aptitude which defies analysis" (57). He claimed that "there can be no prestige without mystery, for familiarity breeds contempt" (58). He added that a leader "must accept the loneliness which, according to Faguet, is the 'wretchedness of superior beings'" (66). He turned to politics and asserted that "the statesman...must concentrate all his efforts on captivating men's minds" (104).

Joan lived these leadership qualities that de Gaulle admired. Like de Gaulle, she wanted French social, moral, and political renewal. Her emergence as a leader and political presence, her voices, her dynamism "defy analysis." There is a mystery to Joan with correlative prestige and also the existential "loneliness" of Rouen. Above all, she continues to "captivate" our minds; she enthralled de Gaulle's.

The relationship between Charles de Gaulle and Joan of Arc began in his childhood. Charles was taught that his family was intricately involved with the Joan of Arc saga. According to family tradition, Sieur Jehan de Gaulle battled at Agincourt and refused to recognize Henry V's claim as King of France. The de Gaulles believed that he was one of the knights who eventually accompanied Joan to the dauphin at Chinon.[2] Though improbable genealogically, they also claimed descendence from Joan.[3] While the family may have been immersed in myth, the reality was that there was a fervent attachment to Joan and an absorption of the ideal France that she idealized and served so selflessly.

De Gaulle read the works of Charles Péguy, an early twentieth century mystic, who would be an important influence in his thought and word. Péguy devoted sixteen years to study and write about Joan of Arc. He envisioned her (like himself) as a religious nationalist. He once reflected: "Everything begins with mysticism and ends in politics."[4] In Péguy's play, The Mystery of the Charity of Joan of Arc, Joan asserts: "Never would the men of this country, never would the saints of this country, never would even simple Christians of our regions have forsaken [Christ]. Never would French knights...Never would the men of the crusades have forsaken him....Never would the king of France have forsaken him. Never would Charlemagne and Roland..."[5] Péguy has "his Joan" ascribe French political and martial leaders with Christian dedication. This linkage is historically convincing, given her piety and her devotion to the dauphin's coronation at Rheims.

Péguy also idealized the French people as a "chosen people," and this mirrored Joan's sentiments. Consider her statement of 17 March 1431: "And you shall see that the French will very soon achieve a great task which God will send to the French, and such that almost the whole Kingdom of France will tremble. And I say it, so that when it comes to pass it will be remembered that I said it."[6] Here we find a shade of difference with de Gaulle. Certainly, de Gaulle's political and personal engagement with the French was undeniable, but, as Maurice Couve de Murville observed: "De Gaulle was assuredly a man of an intransigent passion and his passion was France."[7] He idealized that illusive "certain idea" of his *mère* rather than its people, who disappointed him despite his patriotic exhortations. The French displayed promise but never lived up to a Gaullist potential. Indeed, perhaps like Joan, de Gaulle felt abandoned occasionally by them, leaving him in his "desert" (a Gaullist metaphor). De Gaulle told André Malraux: "When Frenchmen believe in France, oh, yes, then...! But when they stop believing in her....You remember the Pope's remark: 'The French do not love France.' There you are!"[8] De Gaulle, like Napoleon, and perhaps like Joan, wanted to make something out of the French.[9]

Returning to Péguy as our interpretive mediator between Joan and de Gaulle, the poet "held that a brave man, for the sake of truth, must break with his friends not once but as often as truth demanded it. He must accept solitude. Péguy hated weakness, particularly the insidious weakness which induces men to compromise with their enemies or to surrender their principles."[10] This is why he admired Joan's tenacity and solitary strength. De Gaulle found in Péguy's discourse a reaffirmation of his developing, determined personality and perhaps his life's mission. Péguy, Friedrich Nietzsche, and Henri Bergson emboldened him to take those obstinate positions, such as his insistence after World War I that French military strategies be offensive, characterized by the deployment of armor, rather than entrenched and defensive. De Gaulle enjoyed being different, being an individual, and possibly even being alone.

Péguy perished in World War I. For him combat represented "the ultimate test of honesty and courage."[11] The relationship to Joan is obvious. Joan was wounded twice and repeatedly and recklessly threw herself into battle. De Gaulle fought in World War I and was taken prisoner after a firefight isolated his unit. As the Nazis invaded in 1940, his tanks put up a stiff, if brief resistance. In August, 1962, assassins opposed to his policy of Algerian decolonization riddled his car with bullets. De Gaulle's typically wry response to the assault was a criticism of their marksmanship! While courageously if not fearlessly facing the inherent dangers involved in his leadership roles, this particular incident upset him because the gunmen had endangered the life of Mme de Gaulle. He was chivalrous—to André Malraux, a "knight."[12]

The arrival of the Second World War was the most important event in de Gaulle's life and gave his relationship with Joan a dramatic immediacy. France surrendered to Nazi Germany in June, 1940, a victim of its own political and military immobilism. De Gaulle refused to recognize this act or the formation of the collaborationist French government at Vichy. On 18 June 1940, he introduced himself in a broadcast from England as a recalcitrant, a rebel, and vowed to free France from the Nazis. Joan had said: "I must go to war to restore the Kingdom of France."[13] De Gaulle felt compelled to follow her example.[14] He told Eric Hawkins of the *New York Herald Tribune* in late 1940: "'I am like Joan of Arc.' Adding with his little quarter smile, 'Only *I* have no army.'"[15] He later recalled: "Some people reproached me for determining to take France upon myself: what else could I have done?"[16] When headquartered at the Connaught Hotel in London, his visitors saw portraits of Napoleon and Joan of Arc in his office.[17]

De Gaulle mobilized the Free French movement, earning the begrudging admiration of Prime Minister Winston Churchill, who had to endure the General's haughtily obdurate personality, but who, of course, also possessed one himself. Churchill's support forced President Franklin Delano Roosevelt to take notice. The relationship between FDR and de Gaulle was tenuous and tried. When they met for the first time in Casablanca, and upon the recommendation of Admiral Stark, who was engrossed by the Free French leader, de Gaulle

> expatiated upon the greatness of France, emphasising in particular that the capacity for leadership was so widely diffused among the French people that someone had always been thrown up from the masses to give inspiration in times of misfortune. This had been true since the days of Charlemagne, and he instanced among others Joan of Arc, Napoleon, Poincaré, and Clemenceau. 'Perhaps this time,' he added, 'I am one of those thrust into leadership by circumstances and by the failure of others.'[18]

FDR found this laughable, disclosing the President's surprising political and historical myopia, his unappreciation of the ideas and intangibles that often move history. He repeatedly referred disparagingly to de Gaulle's "Joan of Arc" complex. This was insulting to the unforgiving de Gaulle who also possessed an implacable, elephantine memory! On the other hand, Winston Churchill was more circumspect and sympathetic concerning de Gaulle's identity with Joan. Fallen France needed to be reminded of its heroic "Maid" during the Second World War. He wrote:

> [De Gaulle] defied all. Always, even when he was behaving worst, he seemed to express the personality of France—a great nation, with all its pride, authority and ambition. It was said in mockery that he thought himself the living representative

of Joan of Arc....This did not seem to me as absurd as it looked. Clemenceau, with whom it was said he also compared himself, was a far wiser and more experienced statesman. But they both gave the same impression of being unconquerable Frenchmen.[19]

Consider what Philippe Barrès wrote during this time: "When they took as emblem the cross of Lorraine, the Free French expressed clearly their spirit and their deepest feelings. Ever since the time when Joan of Arc carried it on her banner the cross of Lorraine has been the symbol of what is now once more at stake: French national independence."[20] The double-barred Cross of Lorraine was also flown by de Gaulle's tank regiment.[21] Its superimposition on the "Tricolor," however, was not his idea, but he embraced it (perhaps, too, as an indirect statement to his "Anglo" allies).

De Gaulle is primarily remembered during the war for his patriotism and his profound differences and difficulties with his allies. What was crucially important from our perspective today, and often neglected, was how he also had to contend with Vichy France. Both Vichy and the Free French tried to appropriate Joan in their efforts to project a popular legitimacy. Vichy fostered folklore and propagated an idea of "true France."[22] One poster portrayed Joan as "the heroine of national unity" standing in front of Marshal Pétain and French youth. (Indeed, to this day the French Right has attached itself to Joan.) Jacques de Launay related that de Gaulle's identification with Joan of Arc could by psychoanalyically regarded "as a constant struggle to emulate, equal, and then destroy Pétain's image."[23] The growingly certain success of the Resistance could not overwhelm the reality of a France divided, of the imagined "certain ideas of France." As Charles G. Cogan stated: "It was de Gaulle's self-appointed mission to prove that there was a France."[24] It was an existential matter. Was this so different from what Joan pursued?

De Gaulle did his very best to efface the Vichy memory and to project a liberated France. He constantly reinforced the idea that France had freed itself. He thought of Joan and other great French figures as he paraded triumphantly down the Champs Elysées in August, 1944.[25] This procession (which is photographically documented on the Internet), which ended at Notre Dame for a Te Deum, symbolized the political canonization of de Gaulle. Alden Hatch pointed out: "There is a photograph of him looking upward as he walked among a million friends. Even the camera's dull eye caught the ambience of his eyes. So must Saint Joan have looked as she watched her Dauphin crowned at Rheims."[26] Arthur Layton Funk concluded: "De Gaulle's place in French history, by the side of Joan of Arc, is undeniably secure."[27]

After the Liberation came the challenge of fashioning a new French state. De Gaulle commented to a colleague during the time of his short-lived Provisional Government (1944-46): "Charles VII and Joan of Arc did not have to reconstruct the State starting from nothing. Charles VII retained legitimacy."[28] Hatch related that the momentum of the Resistance was hardly decisive. De Gaulle's "legend and leadership were not enough. The same thing happened in Saint Joan's time."[29] As de Gaulle confronted difficulties in persuading France of the necessity of creating a constitution with a strong executive, he thought of retiring. Indeed, one month after the liberation of Paris, he told Robert Aron: "As for me, I shall retire...It is necessary to disappear. France may again have need of a pure image. I must leave her that image. If Joan of Arc had married, she would no longer be Joan of Arc. It is necessary to disappear.[30] Before his resignation, in January of 1946, he similarly related: "Really, one can scarcely imagine Joan of Arc married, the mother of a family—who knows—with a husband unfaithful to her."[31] De Gaulle claimed an oxymoronic political viginity, purity. He thought he would be recalled to power and fulfill his destiny to realize his "certain idea" of France. He would have to wait.

France found itself divided again as a result of the Algerian War (1954-62). In many respects, it was a recodification of the Vichy v. Free French contention since an image of "true France" was at risk. Algeria had been assimilated as part of the *métropole* since 1848. French colonialism was severe in both tangible and intangible ways, producing physical and psychological depravations in the native population. De Gaulle's Provisional Government had been in power when large-scale violence erupted in May of 1945 in Sétif. The native Muslims were brutally suppressed. At this time, De Gaulle identified the restored empire with a recovering France. The outbreak of the Algerian War in 1954, especially after the Diembienphu disaster in Indochina, profoundly affected the essentialist perspective.

Georges Le Beau, a former Governor-General, underscored the popular notion that "the future of Algeria is also that of France."[32] Officially, the Fourth Republic declared that success in the Algerian War would condition "the destiny of France."[33] This conflict was more than a question of secession from the Republic; it increasingly represented a deepening despair that France was in decline. Jacques Soustelle argued that "to abandon Algeria is to condemn France to decadence."[34] Tony Smith analyzed that, during decolonization, "the major stake the French had in Algeria was...intangible: their sense of national identity."[35] Algeria symbolized, as Hanson Baldwin reflected, a "battle for the French soul."[36]

With the Army and European settlers in open revolt against the inert Fourth French Republic, de Gaulle was called back to power. By this time, he had changed his mind concerning imperial France and had already suggested an ambiguous "association" with Algeria.[37] It took three years for de Gaulle to prepare France and himself for decolonization, followed by about a year of intermittent but intensive negotiations with the Algerian nationalists. The personal and convulsive political adversity was intense for the aging statesman, yet he had his way, impressively overwhelming another military revolt in 1961 in a vain effort to preserve *Algérie française*. De Gaulle's successful responses to these events underscored the effectiveness of an inspired "Joan of Arc complex." Concurrently, he established the Fifth Republic with its strong executive, decolonized Francophone Africa, and soon initiated a remarkable program of cooperation with the revolutionary Algerian government. He declared: "If France's history goes by way of independence for Algeria, let it!...Regretting Algerian independence was not pleasant. But the important thing was to know that we had the responsibility for France."[38] Colonialism was anachronistic. France had to be "wed to new realities." France was delivered once more.

Joan reflected: "St. Michael told me that I must be a good child, and that God would help me....He said that I would have to go into France."[39] She was not instructed to go "to France," but "into France." The semantic difference may be minor, but it illustrates how Joan became one-with-France. She claimed: "The voice has told me that it is God's will to deliver the people of France from the calamity that is upon them."[40] De Gaulle did not claim do have divine direction, yet he did know his "certain" France: "I had a contract with France. Things might have gone well or ill, but she was behind me. She was with me all throughout the Resistance..."[41] He added, concerning his return to power in 1958: "When I spoke at Algiers...everyone understood that this time it was France who was speaking."[42] Joan and Charles de Gaulle did not simply identify themselves with France; they became France.

Joan's politics were impelled by mysticism. What about de Gaulle's religiosity? He discussed this with Malraux: "The Resistance had several motives, even the noblest segments of it. I believe France knows that I was not battling one policy for the sake of Christianity. I was the Resistance *of France* against Germany. It won't be possible for people to forget that I welcomed everyone. If I had not done that, I should simply have been chief of a party in exile."[43] How important were de Gaulle's Christian beliefs? Malraux thought they were vital:

I thought about his own faith, which I had never grasped. The Church was a part of his life, but he said to the Pope, "And now, Holy Father, suppose we speak of France?" He very rarely mentioned God, and not at all in his last will and testament. He never mentioned Christ. I was accustomed to his silence on certain ma-

jor topics, a silence born of an invulnerable sense of decency and of great pride—
if the feeling, "this concerns me alone," can be called pride. He took communion at
Moscow for obvious reasons: he was bearing witness. But he took communion not
only at Moscow. I believe his faith was so deep that it ignored every domain that
would put it in question. That is why my agnosticism did not bother him. (And
because I am neither anti-clerical nor anti-Christian....He was intrigued rather
than annoyed by an agnostic friendly toward Christianity, even one who was also
friendly to Hinduism.) His faith was not a question: it was a given, like France.
But he liked to speak of his France; he did not like to speak of his religion. A God,
supreme judge, who inspired him to pardon the condemned, or helped him divine
the fate of France? That faith covered a secret realm which was probably that of
Christ, and also a questioning—not into faith, but into the forms it takes. He had
been struck when I quoted him the Hindu saying, "Each man moves toward God
through his own gods.[44]

Like Joan, de Gaulle linked his religion to France's destiny, to its place in history.
He said: "France was the soul of Christianity—today, let us say, the soul of European civilization." Jean-Marie Mayeur underscored that "De Gaulle never stopped
emphasizing the importance of Christian values in the history of France." This legacy
was "inseparable from the history of France."[45] Mayeur concluded: "Thus de Gaulle,
a keen reader of Péguy, who in the darkest hours of the Free French exalted the
memory of Joan of Arc, the 'girl from Lorraine,' rejected a narrow conception of
secularism which would deny Christian tradition."[46] Alden Hatch reported that at
the small church in Colombey, near his home, de Gaulle and his wife "chose [to
worship] under the stained glass window consecrated to St. Joan. Like Joan, he was
mystically informed of the role he was to play."[47]

There was something Nietzschean in de Gaulle's and Joan's wills to power. Pierre
Lance considered de Gaulle a "Nietzschean Christian" who managed to reconcile
the contradiction. Or was there one? Wasn't Zarathustra an "intrepid" individual
and "missionary?"[48] Wasn't Zarathustra against mediocrity and the Establishment?
(The statement: "God is dead!" is directed at institutionalized religion rather than
at God. It was a promethean plea against the religious establishment.) Wasn't the
"will to power" a creative force? De Gaulle selectively embraced these values. (This
also relates to Joan and her willful character. Imagine what she had to contend
with—especially a political patriarchy.) One biographer (Emmanuel d'Astier) described that de Gaulle "'was to make of Nietzsche, Charles Maurras, and Machiavelli
a very personal salad.'"[49] Nora Beloff added: "There is obviously a good deal of
Nietzsche in the superman de Gaulle created and became. Yet his orthodox Catholic upbringing and convictions always made it impossible for him to accept the cult

of physical violence and totalitarianism adopted by other Nietzsche disciples."[50] Despite his powerful personality, de Gaulle despised Nietzschean elitism (or its corruption) which he contended in his first book, *Discord among our Enemies*, had contributed to Germany's defeat. He preferred "the perfections of a French garden with its geometric harmonies and 'le sens de l'équilibre, du possible, de la mesure'" ('the sense of balance, of the possible, of moderation.'")[51]

What makes more sense here is the intangible importance of Henri Bergson's *élan vital*, the power of an instinctive, intuitive knowledge that marked de Gaulle's decisiveness. He had intensely read the popular, early twentieth-century philosopher. The *élan vital* can be considered a sense of knowing, an epiphany. This is about as close as we can hear the resonance of Joan's voices (though de Gaulle's unique nature may have included acoustic enhancements!).

Are the images of Joan of Arc and Charles de Gaulle creations of elaborate mythmaking, productions of knowledge? As I commented earlier in this celebration of Joan of Arc, her reputation became fused with romantic nationalism. I acknowledge that Joan's providentialism links her to the medieval age, but I find her mission and her trial particularly identifiable as political and modern. Indeed, her popularity emerges from the modern period; it was produced from it rather than from her contemporary one. It took decades to rehabilitate Joan in her own country. Of course, complex political considerations were part of this enduring process, especially the ramifications of the French monarchy's image. Ironically, it was the French Revolution, with its anti-clericalism and republicanism, which produced a consequential romantic nationalism that regenerated Joan's heroic reputation. This was also the time when the ideal of "Liberty" was personified as a woman. Delacroix's famous "Liberty at the Barricades" is a memorable representation as is the Athena-like "Marianne," sculpted on the Arc de Triomphe, who leads the revolutionary armies. Joan's mission was codified as a nationalist metaphor. Her life received the attention of prominent French literary figures such as Jules Michelet, Alphonse de Lamartine, and then, just after the turn of the century, Anatole France, besides the aforementioned Charles Péguy.

Joan acquired even greater symbolic attention at the time of the Treaty of Frankfurt in 1871, where Alsace and part of Lorraine was severed from the mère patrie. Louis Marin, the influential anthropologist-politician, kept a bust of Joan of Arc on his desk as she had become by that time "the heroine of the new right cultic nationalism that had come out of his native Lorraine at the end of the century."[52] Not surprising, a popular song during World War I was entitled: "Joan of Arc, They are Calling You." Undoubtedly, the Great War hastened Joan's being named saint.

Was de Gaulle a myth a personality, or a product? The General commented to Malraux: "In an historic personality, the legendary creative power—you understand what I mean—takes the place of the soul."[53] My friend and colleague in the English Department, Professor Milton Bates, subtitled his book on Wallace Stevens "a mythology of self." Did de Gaulle invent himself and mystify us? (Malraux was right when he said: "For his friends, and for his enemies, there was something of wizardry in him [and for the tribunal of Rouen, if Joan of Arc was not bound to the saints, how could she be bound to anything but the devil?])"[54] De Gaulle reflected: "People want history to resemble themselves or, at least, to resemble their dreams. Happily, they sometimes have great dreams."[55] I submit that Joan of Arc inspired de Gaulle's dreams, impelled his personal perception of historical realities, and compelled a fervent consciousness of himself and his country. Above all, Charles de Gaulle possessed the audacity to live his dreams and his destiny.

Notes

1   Charles de Gaulle, *The Edge of the Sword*, trans. Gerard Hopkins (New York: Criterion Books, 1960).
2   Aiden Crawley, *De Gaulle* (Indianapolis: Bobbs-Merrill Company, 1969), 14.
3   See *Boston Globe*, 10 December 1967. The publication of Maurice David-Darnac's book on Joan in 1965 irritated if not infuriated de Gaulle.
4   Jacques de Launay, *De Gaulle and His France: A Psychopolitical and Historical Portrait*, trans. Dorothy Albertyn (New York: Julian Press, 1968), viii.
5   Charles Péguy, *The Mystery of the Charity of Joan of Arc*, trans. Julian Green (New York: Pantheon, 1950), 181-82.
6   Willard Trask, comp. and trans. *Joan of Arc: Self Portrait* (New York: Stacpole Sons, 1936), 157.
7   Maurice Couve de Murville, *Une politique étrangère, 1958-1969* (Paris: Plon, 1971), 10.
8   André Malraux, *Felled Oaks: Conversation with De Gaulle*, trans. Irene Clephane, rev. Linda Asher (New York: Holt, Rinehart and Winston, 1971), 17.
9   Malraux, 66.
10   Crawley, 22.
11   Crawley, 22.
12   Malraux, 10.
13   Trask, 41-42.
14   Three decades later, he reflected to Malraux: "Joan of Arc was right at Patay, another eighteenth of June, in the year 1429" (Malraux, 122).
15   Alden Hatch, *The DeGaulle Nobody Knows: An Intimate Biography of Charles de Gaulle* (New York: Hawthorn, 1960), 76.

16 Malraux, 47.

17 Crawley, 145.

18 Crawley, 196; quoting Robert E. Sherwood, Roosevelt and Hopkins, 956; referring also to Milton Viorst, *Hostile Allies: FDR and Charles de Gaulle* (New York: Macmillan, 1965), 144.

19 Quoted by Alexander Werth, "Noble Anachronism," in F. Roy Willis, ed., *De Gaulle: Anachronism, Realist, or Prophet?* (New York: Holt, Rinehart and Winston, 1967), 116.

20 Philippe Barrès, *Charles de Gaulle* (New York: Doubleday, Doran and Company, 1941) 258. There is a historical question as to when the Cross of Lorraine first appeared in history. Nevertheless, it has been popularly associated with Joan.

21 Hatch, 76-77.

22 See Herman Lebovics, *True France: The Wars over Cultural Identity* (Ithaca, New York: Cornell University Press, 1992), 171-83.

23 De Launay, 255.

24 Charles G. Cogan, *Charles de Gaulle: A Brief Biography with Documents* (Boston: Bedford Books of St. Martin's Press, 1996), 5.

25 Charles de Gaulle, *The War Memoirs of Charles de Gaulle: Unity*, trans. Richard Howard (New York: Simon and Schuster, 1959), 352.

26 Hatch, 171.

27 Arthur Funk, "De Gaulle and Roosevelt: A Euripidean Drama," in Willis, 31.

28 Alfred Fabre-Luce, "The Rebel," in Willis, 19.

29 Hatch, 193.

30 Philip Cerney, *The Politics of Grandeur: Ideological Aspects of de Gaulle's Foreign Policy* (Cambridge: Cambridge University Press, 1980), 17; quoting Jacques Fauvet, *La IVe République* (Paris: Fayard, 1959), 64n.

31 Don Cook, *Charles de Gaulle: A Biography* (New York: G.P. Putnam's Sons, 1983), 294.

32 "L'Algérie française," *L'Opinion en 24 heures* (Paris: Centre de Documentation Générale, 1956), 31.

33 Ministère de l'Algérie, *Action du gouvernement en Algérie: Mésures de pacification et réformes* (Algiers: Service de l'Information du Cabinet du Ministère de l'Algérie, October 1957), 18.

34 Jacques Soustelle, *Le Drame algérien et la décadence française: Réponse à Raymond Aron* (Paris: Plon, 1957), 69.

35 Tony Smith, *The French Stake in Algeria, 1945-1962* (Ithaca, New York: Cornell University Press, 1978), 28.

36 *New York Times*, 19 March 1962, 12.

37 See Phillip C. Naylor, "De Gaulle and Algeria: Historiography and the Decisions of Decolonization," in *Proceedings of the Twentieth Meeting of the French Colonial Historical Society* (Cleveland, May 1994), 136-147.

38 Malraux, 123.

39 Trask, 29.

40 Trask, 49.

41 Malraux, 16.

[42] Malraux, 27.

[43] Malraux, 47.

[44] Malraux, 101-102.

[45] Jean-Marie Mayeur, "De Gaulle as Politician and Christian," in *Hugh Gough and John Horne, De Gaulle and Twentieth Century France* (London: Edward Arnold, 1994), 101-102.

[46] Mayeur, 102.

[47] Hatch, 76.

[48] See Pierre Lance, *Charles de Gaulle: ce Chrétien nietzschéen.* (Paris: La Septième Aurore, 1963), 21.

[49] Quoted by Nora Beloff, "Enigma," in Willis, 110.

[50] Beloff.

[51] De Gaulle quoted by Beloff, 110.

[52] Lebovics, 12.

[53] Malraux, 60.

[54] Malraux, 36.

[55] Malraux, 25.

Closing Argument:
A Lawyer's View of the Trial of Joan of Arc

Michael Gillick

d'Epinay, Reims

The task that has been given to me tonight is to present a lawyer's point of view on the trial of Joan of Arc. The specific nature of the task that I have set myself is both pragmatic and personal. It is pragmatic because I take a trial lawyer's point of view and the task of every trial lawyer is fully pragmatic in that his or her job is to win over the trier of fact—whether that be judge or jury—to his client's point of view, that is, to the goals that the client has asked the lawyer to attain. It is personal because, being concrete, there are as many ways to accomplish the client's stated goals as there are lawyers.

So the question I have set myself tonight is this. How would I, Michael Gillick, as attorney for Joan of Arc, go about representing her in her trial before the inquisitorial court? The first question, of course, is whether Joan of Arc would have wanted me to represent her at all. And the answer is yes, she would have. Joan asked for counsel and was offered it—from among any one of those sitting in judgment against her. She may have been unschooled and even illiterate, but she was not stupid; she declined that offer. But we may assume that she would have accepted competent counsel dedicated to her interests. Granted, there is some question as to my com-

Atty Gillick is a partner at Murphy, Gillick, Wicht, and Prachthauser.

petency to defend Joan of Arc, but because I would be rabidly devoted to her interests, let us assume that I qualify.

The next question would be: what would Joan of Arc want me to do? She obviously would want me to have the charges against her thrown out. But on what basis? For instance, would she have wished me to establish that she was insane? That is, would she have allowed me to assert the insanity defense? Absolutely not. Joan of Arc insisted throughout that she *did* hear the voices and that the voices were *real* and that the voices came from *God*. An insanity plea would have been tantamount to a denial of this, and Joan would have never put up with such an assertion.

We are left then to defend either on the basis of the facts or on the basis of the law. Would she have allowed me to dispute the facts? That depends on which ones are at issue. She was charged with devil worship and witchery. Joan would certainly have disputed these facts, but these are the minor charges against her. The real charge, the heart of the case against Joan of Arc, is that she claimed that her voices had priority over the institutional Church. Joan would not have allowed me to assert otherwise. She would insist on these facts: that she heard voices, that they were from God, and that she must follow them even if they contradicted the teachings or orders of the institutional church.

The central issue here is whether or not these voices were indeed from God. If they were, the institutional Church would have no choice but to set her free. If they were not from God, but from the devil, then Joan's insistence on following those voices would have to be condemned; she would have to be found excommunicate. So the task assigned me by Joan of Arc would be to announce that she was sane, that the voices she heard were from God, and that she should therefore be set free.

At this point we address the key practicality in the actual case of Joan of Arc: the trial, most likely, was fixed. Let me explain. It was claimed that Joan had been captured within the diocese of Beauvais, which meant that she had to be tried in the ecclesiastical court of that diocese. The bishop of Beauvais, the infamous Pierre Cauchon (who has been viewed by history as every bit the pig that his name suggests), had in fact manoeuvred to get hold of Joan after her capture. He then sold her to the English for a fine sum and made sure that she would be tried under his jurisdiction. Cauchon, whose history and fortunes were intimately bound to the English cause, was determined to execute Joan of Arc for reasons which were unrelated to the sacred mission of the Church. He had stood with the English in rejecting the French pope at Avignon; he was a sworn witness to the Treaty of Troyes, by which France was effectively handed over to the English crown. And now the English needed Cauchon to find that Joan was an enemy of the Church, to discredit her and therefore to discredit Charles II, whose kingship was largely the result of Joan's efforts. Cauchon knew which side his political and fiscal bread was buttered on. He had already been granted several handsome benefices by the English and he knew, if he delivered a verdict against Joan, that he would be rewarded with the rich bishopric of Rouen. There was more. During Joan's victorious march through northern France, Beauvais had fallen to the French. Cauchon therefore lost one of his richest sources of tithed income. Cauchon yearned for revenge.

When Joan was captured, Cauchon positioned himself to control the proceedings against her. As a loyalist with his hand in the English pocket, as a prelate of the Church in whose face Joan had flown, as a vengeful egocentric, Cauchon wanted her condemned and he wanted her executed. He wanted her completely disgraced and he wanted her dead. Given Cauchon's enormous need to succeed and his patent lack of conscience, he could never have allowed Joan's fate to have been decided by unbiased minds, and so he handpicked some sixty church officials—abbots, prelates, doctors and lawyers of the church—whom he was certain he could manipulate to find in accordance with his wishes.

Realizing this, as a trial lawyer, I am close to despair. My client will not allow me to deny the facts upon which the charges are based, nor will she allow me to assert an insanity defense, which, at least from a layman's point of view, seems to have great merit. And the jury is fixed. It appears that all is lost.

There is, however, one chink in Cauchon's armor. It is the jury itself. Cauchon was "certain" that he could manipulate these men. Yet, with the benefit of hindsight, we know that at least twelve of the jurors found in Joan's favor. Whatever influence Cauchon had over these men, it was not sufficient to guarantee their absolute cooperation. After all, the men of the jury were all churchmen; as such, they no doubt believed Catholic doctrine in one important particular—that a human could, by acting against the will of God, surrender his soul to eternal damnation. Furthermore, these men must have known Cauchon for who he was; after all, he had chosen them for their lack of credulity. They understood that Cauchon had already made up his mind.

There is my defense. These are venal men, willing to participate in a fixed jury, either in hopes of a reward or in fear of a punishment at the hands of Cauchon. I must bring them to see that any sway that Cauchon may have over them is absolutely trivial compared to what Cauchon is asking them to put at risk. I must convince them that they must release Joan, not to serve justice, but to serve their own selfish interests.

The Argument

May it please the court. And may it please you, your excellency, Pierre Cauchon, bishop of Beauvais. And may it also please you, members of the jury—abbots, prelates, doctors and lawyers of the Church. And most of all, may it please God our sovereign lord, in whose name you are asked to sit in judgment here. For this is not a civil tribunal in which you are asked to apply the law of man to the facts presented here. As you all know, this is a canonical court, a court of the Inquisition authorized by a duly appointed representative of the one true Church. And you are not being asked to impose any civil punishment. You are not being asked to send this woman to imprisonment, nor even to her death. No, the burden upon you is infinitely greater than that. The onerous, awful, terrible task that you gentlemen have so courageously agreed to assume is to decide the fate of Joan of Arc's immortal soul.

Whatever the circumstances of your agreeing to take on such a frightful burden, I can only assume that you must hold the bishop of Beauvais in the highest of regard. I am only a humble lawyer and have no knowledge of the character of such high personages as his excellency, the bishop of Beauvais, but I can only conclude from your willingness to sit here at his request that his excellency is of all men the most saintly, the most just, the most honest, and the most devoted to the will of God.

I salute you gentlemen of the Church. I stand in awe of you. For my part, I am a cowardly man and could never in my life claim the courage that you demonstrate here, not to mention the courage of the bishop of Beauvais. I, like any other man, would agree, and have agreed a great many times, to lend some earthly possession or sum of money for friendship's sake, knowing that in so doing I risk the loss of that sum or that possession. But you, gentlemen, put any of my actions to shame; your commitment is one that I could never make even for one so great and true and pure as the bishop of Beauvais. For you have agreed to his request that you sit in eternal judgment of this young woman. You have agreed to determine whether it is the will of God that the soul of this young shepardess should be sent to eternal damnation.

No, I am not so courageous, because I would fear the consequences if my judgment were wrong. I would say, "God help me if I were wrong," but I would fear precisely that God would not help me. I would fear that if I wrongly sent the soul of this little girl to hell that God would have no mercy on me. If I sent the soul of this little girl to hell and I was wrong, God would have no mercy on me and he would surely and irrevocably surrender my soul to the eternal fires. No, I could never take such risk myself, nor could I ever counsel another to assume such a frightful burden.

If I were, for instance, to counsel any of you, I would tell you without hesitation to have nothing to do with passing judgment on this young Christian soul, no matter what assurances you might give me of the good intentions of the bishop of Beauvais. I would say, "take care, take care, take great care. You are in jeopardy of the loss of your eternal souls. You, at the risk of eternal damnation, must be absolutely certain of the unredeemable evil of this young girl and of the absolute purity of the intentions of the bishop of Beauvais. Be wrong about one or the other in the slightest degree, and you have lost your soul forever." "No," I would say, "this is not so obvious a case that you should take such a chance. I see no monster here, but only an unschooled peasant girl who thought she had a message from God." "No," I would say, "if she is the devil, she is cleverly disguised, and far too cleverly for me to risk my eternal salvation. She wronged the English; let the English take her life. But as for her soul, if you have any doubts about her or any doubt about the bishop of Beauvais, then take care, take care, take great care. It is your souls, gentlemen. It is your eternal souls. Take care, take care."

Marquette's Joan of Arc Chapel
Her Spirit in Stone

Curtis Carter

Marie d'Orléans, Bois Chenu

Shortly after the First World War, a young architect and historian, Jacques Couëlle, travelling the byways of southern France, happened upon the village of Chasse in the Rhône valley about twelve miles south of Lyon. There he discovered the remains of a small chapel, built in the fifteenth century "or perhaps earlier"[1] and abandoned since the time of the French Revolution. Over five centuries, the structure had fallen into ruin. But Couëlle recognized that the chapel represented an important discovery—an edifice "absolutely unique in its genre."[2] Convinced that it was worthy of reconstruction, he set about studying the structure, taking precise measurements and making photographs and detailed drawings.

A few years later, the chapel at Chasse attracted the attention of Mrs. Gertrude Hill Gavin, the daughter of James Hill, the American railroad builder. In the early twenties, Mrs. Gavin had purchased a Renaissance chateau once owned by the dukes of Orléans-Longueville and had it transferred from France to her Wheatley Hills estate on Long Island. In 1926, negotiating through Couëlle, she acquired the chapel. She arranged that it be shipped from France and reconstructed at Wheatley Hills under the supervision of the American architect, John Russell Pope, who used

Dr. Carter is director of the Haggerty Museum of Art at Marquette University.

Couëlle's drawings as a guide. Mrs. Gavin's decision was well timed. In a letter to Couëlle, written in the fall of 1927, Mrs. Gavin remarked: "It is very good news to know that all the stones for the chapel have left France. I was so afraid that something would happen, and that the government would prevent their being exported."[3] Shortly after the chapel arrived in New York, a Commission of the Monuments Historiques de France halted the exportation of all such historic artifacts.

Joan of Arc Chapel, Marquette University
Watercolor: Charles James Kaiser

Mrs. Gavin had also purchased an early Gothic altar and the "Joan of Arc Stone," both of which were built into the chapel during its reconstruction. The latter, whose authenticity was endorsed by the Monuments Historiques de France, forms the base of a wall niche in the left side of the sanctuary. According to legend, Joan stood on this stone when she prayed to Our Lady for success in her mission to raise the seige at Orléans. As the story is told, she knelt at the end of her prayer and kissed the stone, which was subsequently believed to be colder than the stones surrounding it.

In 1962, the Gavin estate was purchased by the Marc Rojtman family. Five days before they were to move in, however, a fire destroyed the chateau (excepting the façade, which the Rojtmans donated to the Metropolitan Museum of Art) but did not reach the chapel. In a letter dated May 12, 1964, addressed to Father Edward O'Donnell, S.J., who was then Chancellor of Marquette University, the Rojtmans offered the Chapel to Marquette—notwithstanding the fact that "several [other] institutions ...[had] been most anxious to acquire it for some time." Mr. Rojtman wrote: "I am sure you fully understand that this chapel means far more to me than any donation I have ever made and transcends by far any mere monetary value. Naturally therefore I trust that the choice of location and the use of the chapel will be commensurate with its importance."[4] In accepting the chapel, Marquette chose to place it in the heart of the campus, to serve as a living center of religious faith and not as a museum.

It took nine months to dismantle the chapel; each stone was carefully marked on three sides and coded into an overall plan. The first of a fleet of trucks carrying thirty tons of stone, terra cotta tiles, and stained glass arrived in Milwaukee in November of 1964. Reconstruction began the following summer, closely following the original plan of Couëlle. At Marquette, however, some modifications to the original were made, including a longer nave to accommodate more visitors and in-floor heating to avoid unsightly pipes. Among the treasures arriving at Marquette that spring were the stained glass windows designed for the chapel by Charles J. Connick, who modeled them on the vibrantly colored vitraux of Sainte Chapelle in Paris. The crates also included a twelfth century baptismal font and numerous furnishings for the chapel—additional gifts of the Rojtmans.

True to their promise to erect the chapel as soon as possible, Marquette workers affixed the cross to the chapel spire in the spring of 1966. On May 26 of that year, four days before the 535th anniversary of her death, Marquette dedicated the chapel to Joan of Arc.

In the thirty years since, the chapel has been used for weddings, memorial services, ordinations, first communions, confirmations, and even social protest. On April 23, 1969, fifty students locked themselves in the chapel to boycott the Marquette University ROTC program. Police kicked down the sacristy door and forcibly expelled the students. The following week, dozens of students staged a peaceful rally on the chapel steps. In October of the same year, hundreds more assembled at the chapel to march in support of fourteen Milwaukeeans charged with burning their draft cards.

The subject of this essay, "Her Spirit in Stone," recognizes the historic fact that after five centuries, Joan of Arc is memorialized in a building on the Marquette University campus. But beyond the metaphor, how does the chapel evoke Joan's spirit?

First, linking the terms "spirit" and "stone" extends our understanding of them beyond their ordinary use. In speaking of the material elements of the chapel as being permeated by spirituality—by which I mean the highest qualities of mind or soul—one is speaking of a work of art. The Joan of Arc chapel at Marquette is undeniably a work of art. It is aesthetically pleasing, it has a conceptual focus, and it is able to inspire in visitors a sense of the spiritual. As a chapel, it also has a societal function beyond pleasure or understanding.

According to the philosopher of art, Nelson Goodman, a work of art can both denote—that is, represent someone/something—or it can exemplify—that is, present formal and expressive qualities.[5] The painting by Andrew Wyeth, "Christina's World," represents a woman named Christina; at the same time it exemplifies certain textures, light, and perspective as well as a sense of tenuous hope. While traditionally pictorial works of art such as the Wyeth both denote and exemplify, modern abstract art tends only to exemplify. An abstract painting by Kandinsky, for example, does not denote (nor does it intend to), it simply exemplifies particular qualities of form and color. In the case of architecture, which is essentially an abstract art form with additional functions to perform, the relationship between denotation and exemplification is unique. For example, a 555 foot high obelisk in our nation's capitol is named "The Washington Monument." It is, of course, not a pictorial representation of our first president. However, it evokes an awareness of his place in American history. The qualities it exemplifies—whiteness, strength, height—are thus translated into qualities that we associate with Washington: purity of character, strength of purpose, single-minded devotion.

So it is with the Joan of Arc chapel. When Coëlle found the chapel in France, it was named St. Martin de Seysseul. The story of this particular St. Martin was unknown to the villagers and the modifying "de Seyssuel" had been a matter of political contention for many years as locals unsuccessfully fought to call the chapel "St. Martin de Chasse." When Mrs. Gavin installed the "Joan of Arc Stone" in the building, she began informally to refer to the edifice as the "Saint Joan chapel." Reconstructed at Marquette University, it was officially dedicated to the saint as the corner stone indicates. The rough hewn character of the chapel brings to mind the simple, steadfast, peasant saint of Lorraine.

Aura is a term used by the aesthetician, Walter Benjamin, to refer to the uniqueness and the authenticity of an original work of art, as well as to our experience of those qualities. Aura here helps explain the symbolic power of the Joan of Arc Chapel. The aura of a work suggests the mysterious presence of the artist-creator, of creativity and genius; these features inspire a sense of awe and a feeling of respectful distance in the viewer. Aura embraces as well the permanence of a work, its timeless value.

The Joan of Arc chapel is unique, not only at Marquette University and in Milwaukee, but in North America. Even in Chasse, Coëlle attested to the chapel's uniqueness of style, to the unusual accretion of details in the chapel's form which reflect its cultural history. A sheaf of official documents housed in the Marquette University Archives attest to the chapel's authenticity. It is a Gothic chapel from a Gothic age as opposed to a replica. Several practical details, such as the lengthened nave, have been added in the Marquette reconstruction, but these remain faithful to the dominant style of the original structure. Apropos of this, a comparison of the chapel with Gesu church, a Gothic replication which stands across campus from the Joan of Arc chapel, reinforces the chapel's authenticity. Benjamin includes permanence as a part of aura. Perhaps he would object to the fact that the chapel has been dislodged from its original context, considering its permanence to have been thus compromised. I would answer that the meticulous stone-by-stone re-construction of the chapel and the respect shown for the original underscore its permanence—that it has remained essentially unchanged in its transfer from Chasse to Marquette University.

Aura, as Benjamin points out, is directly related to history: "the authenticity of a thing is the essence of all that is transmissible from its beginning, ranging from its substantive duration to its testimony to the history which it has experienced."[6] It is through its history that the aura of the chapel is connected to Joan of Arc. The chapel was built in rural France around the time of Joan's life, in the early years of the fifteenth century. While it is improbable that Joan ever visited Chasse—her home lies some 250 miles north of Lyon and her journeys led her mainly to the east (to Orléans and Chinon) and north (to Reims and Rouen)—she likely prayed in dozens of similar small oratories. We know that during her journey from Vaucouleurs to Chinon in 1429, Joan could not attend Mass for fear of being recognized. Instead she prayed in small, unattended chapels along the way. The "Joan of Arc Stone" is said to have originated in one such chapel. Although not originally from the Chasse structure, it may have come from a similar building.

One final point, again from Benjamin, and perhaps the most important: "It is significant that the existence of the work of art with reference to its aura is never entirely separated from its ritual function."[7] For centuries, art was associated primarily with the practice of religion. This was true not only overtly, as in mosaics having religious subjects, but also in the formal qualities of Gothic churches, with their heavenward soaring vaults and their dependence on "divine numbers" for their proportions. Benjamin makes the point that *any* work of art traces its power of spiritual evocation to religious ritual, no matter how apparently disconnected from religion the work seems to be. With respect to a chapel that is a work of art, Benjamin's point is especially clear. Here are two cases. The Sainte Chapelle in Paris, built by Louis IX to house the religious relics that he had collected, is a great work of art, boasting magnificent stained glass windows. Sainte Chapelle no longer functions as a church: the lack of predieux, altar fixtures, and sanctuary lamp and the thirty-two franc admission fee attest to this claim. It is a museum and, as such, is perceived differently from a functioning church. The Joan of Arc chapel, modest in scale and significance by comparison, is nevertheless a work of art which continues to honor its primary mission as a chapel. The Rojtmans specified, as a condition of their gift, that the chapel should continue as a place of worship. Marquette's Joan of Arc chapel is, in fact, the only medieval structure in North America which still serves its original purpose. In this chapel, whose aura expresses the confluence of art and the holy, we are reminded of Joan of Arc. Of all the things to be said of her—that she was a peasant, a politician, a soldier —she was above all a woman of the spirit. She knew herself as a "daughter of God;"[8] we know her as a saint. In this chapel named for her, in its simple aesthetic, its historic and religious aura, its daily use as a place of worship, we are reminded of Joan of Arc—we perceive "her spirit in stone."

Notes

[1] "peut-être plus tôt." Document letter from M. Bertholony, mayor of Chasse, February 18, 1927. Unprocessed material, Marquette University Archives, B9.2, Series 1.

[2] "ce monument absolument unique en son genre." Jacques Coëlle in a letter to Mrs. Michael Gavin, July 1, 1927. Unprocessed material, Marquette University Archives, B9.2, Series 1.

[3] October 25, 1927. Unprocessed material, Marquette University Archives. B9.2, Series 1.

[4] Unprocessed material, Marquette University Archives. B9.2, Series 1.

[5] See Nelson Goodman, *Languages of Art* (New York: Bobbs-Merrill, 1968), 3-6, 52-57.

[6] Walter Benjamin, "The work of art in the age of mechanical reproduction," in *Illuminations/Walter Benjamin*, ed. Hannah Arendt, trans. Harry Zohn (New York: Schocken Books, 1968), 221.

[7] Benjamin, 224.

[8] Raymond Oursel, *Le Procès de condamnation et le procès de réhabilitation de Jeanne d'Arc*. (Paris: Editions Denoël, 1959), 66.

"Hommasse": Joan of Arc as Feminist Model

Helen M. Sterk

Bergot/Lavalley, Orléans

"Hommasse" is a French term, in use since the Middle Ages, to describe a mannish or masculine woman. Unfortunately, it is a term of derision, one which suggests that the "pure" gender attributes of a woman have been tainted by the addition of male characteristics. I would rather think of the term as "femme-homme" or "woman-man"—a balanced pair. That would allow us to think of a person whose primary gender orientation is womanly, yet whose life choices resonate with what is considered manly. Explore with me the synthetic quality of the gender of Joan of Arc, using the frame of "femme-homme." First, we will consider exemplars of the femme-homme, next develop some characteristics of the femme-homme, and finally consider the case of Joan of Arc.

Other femme-hommes that I can think of include Athena, the warrior goddess; Jael, who saved the Israelites from Sisera by pounding a stake through his head as he slept after she had fed him dinner; Deborah, who judged Israel; Rahab, who saved the lives of the Israelite spies in Canaan; Judith, who killed Holofernes to save her city of Bethulia; Sappho, the wise Greek woman; Aspasia, who taught Plato; the warrior queen Boadicea; Pocahantas, who mediated between Native

---

Dr. Sterk teaches Communication Studies at Calvin College.

Americans and the British; Sacajawea, who guided Lewis and Clark; Anne Hutchinson, who became a spiritual leader among the Puritans; Clara Barton, the angel of the battlefields in the Civil War; Anna Howard Shaw, the first ordained American woman minister; Susan B. Anthony, stalwart fighter for female suffrage; Eleanor Roosevelt, who provided the model for a modern First Lady; Hillary Rodham Clinton, who is expanding our understanding of the possibilities for women; and Janet Reno, who makes tough decisions on American justice.

What I find especially intriguing in this list is the fact that each woman exhibits a clear sense of her own value. Each embodies a kind of heroism that expresses itself in not allowing external forces—whether people or cultural norms—to determine their behavior. While the women acted in ways that indicated their deep care and connection to others, they also refused to acquiesce to traditional definitions of womanhood, displaying a secure self-confidence.

The way these femme-hommes lived out their lives reminds me of the biblical injunction to love your neighbor as yourself. The injunction bridges the poles of self-sacrifice and selfishness. It takes strength of will, character, and self to stand on such a bridge. Standing demands that one live a life of responsibility, which I see as literally requiring a response to a particular call in a particular situation. Sometimes, those situations are private, such as when a woman answers the call to become a mother. In such a situation, she weighs her own health and life possibilities against her connections and responsibilities to partner and child. And, if she decides to get pregnant and to bear the child to term, she changes her life forever. Sometimes, those situations are public, such as when a woman answers a call to serve a cause. That cause could be exploration and discovery, protection of one's country, righting injustices, or even weighing in on the intellectual issues of the time. Answering a call, whether private or public, bears consequences that a hero sees through to the end.

While it would be anachronistic to call all these women feminists, since the term didn't come into common use until the nineteenth century, perhaps they can be seen as exhibiting a consciousness that we now term feminist.

Gerda Lerner, historian, in *The Creation of Feminist Consciousness: From the Middle Ages to Eighteen-seventy*, sees these characteristics as marking a feminist consciousness:

1. an awareness by women that they belong to a subordinated group and that, as a member of such a group, they have suffered wrongs;
2. a recognition that their subordination isn't natural, but is socially imposed;

3. the development of a sense of sisterhood;
4. an autonomous definition of what they want to accomplish and how they will do it;
5. the development of an alternative vision of the future.[1]

What Lerner calls feminist consciousness, I think of as being a femme-homme. A femme, woman, acts in ways that her culture deems acceptable to women. An homme, man, acts in ways that his culture stamps as masculine. However, a femme-homme blazes new trails, neither traditionally feminine or masculine, but providing a path to an authenticity and authority that are essentially female.

In western culture, authenticity and authority have been claimed for the public realm, reserved for men. Of the two sexes, men have been able to assume a larger measure of individually initiated action, while women have been remanded to prescribed actions. Men have been allowed, even encouraged, to leave home to find their destiny, while women have been told bluntly that their destiny is found in the home. Women's destiny has been to become the property of one man, to whom she will relinquish her autonomy. In order to become a femme-homme, a woman traditionally had had to resist marriage. The customs and traditions of marriage, as well as the assumption that her husband will represent her in public, have made it all but impossible for women to operate with even limited autonomy. A good example of what I mean is Angelina Grimke, a passionate and gifted nineteenth century speaker against slavery and for women's rights. When she married, her domestic duties so pressed upon her that she could not continue an active public life. It is no surprise and no mistake for our list of femme-hommes to include very few married women, instead featuring single or widowed women.

Joan of Arc strikes me as a clear example of the joys and sorrows of a femme-homme, a woman whose chosen way of caring for others necessitates alienation from her culture's prevailing definitions of what is womanly, and therefore, makes her both extraordinarily memorable and also vulnerable to the consequences of gender difference.

For the purposes of this analysis, I will refer to the characterization of Joan in Jean Anouilh's play, *The Lark*.[2] Anouilh makes it clear that Joan's expression of a femme-homme gender both benefitted her and cost her greatly.

Lerner's first characteristic of a feminist consciousness is the woman's knowledge that she belongs to a subordinated group and that as a member of that group, she has suffered wrongs. While Joan does not use this sort of language, it is clear she understands that her status as a woman puts her under male authority and leaves her at the mercy of men. For example, Joan's father becomes enraged, believing she has been with a man. After she explains her divine call to war, he beats her, saying, "For ten years, I have dreamed that you would disgrace us with men. Do you think I raised you, sacrificed everything for you, to have you run off with soldiers?"[3] Joan submits to his blows, later responding to her mother's reminder, "He's your father," with "Yes. He is my father,"[4] tacitly recognizing his right to beat her if he pleases. Further, when Joan is questioned about why she insists on wearing men's clothes in prison, she blurts out, "One doesn't have to be an educated man to understand what I am saying," explaining that the two English soldiers guarding her in her prison cell threaten her virginity. She realizes she alone has been responsible for safeguarding her chastity, pointing out: "In this uniform it is easier for me to defend myself."[5] Joan understands that being a woman places her at risk, and that it is up to her to take punishment, to figure out ways to avoid rape, or as other scenes show, to use manipulation to convince men to believe her (as when she flatters Beaudricourt by calling him intelligent[6]) and to suffer condemnation for dressing and living as a man.[7]

Lerner's second characteristic of feminist consciousness, a woman's recognition that her subordination is not natural but rather socially imposed, does not find explicit expression in what Joan says. However, her knowledge that social norms are just conventions and not of the essence of her sex comes through in the very pragmatic way in which she chooses to dress in men's clothes in order to accomplish her task. She does not seem to feel her womanly self is denied by wearing such clothes. And Joan does identify herself as a woman who, like Deborah, is called to do a task that God has fitted her for in disregard of her sex. One indicator of that is the choice of metaphors she uses. For example, in *The Lark*, she refers to an everyday womanly task, saying it was as easy for God to bring Lazarus back to life as it was for her to make thread for her loom.[8] One biographer quotes her as saying, during her trial, "I learned to spin and sew; in sewing and spinning I fear no woman in Rouen."[9] In presenting herself as a woman simply doing what needs to be done, Joan implicitly rejects the idea that subordination of women is in the nature of things.

Joan is not shown in *The Lark* as participating easily in Lerner's third marker of feminist consciousness, the development of a sense of sisterhood. Indeed, in the play, she is rarely seen in the company of women. However, other sources suggest that she had close female friends before she left Domremy and, further, that she found comfort in her occasional short stays at women's homes during the time in which she led the French army.[10] While Joan's connections with other women may have been somewhat hard to ascertain, it is clear that she welcomed the divine presence of Saints Margaret and Catherine, two of her principal voices. *The Lark,* as well as scholarly biographies of Joan, portray these female beings as her most constant and trusted companions.

The fourth sign of feminist consciousness is the one most clearly displayed in Joan's story. Her story rests upon her autonomous definition of what she wishes to accomplish and how she will do it. In the face of derision and ridicule, Joan followed the course set by her voices. Her every statement indicates a serene and absolute belief in the rectitude of her demands to be given a horse, horsemen, and the French army. No human voice can dissuade her. When accused by Cauchon of the sin of pride, Joan denies its sinfulness. She says, "I know that I am proud. But I am a daughter of God. If He didn't want me to be proud, why did He send me His shining Archangel and His Saints all dressed in light.... If He had left me alone, I would never have become proud."[11] And, in the end, she recants her confession, finding herself in her integrity. She tells Cauchon she discovered a state of grace, "when, at the very last minute, I gave myself back to myself."[12] For Joan, the cost of denying her integrity was greater than she was willing to pay. Not once but twice she says, "What I am I will not denounce. What I have done I will not deny."[13] She counted death as the lesser cost.

The final sign of feminist consciousness, development of an alternative vision of the future, finds expression in the life of Joan of Arc. It is unfortunate that Jean Anouilh chooses not to weave this aspect into *The Lark.* Joan spoke powerful prophesies just before her death. As Cauchon visited her in her cell, she said to him, "Bishop, I die through you."[14] And later, when she was tied to the stake, she is reported to have said of Rouen, "Ah, Rouen! I have great fear that you will suffer for my death."[15] Just before the fire is lit, Joan is said to have looked at the bishop and repeated her charge, "Bishop, I die by you."[16] Her lack of resignation to her death indicates her belief that she had been wronged; her charge of the bishop suggests her vision of the future is one in which she is vindicated. Anouilh allows her no last words. Instead Warwick presents an alternative vision when he says, "We made a lark into a giant bird who will travel the skies of the world long after our names are forgotten, or confused, or cursed down."[17] Also, by silencing Joan at this climactic moment of her life, Anouilh turns Joan's power to define the meaning of her own life, death and its trajectory over to others.

A woman with a feminist consciousness, whether alive today or many years ago, stands out because she is a femme-homme, a woman-man. Her gender synthesizes feminine and masculine without diminishing or trivializing either. And I find it no surprise that Joan is a devout Christian. For centuries, women have found resources of authority through mystical connection with Jesus Christ. It seems Christ's unconditional love makes it less important to seek a man's often conditional love and to give up one's autonomy to that man. And while the Church through the centuries has served a patriarchal ideology through endorsing wars, burning heretics and witches, and excluding women from places of authority within the Church, the Bible has been a rich source of strength for women. Further, the woman-mystics Hildegard of Bingen, St. Catherine of Siena, St. Teresa of Avila, Anne Hutchinson, and Julia Foote[18] have taken direct revelations from God as authorization to write and speak, breaking all cultural injunctions against their public speech.

Christianity is radical; it transforms culture—including the culture of gender—root and branch. As the example of Joan shows, it presents a warrant for synthesizing feminine and masculine genders. When God calls a woman, asking her to love God above all else and to love others as she loves herself, her knowledge of her own value enables her to answer the call boldly. Nothing on earth matters more than God's call. If God wants her, then the opinion of people on earth is of no consequence.

And I might suggest that Christianity likewise provides warrant for transforming men. When God calls a man, asking him to love others as he loves himself, he learns that others matter as much as he does. While a woman's call leads her to an increased sense of self-worth, a man's call encourages him to an increased sense of the worth of others. All its flaws and potential for abuse aside, Promise Keepers is a contemporary example of taking the second great commandment seriously. Promise Keepers holds men to a high standard of respect and honor for others, especially the women in their lives. Essentially, it seems to me that Promise Keepers encourages men to become homme-femmes, people who care as well as protect. The good news and continuing influence of Christ upsets the taken-for-granteds of western standards of gender.

Consider the remarkable case of Joan of Arc, a woman who led France to victory against the English. Ask yourself not just the definitional question of what sort of woman she was, but the more interesting question, why was she the woman she was? Not an hommasse, but a femme-homme, Joan of Arc went with a fuss.

Notes

1 (New York: Oxford University Press, 1993), 274.
2 Adapted by Lillian Hellman. (New York: Dramatists Play Service, 1957), 12.
3 Anouilh, 12.
4 Anouilh, 13.
5 Anouilh, 50.
6 Anouilh, 16ff.
7 Anouilh, 49ff.
8 Anouilh, 38.
9 Mary Rogers Bangs, *Jeanne D'Arc: The Maid of France* (Boston: Houghton Mifflin Company, 1910), 284.
10 Edward A. Lucie-Smith, *Joan of Arc* (New York: W.W. Norton Company, Inc., 1976).
11 Anouilh, 9.
12 Anouilh, 10.
13 Anouilh, 45-46.
14 Bangs, 345.
15 Bangs, 350.
16 Bangs, 351.
17 Anouilh, 56.
18 Lerner, 88-115.

Joan of Arc, the Hundred Years' War, & French Gothic Architecture

Lawrence Hoey

Larrivé, Bourges

If Joan of Arc represents for many French people the very best in heroism, piety, and nobility left to them from the annals of their medieval history—as countless devotional images of Joan in small French churches attest—there is no doubt that their Gothic architecture occupies a similarly high position in the French cultural memory. One might think, given their contemporaneity, that the two should be linked in significant ways, but there is little evidence that they are or were. There are two basic reasons for this. Although Joan swept past several major Gothic monuments during her brief and tumultuous career, in cities such as Orléans, Poitiers, Compiègne, or Rouen, there is no evidence for what this peasant girl from the eastern borderlands thought about such architectural prodigies. Her singleminded concentration on the defeat of Charles VII's enemies might lead us to doubt whether she much noticed them at all.

If Joan may not have had time or inclination to have fully appreciated the Gothic churches of her day, neither is there evidence that the builders of such churches took any notice of her. For this there are also two reasons. The first is that, for all her present notoriety, Joan was not big news in the later Middle Ages. Although

Dr. Hoey teaches Art History at the University of Wisconsin-Milwaukee.

King Charles, having done nothing to prevent her trial and execution in Rouen, did go to the trouble of having its verdict reversed in 1456, he and his court did little more to foster her memory, much less any cult. There is nothing to compare, for example, to the outpouring of popular piety and miracle working that followed the murder of Archbishop Thomas Becket at Canterbury in the late twelfth century. There were thus no chapels or churches built in Joan's honor in medieval France. Her memorials are almost all of the last two centuries.

The second reason for this disjuncture between Joan and the history of French Gothic architecture is still more significant. The years of Joan's public life, 1429-31, represent the nadir in architectural production of the entire Middle Ages in France. The reason for this almost complete lack of building activity is, of course, the same reason that inspired Joan's mission: the Hundred Years' War and its pernicious effects on the economy, politics, and society of medieval France. Churches, especially

1. *Reims Cathedral (photo: Hoey)*

great churches such as cathedrals, were very expensive and required masons trained in stable workshops over long years. With much of the French countryside laid waste by the depredations of war bands from both sides, many church fabric accounts found themselves deeply in the red by 1430. Nor do Joan's victories change things, at least not in the short term. It took twenty more years for Charles to expel the English, and serious architectural production took longer still to recover. It is really only in the last quarter of the fifteenth century that one can discern a new burst of church building—or rebuilding—in France. Buildings destroyed or damaged by the wars are reconstructed, cathedrals left unfinished because of the war are completed, and a few completely new foundations are begun. But all this takes place long after Joan.

Rather than using this vacuum in French Gothic architecture as an excuse to end my talk early and go home, however, I'd like to discuss some buildings from sites associated with Joan to try and convey some idea of the state of French Gothic in the time of Joan and of its recovery in the later fifteenth century.

We begin with Reims Cathedral, where Charles was crowned in Joan's presence in July, 1429. Reims was, of course, the traditional site of kingly coronation in medieval France, an honor it owed to the early medieval story of the baptism of Clovis there by Saint Remi in the year 497, as we have all been recently reminded by the Pope and quarreling French politicians. Reims is without question one of the great

Gothic cathedrals of France; in my personal opinion its only peer is Bourges. Gothic cathedrals are all meant to be earthly visions of the heavenly Jerusalem; their deeply glowing windows and long vistas of arching rib vaults suggest transcendence and spiritual exaltation. At the same time, they are buildings of great aesthetic sophistication and control, made possible by superb stone cutting, careful geometry, and imaginative structural engineering. Reims represents the most popular type of French Gothic design: an elevation with three stories—an arcade, a band of small arches called a triforium, and an upper zone of very large windows called, logically, a clearstory (figure 1). The scale is immense—the bases on the massive nave piers are about six

2. Reims Cathedral (photo: Hoey)

feet high. The vaults at Reims crest at 142 feet above floor level. The great clearstory windows, which one sees here from the outside (figure 2), were originally filled with stained glass to provide that heavenly vision. They are made possible by that most famous of Gothic structural devices, the flying buttress, several of which you see here sailing elegantly over the double aisles of the Reims east end. By externalizing the structural support system, French masons no longer needed to build massive walls to support the interior stone vaults. Such formerly massive walls could be thinned and turned into glass screens. The west façade of Reims (figure 3), which still towers over the town as it did in 1429, has a large rose window and two tall flanking towers. The three immense portals are encumbered with some of the greatest sculpture of medieval France. High above the western rose is the gallery of kings, to which Charles and Joan may well have raised their eyes with strong emotion on that July day more than five centuries ago. What one sees in these illustrations, they, too, would have seen.

3. Reims Cathedral

And that, of course, is my point—Reims Cathedral is a building almost entirely of the thirteenth century, already almost two centuries old in 1429, as far removed in time from Joan and Charles as Independence Hall is from us. Reims was begun in 1210 and more or less complete by the 1280s except for the tops of the towers, which were built in the early fourteenth century, but still before the start of the Hundred Years' War. The great century of French Gothic lasts roughly from the 1150s until 1250, with various large projects like Reims continuing on to slow completion in later decades. The Hundred Years' War was certainly important in retarding construction, but the decline had begun half a century before the 1330s. Most cathedral or abbey chapters who could afford to rebuild their churches had already done so by 1275; the vast expenditure of money, skill, and labor on the building projects of the twelfth and thirteenth centuries led inevitably to a cessation afterwards. Like Chicago office towers in the 1990s, many parts of France had more large churches than they needed by 1300.

4. Rouen Cathedral

Another interesting case is Rouen, the capital of English Normandy, where Joan met her end. Rouen has three great Gothic churches: the Cathedral, the abbey church of Saint Ouen, and the parish church of Saint Maclou. It is likely, given the site of Joan's imprisonment in the castle on the southeast edge of Rouen, that her first glimpse of the cathedral would have been on the day she was led to the marketplace to be burned. What must her thoughts have been, especially as the west façade of the cathedral so closely resembled that of Reims, the scene of Joan's greatest triumph. Rouen cathedral is also largely a building of the thirteenth century, and, although the nave has four stories instead of three, and the details conform to a local Norman version of Gothic, the overall effect is very similar. But it also has work of the later Middle Ages, work much closer in date to Joan's fateful sojourn there. The west façade is particularly interesting in this regard. It is a work of many dates and lacks the tight organization of the Reims west front because, at Rouen, the two towers are set beyond the line of the aisle walls and are disparate in height and style. The north tower is essentially late Romanesque, while the south is latest Gothic. The part between (figure 4), with its three portals and complex screen work above, is, of course, the façade that fascinated Monet centuries later, when he lived not far away at Giverny. The light-catching gables and crockets that so entranced the painter were built in an extended period beginning in the 1370s. The first level of the façade is the same date as the north tower—late Romanesque, although the central door has been rebuilt at the very end of the Middle Ages, in the early sixteenth century. The screenwork above the door, although begun in the late fourteenth century, was not completed until long after

Joan's death in 1431. A close examination of the tracery under the gables shows that the patterns change from geometrical designs of circles and pointed arches to more complex curvilinear designs that look like exotic leaves—testimony to the slow progress possible during a time of war and political uncertainty. The great rose window and the immense south tower were only built in the period of real recovery toward the end of the century—the south tower was begun in 1485, and the portal, as I have said, is later still.

It was in the cemetery of St. Ouen in Rouen that Joan's sentence was publicly read, that she abjured. At that time, in 1431, Joan would have seen only the elegant fourteenth century choir; the nave of the abbey church was yet to be built. In fact, the monks of St. Ouen were so notoriously intent on their con-  struction that they had refused funds to help fortify the city against the English. It is important to underscore here the simi- larity between the early choir and the much later nave, com- pleted toward the end of the fifteenth century. In fact, in many of the large churches completed after the end of the war, the fifteenth century masons decided, or were ordered, to adhere to the earlier thirteenth century design.

Before we leave Rouen, let us note the west façade of Saint Maclou, the great fifteenth century parish church in the city (fig- ure 5). This façade, with its folding-screen-like portals, is unique in French Gothic. All of Saint Maclou is a building of the high- est quality and imagination. At Saint Maclou, the fifteenth cen- tury masons did not have to deal with an earlier building and so could be more original. What is particularly interesting about Saint-Maclou is that it was begun in 1434—only three years af- ter Joan's immolation and long before Rouen was "liberated" by Charles. Indeed, Rouen, and Normandy in general, were rela-

5. Saint Maclou (photo: Hoey)

tively prosperous during the decades of English occupation, and their inhabitants were by no means overjoyed to see the English leave and Charles and his tax collec- tors arrive. Whatever they may have privately thought of her, Joan's execution in Rouen had little effect on the progress of French Gothic architecture in the city.

Troyes is another city closely associated with Joan and the Hundred Years' War. It was here that the Treaty of Troyes was signed in 1420, a document which denied accession to the throne to Joan's beloved dauphin, Charles of Valois. Troyes was among the cities that Joan captured for Charles in her victorious march toward Reims in 1429. Troyes Cathedral is another building begun in the thirteenth century, but only completed in the fifteenth and early sixteenth. Unlike Rouen Cathedral, in which only façades and towers remained to do in the late Middle Ages, at Troyes, most of the nave had yet to be constructed. Again, as in the screen on the Rouen west front, it is only in the details of the tracery patterns that one can chart the passage of centuries. When one stands in the nave of Troyes and looks east, then, the vista is one of a unified design, more or less, from one end of the building to the other. Such aesthetic unity is common in France, but there is more to it than that—it seems clear that the builders and patrons of the later fifteenth century saw the thirteenth century cathedrals just as we do—as the paradigmatic buildings of a

6. Montargis (photo: Hoey)

golden age when French political and cultural dominance had been unquestioned in Europe. The painful collapse of that double hegemony during the long war with England could best be forgotten by returning to the architectural verities of two centuries earlier.

This doesn't mean, however, that late medieval French designers were merely copyists. On the contrary, late French Gothic, usually known as Flamboyant after the flame-like forms of its tracery, can be highly original. Nevertheless, its genius is most apparent, not in great cathedrals, but in smaller buildings, such as the many parish churches that had to be rebuilt or repaired all across northern France after the ravages of the war. For example, in Pithiviers (near Orléans), arch moldings and vault ribs spring out of tall cylindrical piers without any intervening capitals—a kind of architectural elision that has no parallel in the thirteenth century.

In smaller buildings, late medieval masons were not so intent on matching their new designs with surviving older parts. In Montargis, an important city south of Orléans, for example, a simple two-storied church of the twelfth century has been given an immense choir of the hall-church type where aisles and central vessel are all vaulted at the same height (figure 6). That means a forest of high thin piers with exciting vistas in all directions. Here the vaults have become quite ornate, with fancy pendants hanging from their central keystones. Pier forms as well are now more finely divided, a design practice that requires the greatest precision in stone cutting.

One of the most interesting and impressive buildings from the new burst of French church building in the later fifteenth century is King Louis IX's funerary church at Cléry on the Loire, not far from Orléans and other sites associated with Joan's ex-

ploits. Why Louis should eschew being buried in Saint-Denis
with his predecessors and successors is something of a mystery,
but Louis was in many ways an unusual king. The older church
at Cléry had in fact been destroyed in the war, so its reconstruction might in some ways be taken as symbolic of the reconstitu-
tion of France that was begun with Joan and completed, in many
ways, by Louis. Although a large church designed for a king's
burial, Cléry is a very different building from the thirteenth century Gothic cathedrals discussed earlier (figure 7). It has only
two stories, simple four-part vaults (none of those fancy pendants), and relatively simple tracery; its elegant austerity stands
in sharp contrast both to the filigree façades of Rouen and to
the earlier multi-storied elevations of the thirteenth century. Of
course, Louis was notoriously cheap and perhaps Clery reflects
his reluctance to spend money. On the other hand, it clearly demonstrates the variety of expression possible in the Flamboyant
style of the later fifteenth century, whose flaming lines can also
be caught and subordinated in a design of relative simplicity.

7. *Cléry (photo: Hoey)*

I would like to close with an example which I think illustrates
the undiminished creativity of Gothic architecture in France at
the end of the fifteenth century: the parish church of Saint
Severin on the left bank in Paris. Saint Severin was originally a
thirteenth century church, as was so often the case in late medieval France. The parishioners decided to rebuild it around 1450,
at the end of the war, but they also decided to keep intact the
two thirteenth century west bays of the nave. In the reconstruction east of these, the patrons and masons evince a remarkable
fidelity to the preserved western bays; only the more complex
pier forms and differing tracery patterns demonstrate the two
century gap between them. As at Troyes, the visual continuity of
the elevation was a prime consideration. The apse of the building, however, demonstrates a marked discrepancy in levels, and,
looking to the vault, one sees that the simple forms copied from
the thirteenth century west bays have been replaced by a stun-
ning multi-ribbed vault over the high altar (figure 8). We know
from documents that this easternmost part of Saint Severin was
not begun until 1489 because, until that time, a town house or

8. *Saint Severin (photo: Hoey)*

hôtel occupied the site, facing onto the Rue Saint-Jacques. After the church had bought and demolished the hôtel, a new apse and ambulatory could be built. Where the main vessel of the nave was felt to require a treatment consistent with the thirteenth century fragment, the eastern climax of the church was seen as another matter. Not only do the vault and elevation change, but the aisles of the church now meet in a magnificent double ambulatory, whose plan is copied from the cathedral of Notre-Dame just across the river, but whose forms are entirely flamboyant. Thus we have this spiral pier between the two ambulatories at the apse apex supporting a vault of great complexity; adjoining this pier, others are arranged in a symmetrical pattern moving outwards in both directions. Such piers and ribs form one of the great spaces of medieval France. Saint-Severin is one of the best indications of the new energy and experimentation made possible by the end of the Hundred Years' War.

Although Joan of Arc and French Gothic architecture seem at first to have little to do with one another, Joan's role in bringing the war to a triumphant conclusion was important in allowing the growth of a powerful new French kingdom, one of whose manifestations was this new burst of creativity in Gothic church architecture.

Burned by Celluloid: Joan of Arc in Film History

Dominique Paul Noth

Saupique, Rouen

From the start, the movie industry's relationship with Joan of Arc was uneasy. Not as uneasy as the Catholic Church's, which first validated her, then condemned and burned her, and then redeemed her with full canonization as a saint in 1920 (releasing a flood of archival documentation that served as motivation to artists and film makers). But uneasy nevertheless. With the understandable exception of France, the commercial film world's interest in Joan is marked by fits and starts but mostly stops—long stretches of time when the story has been virtually ignored.

Consider some of the dilemmas. There may be a worldwide fascination and hence a built-in audience for the story of Joan, and yet it defies conventional commercial wisdom. First of all, here is a woman surrounded by men—battalions and legions of them. She travels with men, camps with them, leads them, confuses them, consorts with known womanizers (Dunois, Bluebeard, *et al.*)—and yet, there can be absolutely no sex and no love story except in a spiritual sense. Then, look at how many of the key issues in Joan's life are mired in arcane concepts of feudal law, medieval methodology, and inquisition theology. And this heroine hears voices.

Mr. Noth is former film critic for the Milwaukee Journal-Sentinel.

Voices! This is a concept Hollywood associates more with Freud than with God. To top it off, there is no happy ending, no army galloping into the town square to save a Guinevere from the flames, nor could movie studios accustomed to playing loose with historical truth concoct such a conclusion in so famous a religious context, tempted though they clearly would be. No, Joan sure doesn't sound box office, even in an era when films for and about women are more easily financed.

Still, there are elements in Joan's story made for the cinema. The story itself is wonderfully dramatic. Here was a girl of no means, education, or stature who was surrounded by pageantry, intrigue, and war. She led the dauphin's army through harrowing times to great victories. She helped shape the geographic, social, and political world of Europe—in the process making those about her so uncomfortable that they put her to death. By comparison, the stories of Ulysses, El Cid and King Arthur were mild; besides, they were just men. Moreover, what a performance challenge for an actress! It is more than the allure of short hair and male dress, more than the transformation of a peasant girl into a general and then a martyr. The role invests actresses with a special aura, even icon status. There is a cruel side to this, however, as we will demonstrate. The public irresistibly intertwines the performance and the performer's personal life. The role of Joan has come to haunt the lives of those who have played her; perhaps more than any other role, this one has revealed that our ferocity over celebrity sainthood is more extreme than the religious variety.

The Films

Out of this cauldron of conflicting concerns, about twenty films have emerged over the span of ninety years which focus on the story of Joan. Nearly half were made or financed in France, where Joan is patriot, holy woman, and tourist industry. Nearly half are silent films, including two attempts (now lost) by America's master of the Biblical Epic, Cecil B.de Mille. Only a few of these Joan films are revived or remembered today—or even available. (It is a sad comment that the availability of films more than their merit dominates so much of our exploration of film history.)

The best known are those directed by Victor Fleming (*Joan of Arc*, 1948), Otto Preminger (*St. Joan*, 1957), and Carl Dreyer (*La Passion de Jeanne d'Arc*, 1928), all of which we will explore in depth. Others include a Joan-on-trial film (*Le proces de Jeanne d'Arc*, 1962) by a noted French filmmaker and narrative experimenter, Robert Bresson, who revered Dreyer and sought to put his own stamp on the same basic subject matter; even Bresson's ardent fans, however, find the results difficult to venerate.

There are also curiosities, such as a World War II B-movie called *Joan of Paris* about a young girl who rescues RAF pilots. And there is *The Miracle of the Bells*. This is a sentimental film that is really more about Hollywood legend-making than about the maid of Orleans. It still shows up on television at Christmas time and has noteworthy, albeit odd, historical elements. While *The Miracle of the Bells* stars Fred MacMurray, there is a young priest in the film who must deal with an apparent Joan-connected miracle. The part is played by Frank Sinatra (trying to do for his career what *Going My Way* did for Bing Crosby's—there's nothing like playing a priest to validate a singer's dramatic capabilities). The plot involves a movie version of Joan's life in which the unknown actress who completes the film promptly dies. MacMurray, a press agent who was in love with her, vainly tries to get the studio to release the film anyway, but it takes the apparent post-mortem miracle in her hometown church to get the studio on his side (they now have all that free publicity). The film contains several straight scenes from a mythical Joan film in which the role is played by the Italian actress, Alida Valli, whose intensity and mystique briefly made her an American star in the 1940s and who desperately wanted to play Joan in a better film. Made in 1948, the same year as Fleming's Joan film (with Ingrid Bergman), the movie today looks almost like a bizarre audition for the part, or an effort by one studio to capitalize on the Joan publicity being generated by another.

Only two commercial heavyweights, Victor Fleming and Otto Preminger, dismissed the risks inherent in the Joan story and threw their talents behind major productions. Fleming had directed two of the greatest box office hits in American film history, *The Wizard of Oz* and *Gone with the Wind* (in the same year in fact) and was so enamored by Bergman that he agreed to use the rather pedestrian script adapted by Maxwell Anderson from his stage play, *Joan of Lorraine*. That play survived on stage largely on the strength of Bergman's appeal, but it is seldom revived today, the theater world having recognized that Bernard Shaw's *St. Joan* and Jean Anouilh's *The Lark* (in Lillian Hellman's adaptation) are the deeper, more potent vehicles. A usually no-nonsense director in terms of dramatic development, Fleming never came near the promise of the story or of his own usual competence in the film. He had no perspective on what made Bergman so special for the part. Lost in the inadequacies of the script, he simply threw in more spectacle. This sad final chapter in Fleming's professional life was compounded by his own poor health and the fact that he had fallen in unrequited love with his leading lady. Bergman herself realized many of the problems with the film: "It had the smooth glossy quality of

Hollywood," she wrote, "I didn't think I looked like a peasant girl at all. I just looked like a movie star . . . when the part called for an appearance not a quarter as glamorous."[1]

Preminger took a different approach for his 1957 *St. Joan*: don't cast a star, cast an unknown. Armed with Shaw's brilliant script in a skilled adaptation by Graham Greene and graced with workmanlike performances from established actors such as Richard Todd and Richard Widmark, plus the almost redemptive presence of John Gielgud wielding Shaw's language with wicked ease, Preminger chose to commingle Hollywood's own legend-making machinery with the legend of Joan. Just as God plucked Jeannette of Arc from the sleepy village of Domremy to be His emissary, Preminger plucked Jean Seberg from an Iowa campus (after an ostensibly worldwide talent search) to be his Joan. Again, think of all the free publicity. Prettied up and romanticized by Preminger (much as Bergman had been by Fleming), Seberg was vilified by the critics. Though clearly an intelligent, self-possessed teenager with solid oral interpretation skills, she would have needed the Joan-like voices of St. Stanislavsky and St. Strasberg whispering in her ear to rise to the challenges of a role that had sunk many an established actress on stage. Rise she did not, and without a Joan of consequence, no Shaw St. Joan endures.

One Joan film is a masterpiece: Carl-Theodore Dreyer's *La Passion de Jeanne d'Arc*. Though made in 1928, this work remains among the top artistic achievements in cinema, certainly among the top ten silent films ever made. Using Joan's own words and the trial transcripts as a starting point for his invention, Dreyer compresses the long months of Joan's imprisonment, interrogation, and burning into one claustrophobic day. Granted, the film is not an easy sit-through for modern audiences. We are no longer used to the acting conventions and pacing of silent films, where action is often subordinate to reaction. We have a problem with black and white films in general, even more so with a seventy-year-old silent, black and white film. We wag our heads at the background organ music and title card dialogue. We do not appreciate, despite the eyes bugged toward the camera and the extreme time taken with many close-ups, that this was the epitome of "realistic acting" in silent films. No matter. The artistic merit remains. Through montage and moving camera, by invading the tranquillity and spiritual agony of Joan with animatedly gross and twisted male faces, Dreyer creates a vision of ecclesiastical spiders scuttling to and fro, seeking to snatch at and mentally unravel a significant innocent. Amid all this unfriendly human motion toward her, Joan seeks to reconnect her strength through the objects around her. In effect it is her eyes—what she sees and how she sees it—that become our gateway to her higher soul and higher suffering.

To date, no film maker has approached Dreyer's power in handling the burning of Joan. The scene progresses from her last Holy Communion, through soaring doves and a suckling baby, to an unrelenting progression of flames that appear to destroy her as townspeople riot—all intercut at dynamic speed before a warped Caligari castle created just for the film. The sequence remains one of the significant pieces of pure movie-making in the annals of cinema.*

The Actresses

Granted that film has the power to elevate actors into icons and that audiences have difficulty separating actor and part, it is still remarkable how relentlessly the ghost of Joan pursued the private lives of the actresses in all three of these films. Part of this may be a natural outgrowth of our modern media: expecting those who play a beloved saint to somehow assume her persona in real life, we more hysterically record any fall from grace. But even so, the tenacious connection of Joan to these actresses' private lives—the way each case fomented a subindustry of rumor, rumination, and often ruination—seems startling.

Consider the most successful screen Joan, Marie Renee Falconetti, who starred in Dreyer's silent film. Soon after the film appeared, both Europe and the Americas were swept with strange stories—that Falconetti had been cast because of her saintliness, that the villainous Dreyer had tortured her, that she had actually been burned and terribly scarred in the final scene, that she had become so much like Joan as to enter the cloister after filming and there lose her mind. None of these stories was true. Certainly, Falconetti endured hardships to make the film: she knelt for hours on stone floors; she had her hair shorn on camera; she was subjected to exhausting months in physically arduous circumstances and was constantly berated by the director in his desperation to fulfill his vision. But throughout, she was completely in sympathy with Dreyer's desires, willing to endure these difficulties for the sake of the film. She was in no way harmed, not even during the final scene—though a cameraman was accidentally burned and a camera melted during the filming.

Falconetti had come to the film as an established and mature stage actress, trained at the Comédie Française. But after the arduous experience with Dreyer, she chose

---

* Dreyer's film has also won new attention due to a moving oratorio, *Voices of Light*, inspired by the film and composed by Richard Einhorn. Although the oratorio is not a score for the film—it actually uses texts from medieval women poets and mystics—a screening of the film typically accompanies public performances of the music.

not to make another film. Though she continued to act—even running her own theater company in Paris for many years—she was beset by financial problems and finally decided to emigrate to America in the late 1930s. However, immigration authorities here found her lacking funds, connections and "special skills" (obviously no film buffs among them) and rejected her request. She was forced to travel on to Buenos Aires, where she spent her final years teaching drama to French school children. She died there in obscurity in 1946.

Seberg's story was tragic, perhaps because Hollywood had deliberately conflated her personality with that of Joan from the outset. Studio hype machines ground out miles of news footage about this authentic naif from Iowa, a Joan of the heartland. But even as she was heroized, she seemed driven to break the stereotype forced on her. After the film was made, Seberg expatriated to France, where she became the darling of the new cinema and also a supporter of the Black Panther movement. Her interest in radical causes earned the enmity of J. Edgar Hoover's FBI and the American and even European press. Vicious stories spread that the child she and French author Romain Gary were expecting had actually been fathered by a Black Panther. The infant died, and Seberg insisted on burying the child in a glass coffin to lay to rest those stories. A deeply troubled neurotic, she committed suicide at age forty—an image progression that bewildered those who had known her as a teenager in America. Seberg's journey from Joan to suicide has itself has inspired a film, *From the Journals of Jean Seberg*, whose ironies parallel those of her own life. Director Mark Rappaport based his film on wholly invented dialogue and manufactured diaries that he used as sources for his "biographical" work.

The actress who was most spectacularly associated with the role of Joan was Ingrid Bergman. From her earliest recollection as a child in Sweden, she had wanted to play Joan. In fact, Producer David O. Selznick (who feared that the impending war would make her unavailable for his other projects) coaxed her back to America in 1940 with the promise that Joan would be her next film. When she arrived, however, Selznick pointed out that this was hardly the time for the topic; a film about an aggressive English war machine overrunning France and burning maidens did not exactly mesh with Dunkirk and the blitz. While she waited, Bergman starred in *Casablanca*, *For Whom the Bells Tolls*, *Gaslight*, *Notorious* and another inspirational blockbuster, *The Bells of St. Mary*, in which she was the captivating nun who believed, like Joan, that prayer would answer any difficulty. During this interim, Bergman emerged as the film world's most popular actress, not only praised for the sincerity and passion of her acting but respected as a wholesome human being (even

Bergman's "bad women" were morally good). And while she rose to stardom, her passion for Joan remained.

In 1947, she agreed to play Joan on Broadway in Maxwell Anderson's *Joan of Lorraine*. Though troubled by Anderson's script, which was more of a pulpit for his social theories than the story of Joan, Bergman rose to the difficulties; it was her performance that kept the play alive. It was also her personal, social pulpit that made news when the play was on tour before its New York opening. In Washington, Bergman discovered that black people were not allowed to attend the theater. She was furious. Ignoring the pleas of director, playwright, and publicity agent, she spoke up—but very cleverly. At the end of a polite press conference, she dropped the bombshell that she would never again perform in the nation's capitol. Citing Joan's words from the play, "Every woman gives her life for what she believes," she explained: "I will not come back here again until black people, just like white people, can come to the theatre. We play for everybody. Everybody!"[2] The words of this icon of American filmdom led the next day's headlines and caused legislators considerable embarrassment. Within two years they would have a chance to get even.

It was seeing Bergman on stage as Joan that led director Victor Fleming to burst into her dressing room exclaiming, "You should play Joan forever and ever . . . You must play Joan on the screen."[3] Bergman (listed as co-producer) dove into the project, pressed Anderson to replace his polemics with Joan's simple words, worked closely with Fleming (who was now desperately in love with her), and even traveled to France to trace Joan's path from her birthplace in Domremy to the market square in Rouen where she had been martyred. Bergman was amazed and moved by the experience. All along the route, large crowds gathered to welcome her as the reincarnation of Joan. (For years afterward, despite scandals and other factors, Bergman's reception in France was always the same; passport agents would say, "Ah, Jeanne d'Arc . . . welcome home."[4]) But despite Bergman's devotion to the role, despite the image in her heart of Joan as peasant and clarion voice of the people, despite her radiant central presence, the film was a failure. And that failure spurred a change in Bergman's artistic vision. Later, she speculated that it was her disappointment over the glossy Joan Hollywood had to perpetrate that propelled her into artistic migration and controversy: "I suppose when I look back this is where my instinctive rebellion and resentment began . . . I just wanted to get out of the back lot."[5]

Bergman's disillusionment with conventional Hollywood led to her enchantment with new realism, especially in the films of Italian director Roberto Rossellini. Though she had never met him, she wrote him and offered to work with him and he responded eagerly. It was not just his films that she found irresistible. Within months of their meeting, though married to Peter Lindstrom and the mother of his daughter, Bergman was living with Rossellini (also married with children) and pregnant with their son.

The reaction of the public was swift and unforgiving. Boatloads of hate mail and death threats reached her on the volcanic island of Stromboli, where she and Rossellini were making their first film together. She was pursued by press and photographers in an inquisitional manner that would have done the bishop of Cauchon proud. She was denounced, not just from America's pulpits but from the floor of the U.S. Senate. In 1950, a Colorado senator, Edwin C. Johnson, described Bergman and Rossellini as "disgusting, nauseating, vile;" he cited their behavior as an "all-time low in shameless exploitation and disregard for good public morals" and branded Bergman as a "powerful influence for evil."[6] Johnson even proposed a bill that would require producers, films, and actresses (he didn't mention actors) to be licensed by the Department of Commerce, based on a rigorous examination of their personal as well as artistic standards.

Even recognizing the fever of political witch-hunting in Congress in the late 1940s and early 1950s (much of it focused on film and theater artists), even accepting the righteous attitudes of American media of the time, the pillorying of Bergman was extraordinary. Other high profile actresses—Paulette Godard, Viveca Lindfors, Ginger Rogers, Joan Fontaine, Alida Valli (another Joan)—had been involved in divorces and scandals without such fury. Why make an exception of Bergman? Her immense popularity was certainly a factor. But so was Joan. Bergman's public expected of the actress the blazing honesty, personal courage, and impassioned conviction that she had created on the screen. The maid of Orleans would never behave this way; neither could Bergman. Once idolized in America, now ostracized, Bergman was shunned by Hollywood studios and did not return to America for a decade.

Whatever match Bergman and Rossellini were in private, on screen they proved incompatible as artists. The films she made with him in the fifties deserved most of the obscurity they received; their fortunes as well as reputations were at an ebb. Ironically, it was Joan of Arc that came to the rescue in the form of an oratorio created by the French dramatist, Paul Claudel and noted composer, Arthur Honnegger. The work required a dramatic Joan in stage performance surrounded by operatic voices. Bergman became that Joan and toured the oratorio to critical acclaim—Rome, Paris, London, Stockholm—though never to America. (Rossellini recorded the event on film, but it is seldom shown.) Bergman's skills and still-vibrant star power revived her international film career, leading to *Anastasia*, an Oscar, and a triumphant return in the 1960s to Hollywood, although she never returned to the U.S. to live.

Postscript

In the late summer of 1948, George Bernard Shaw invited Ingrid Bergman to tea, intending to chastise her for not doing his *St. Joan*. He was startled when she forthrightly told him she didn't like the play, though she admitted it was probably a masterpiece. "I made Joan a simple peasant woman," she said. "Your words are marvelous but they are Shaw's words, not Joan's. She had no education and only her inborn common sense to give her courage. You made her far too clever."[7]

In cinematic terms, Bergman had a point. Had she ever had a script that totally captured her image of Joan, she may well have done it justice. Had there been a modern visionary director, as there had been a Dreyer in the silent film era, who could find a creative way inside the heart and soul of Joan, free of glamour and press-agentry, we might well have a modern Joan on screen to match the power of Joan in music and Joan on the live stage. Bergman clearly identified with the audacity, clarity, and humanity of the historic Joan. In the theater, the Joans of Shaw and Anouilh are the more intelligent, poetic creatures of nature and spirit; on the stage that is what triumphs. So far in film, it is the peasant image of Falconetti and Dreyer's intense vision of the destruction of an innocent that have triumphed.

However, Shaw also has a point, or rather his play makes one when Joan asks those whose lives she has changed (mostly for the better) if they would like her to come back and help them again. They all move away. Saints are not easy to live with. Visionaries force us out of our shells, challenge our comfort zones. No actress can live up to the image of Joan—as Falconetti, Seberg and Bergman could all attest—and yet somehow our society insists that they try. If we are so critical with the actors—if, abuzz with rumors about them we hold their feet to the fire—how indeed would we treat the saint? Is it only the celluloid Joans we would be tempted to burn? Shaw's Joan asks: "How long before the world is ready to receive they saints? How long, oh, Lord." For the world, perhaps never. For the movie industry, even longer.

Select Filmography

1898   *Jeanne d'Arc*. Pathé. France. Georges Hatot.

1900   *Jeanne d'Arc*. Star Film. France. Georges Meliès.

1900   *Vie de Jeanne d'Arc*. Caserini Productions. Italy. Mario Caserini.

1905   *Jeanne d'Arc au Bûcher*. France. Mario Caserini.

1908   *Jeanne d'Arc*. Pathé. France. Albert Capellani.

1909   *Béatification de Jeanne d'Arc*. Cine. Italy. Mario Caserini.

1916   *Joan the Woman*. Paramount. USA. Cecil B. de Mille.

1921   *Sheltered Daughters* (Joan segment). Paramount. USA. Cecil B. de Mille.

1928   *La Passion de Jeanne d'Arc*. SGF. France. Carl Dreyer.

1935   *Das Mädchen Johanna*. UFA. Germany. Gustav Ucicky.

1948   *Joan of Arc*. RKO. USA. Victor Fleming.

1954   *Giovanna d'Arco al Rogo*. ENIC. Italy-France. Roberto Rossellini.

1957   *Saint Joan*. United Artists. USA. Otto Preminger.

1961   *Jeanne au Vitrail*. Films. C.A. France. Claude Antoine.

1962   *Le procès de Jeanne d'Arc*. Delahaie. France. Robert Bresson.

1967   *Joan of Arc*. USA. Peiro Heliczer.

1970   *Le Début*. USSR. Gleb Panfilov.

1977   *Saint Joan*. Britain. Stephen Rumbelow.

1990   *Le Pouvoir et l'Innocence*. SFP. France. Pierre Badel.

1993   *Jeanne d'Arc*. BAC Film. France. Jacques Rivette.

Notes

[1]   Ingrid Bergman with Alan Burgess, *Ingrid Bergman: My Story* (New York: Delacorte Press,1980), 174.

[2]   Bergman, 162.

[3]   Bergman, 166.

[4]   Bergman, 172.

[5]   Bergman, 174.

[6]   Bergman, 263.

[7]   Bergman, 180.

The Inquisition and Joan of Arc

Ronald E. Zupko

Mehun-sur-Yèvre

Joan of Arc was captured by the English at Compiègne on May 23, 1430. The surprise assault by her troops on the town of Margny, which lay just across the river from Compiègne, had been seen by the Burgundians from the heights above the Oise; they quickly sent reinforcements into Margny and repulsed her attack. Although Joan's troops streamed back across the bridge into Compiègne, the governor of the city, fearing that the English would follow, gave the order to raise the drawbridge and close the gates. Joan herself was cut off. An archer in the service of the Bastard of Wendomme pulled her from her horse and took her captive. Joan was a prisoner of the English; there was no question of that. Wendomme was in the service of Jean of Luxembourg, who was a vassal of the duke of Bedford and therefore in the service of the king of England. How then, or why, was this most prized prisoner handed over to Pierre Cauchon, the French bishop of Beauvais?

The answer is as interesting as it is important. Joan had turned the recent tide of the war against the English, raising the siege of Orléans and capturing Jargeau, Beaugency, and Patay. She had made possible Charles VII's crowning as king of

Dr. Zupko teaches History at Marquette University.

France. But more than her victories, it was her methods that drew the English wrath. In their eyes, Joan hadn't won fair and square. She had used sorcery to beat the unbeatable English. The only tribunal that could deal with these matters—that could accuse her of witchcraft and heresy and therefore discredit her and her victories—was the Inquisition. And Pierre Cauchon, an English sympathizer in whose diocese Joan had supposedly been taken, could be relied upon to find Joan guilty and to dispatch her.

Two days after Joan's capture, the theology faculty of the University of Paris wrote a letter to the duke of Bedford demanding that Joan be turned over to the Church courts. He was pleased to do so. Thus Joan joined a long procession of official heretics; her death became one of the most infamous "products" of the Inquisition.

To provide a background for the Inquisition, let me back up a to the early days of Christianity. The Church grew very slowly during the first four centuries of its existence throughout the Roman Empire. In the first two centuries of the Christian era, the Empire's population peaked at approximately sixty million people; thereafter, it declined due to invasions, wars, famines, soil exhaustion, disease, plagues, and many other factors until it stood at about fifty million by the end of the fourth century. By the time Theodosius declared Christianity the official state religion in 395, Christians comprised only around ten percent of the total population of the Empire. One clear benefit to the Christian situation in this was that heresy—defined by the Church as willful deviation from orthodoxy—was very slow to develop. The early Church demanded doctrinal consensus and doctrine was interpreted exclusively by the Church's teaching magisterium. Attention to heretical individuals and movements began initially in the third century and slowly gained momentum during the remaining centuries of the first millennium. The new millennium brought with it many radical changes in Europe. Among these, the Commercial, Agricultural, Health, and Urban Revolutions particularly influenced population growth in Europe, which tripled between the eleventh and fourteenth centuries from twenty-five million to seventy-five million people. In particular, increased urbanization meant a more heterogeneous, cosmopolitan, and diversified amalgamation of peoples; with this came greater freedoms of expression, which oftentimes translated into doctrinal positions inimical to the medieval Church.

As population expanded, the older "learned" heresies—those limited to discussion among Church scholars —began to affect popular movements. For example, aspects of Pelagianism, a third century heresy which insisted on the individual's duty and right to take responsibility for his own salvation, appeared in mainstream heresies in the new millennium. In fact, the notion of the primacy of individual conscience (and the many variants on this idea) gained ever greater currency in the Middle Ages.

Among the most important heretical movements (actually not an organized movement, but a group of loosely related heretical sects) of the thirteenth century was the Free Spirits. The essence of Free Spirit thought was that the soul is above the moral law when, through a mystical encounter, it attains union with God. Further, they believed that whoever was thus moved by the Holy Spirit was without sin and had no need of the Church or its sacraments. At the center of the Free Spirit controversy was a sect which became very widespread throughout Europe in the 1200s, that of the Beguines and Beghards. Predominantly women (the men, Beghards, represented only a small percentage of the movement), they led lives of chastity, poverty, and piety without taking vows or belonging to an approved religious order. The Beguines were the only female religious movement in the Middle Ages that owed neither their founding nor their inspiration to male clergy or religious. While the Beguines flourished in northern Europe in the thirteenth century, by the early fourteenth century, the Church, which had long honored and protected them, began to question their lifestyle. The name "beguine" is thought to have developed as a term of derision for "half-religious" women. Though untraditional (not part of "regular" orders), they were stricter and more pious than most nuns—"holier than thou," according to their detractors. More serious, they practiced an unrestrained style of mysticism, striving for ecstatic religious experience which they considered "liberating." According to Marguerite Porete, a widely read Belgian Beguine, the liberated soul does not need to pass through death, or through the Church, in order to experience the Beatific Vision. Porete was burned as a heretic in Paris in 1310. In 1312, The Council of Vienne, naming the Beguines a heretical sect, forced them to disband.

In most cases, popular heresies had begun with a desire to return to a simpler, more authentic form of Christian life. Many of these, however—groups whose practices, although radical were still orthodox—were forced into schism by the Church's unwillingness to make room for them in the fold.

It wasn't long after the appearance of heresy that the Church took pains to stamp it out. In the beginning, the local or regional bishop was the chief official entrusted with the task of maintaining doctrinal purity. In fact, this was one of the major reasons for the creation of this office in the early Church. These bishops would continue to exercise this duty, almost exclusively, throughout the first millennium and into the early centuries of the second. However, the magnitude and profundity of new threats to the established Church overtaxed the abilities and resources of the bishops to keep heresy under control. Besides, what was deemed heresy to one bishop might be considered only a nuisance to another. So the Church needed a more centralized system to root out the new threats to its orthodoxy.

The first Inquisitors, appointed by Pope Gregory IX in 1231, were Conrad of Marburg, a German priest, and Robert le Bougre, a Dominican friar who was given a roving commission in northern France. Marburg was murdered for his zeal and le Bougre suspended for excesses. In 1233, the pope sent several groups of Dominicans (whom he had earlier ordered to preach against heresy) to France as Inquisitors. As originally conceived, the Inquisition divided Europe into approximately forty zones, the entire organization being headed by the Inquisitor General in Rome. The latter oversaw the Grand Inquisitors who were responsible for the various zones; they, in turn, appointed the hundreds of Inquisitors trained in Canon Law who actually interrogated and tried heretics.

Although the procedures varied over time, those of Languedoc in southern France, considered typical, went like this: Two Inquisitors traveled together to the various villages and towns in their territory with a retinue of attendants and notaries. The itinerant route was soon found to be unsafe, so courts of inquiry were established in larger cities and the heretics came to them. A sermon would be given, both in the city and in surrounding parishes, "calling" for heretics. The priests then delivered summonses to those named. You might ask how their names got on the list? As early as 1184, Pope Innocent III had instructed bishops to search their dioceses for heretics and to ask the "good men" of the parishes to act as informers. In 1229, the Council of Toulouse established the precedent of protecting the identities of those informers, which greatly increased their ranks. The Church also hired professional heretic hunters to help ferret out the guilty. The intention was less to examine heretical beliefs than to reveal and get rid of heretics. Once rounded up, the accused were pressed to name names. In many cases, even when they were contrite and recanted, they had to name other heretics in order to receive absolution. The only hope a suspect had was to name his personal enemies; if they were the same as those who had accused him, their testimony was discredited.

Decisions were announced publicly, so were penalties. Voluntary (not coerced, as through torture) confessions earned milder punishments such as public scourging, or the wearing of a yellow cross on the front and back of one's outer garments as a badge of shame. The guilty were forced to undertake long (sometimes years) and expensive pilgrimages, or to join a crusade. Fines were imposed, houses destroyed. Even the dead could be found guilty and punished by being disinterred from holy ground and incinerated. Heretics, though repentant, might also be imprisoned for life. Unrepentant, they were burned. Because the Church was not allowed to administer the death penalty, it was the policy of the Inquisition to hand over uncontrite heretics, with an obligatory but empty plea for mercy, to secular authorities, who sent them to the stake.

Officially, appeals were forbidden, but early Inquisitors were known to be lenient. Recalling Pope Alexander III (and Roman law), they believed that it was better to acquit a sinner than punish an innocent. There were also practical reasons for their tolerance : it was the bishops who had to pay for the room and board of prisoners and, added to the cost of the Inquisitors and their retinue, this could be prohibitive. As secular authorities took over the costs, Church judges could afford to be stricter; they also managed to master their scruples. So in time, those Inquisitors who had merely aroused suspicion among the laity inspired hatred: an Inquisitor and his whole band were killed in Toulouse in 1242.

By the beginning of the fourteenth century, the Inquisition had evolved into an institution, its continuance guaranteed by the constant danger of heresy (especially now Beguines), the generally insecure conditions of the 1300s, and especially by the secular governments' recognition that heterodoxy could be politically and socially disruptive. While the Church depended on the support of the State, the State recognized the status and potential usefulness of the Church, particularly in France. In 1311, Philip the Fair persuaded the Inquisition to condemn the Knights Templars, a religious group which had become politically unacceptable. Thereafter, French kings regularly made bold to overturn Inquisition verdicts, again for political reasons. By the beginning of the fifteenth century, the Inquisition in northern France had become less an institution than a ceremonial convenience of the State, ready and ripe for the proceedings against Joan of Arc.

Joan fits squarely here because she was politically dangerous, not for reasons of birth or military prowess, but by virtue of her "saintliness." And as a "saint," she was an easy mark for the charge of heresy. The judges of the Inquisition, aided by juridical scholars from the University of Paris, indicted Joan as a "sorceress, diviner, false prophet, invoker of evil spirits, conspirator, magician...as superstitious, schismatic, sacrilegious, idolatrous, apostate, blasphemous, scandalous, seditious...as a disturber of the peace, inciter of war...as blood-thirsty, indecent, immodest in dress...as a traitor, a seductress" and most important, of course, as a "heretic."[1]

Joan was indeed a heretic according to the Church's definition of it. The Church expected simple, unquestioning obedience of its members. Joan concurred, but only so far; while embracing the Church triumphant, she sidestepped the dictates of the Church militant. Her position is clearly set forth in the trial record: "She fully believes that our Holy Father the Pope of Rome, the bishops, and other churchmen are appointed to guard the Christian faith and to punish those who transgress it, but, so far as her own actions are concerned, she will submit herself only to the church in Heaven—that is to say, to God, to the Virgin Mary and to the saints who are in Paradise."[2] From the beginning, Joan could have invoked Church support for her mission: she lived next door to her parish church; the diocesan seat in Toul was well within traveling distance of her home in Domremy. Yet she never spoke of her voices to the local priests or the bishop. Instead, on the advice of her voices, she sought the help of Robert de Baudricourt, the civil governor of Vaucouleurs. This point—that she revealed her mission to civil authorities rather than to the Church—was a stumbling block even in the much later process of her canonization. Joan's insistence "as far as her own actions [were] concerned" to turn a deaf ear to the earthy church linked her to other heretics—particularly the Beguines—who espoused the primacy of individual conscience.

Joan's similarity to the Beguines goes further. An intensely religious woman, she had taken no religious vows (except privately, to remain a virgin); her life was untraditional to say the least (a military leader, dressed as a man). Most of all, there was the business of her voices. Although Joan never claimed to be a mystic, her supporters maintained that her intense mysticism was the source of her prophecies. While the Church recognized holy mystics, the question of personal divine guidance was a thorny and dangerous one. Unholy mysticism was the source of the heresy of antinomianism or sinlessness, an accusation which had brought about the burning of Margaret of Porete and the eventual crushing of the Beguines. The Inquisition pressed this issue to Joan—hence the famous question put to her: "Are you in the state of grace?" to which she so wisely answered: "If I am, may God keep me there; if I am not may He put me there."[3] It was to the end of discovering whether Joan was a holy or false mystic that her judges urged her to describe the concrete sense experience of her voices. What did they smell like? What were they wearing? What language did they speak? Had she touched them? According to mystical tradition, visions could not be described in corporeal terms; genuine mystics usually spoke in obscure language. At first, Joan had done this. She was vague about the particulars of her visions, or poetic: "The light comes in the name of the voice,"[4] she said. Often she refused to answer, fearing to offend her voices by trying to delineate them. Gradually, however, exhausted and confused, Joan began to answer literally. "They smelled good; they had wings, crowns and long hair; they spoke French; yes [she] touched them when [she] embraced their feet."[5] In making her visions real, tainted with physicality, Joan condemned herself as a false mystic. The Church believed that saints and angels were incapable of assuming material form, that only demons could appear "in the flesh." Joan's visions were pronounced demonic; she was a blasphemer and a heretic to say they were saints.

It is worthwhile to backtrack a moment as an introduction to my final point in connection with Joan's heresy. More than four hundred years before Joan's death, in 1022 in Orléans (the city whose siege she had raised in 1429), several canons and lay nobles were condemned for heresy in the first case of burning as punishment in the medieval west. They claimed to have been inspired directly by the Holy Spirit and so were able to avoid the gospels and the Church. That was the formal charge against them. In fact, they were accused of holding sex orgies, of burning children so conceived in a baptism-mocking ceremony, of making bread with the ashes in a parody of the Eucharist, of desecrating the cross. In other words, of witchcraft. But witchcraft at that time was not a heresy. When it was a crime, it was a civil crime. By Joan's time, witchcraft was associated with devil worship, hence with a formal repudiation of Christianity and thus securely on the rolls as a heresy.

For her admirers then as now, it is shocking to think of Joan of Arc as a witch. Courageous, simple, human she was, but her remarkable gifts stood her outside the realm of the ordinary. To her enemies, it was outside the realm of the natural. Long before her trial, some had wondered if she was a witch. The priest who examined her at Vaucouleurs shook holy water on her to see if she would fly (had she been a witch, she would have). When Brother Richard, the famous holy man of Troyes, met her outside the gate of the city, he gave her the holy water test as well. While Joan, like the heretics at Orléans, was never accused of witchcraft, intangible advantages can readily be understood as evil by those who are jealous or suspicious; it was natural for Joan's enemies to see diabolical power in her apparent ability to suspend the natural order. Joan had caused the wind to change at Orléans; she divined the existence and site of the sword of St. Catherine de Fierbois; she seemed invulnerable to injury and insensible to pain; she jumped (or did she fly?) sixty feet from the prison tower at Beaurevoir, landing unhurt; she resuscitated a dead child at Lagny. Moreover, she accurately prophesied several events, including her own wounding and capture. It was charged by scholars at the University of Paris that these unnatural events were generated by Joan's conjuring of Belial, Satan, and Behemoth. When the Inquisition tried to impugn Joan's virginity, using male dress as proof, they failed. So they used this issue—one which particularly vexed them—to establish her unnatural (therefore diabolical) bent.

On May 29, 1431, Joan of Arc resumed the male garb that had been taken from her and recanted a confession that had been extorted a few days earlier. The next morning, wearing a tall paper mitre on which was written "Heretic, relapsed, apostate, idolatress," she was led to the marketplace at Rouen and burnt to death. In doing so well what she had been sent to do, Joan invoked political enemies strong enough to bring down on her the weight of Church history and the terrible power of the Inquisition.

A Classification of some Heresies after the year 1000

1. Free Spirits: Adamites, Blood Friends, Brethren of the Free Spirit, Spiritual Libertines, Quintinists, Turlupins.
2. Beggar Cults: Beghards, Beguines, Tafurs.
3. Apocalyptic Cults: Millennianists, Joachism, Salvationists
4. "Communist" Cults: Taborites, Wyclifites, Egalitarianists, Waldensians, Pastoureaux.
5. Witchcraft: Black and White witches.
6. Pantheistic Cults: Anabaptist forerunners.
7. "Offbeat Cults": Flagellants and Antichrist groups.
8. Individuals: Tancelm, Arnold of Brescia, Peter of Bruys.

Notes

1 Jules Quicherat, ed., *Procès de condemnation et de réhabilitation de Jeanne d'Arc, dite la Pucelle d'Orléans*, (Paris: J. Renouard et cils, 1841-1849; New York: Johnson Reprint Corp., 1965), 201-5.
2 Quicherat, 304.
3 Quicherat, 122.
4 Quicherat, 122.
5 Quicherat, 122.

Torture in European Justice
and the Trial of Joan of Arc

Julius R. Ruff

Réal del Sartre, Orléans

Torture was an essential aspect of Inquisition tribunals. While Joan of Arc was a victim of judicial torture only to a limited degree, as we will see, the practice was very much a part of the justice administered both by the State and the Church in western Europe from about the thirteenth century until the late eighteenth century.

Let me explain what I mean by torture. Amnesty International tells us that perhaps one third of all the world governments today engage in some kind of torture. The media remind us regularly that dictators such as Saddam Hussein use some kind of torture to cow the opposition into submission or to extract information from them. But the totalitarian regimes which typically use torture do not publicly own up to the practice; they are unwilling to admit that it is part of their system of trial and punishment. What I will discuss here is a practice that was an admitted part of a legal system, a recognized means for gathering information within the process of a trial.

To our standards today, the practice of torture seems bizarre and inhumane. In the first place, it violates our sacred Fifth Amendment protection against self-incrimination to torture someone, extract information from them, and then convict

Dr. Ruff teaches History at Marquette University.

them based on what they have been forced to say. Furthermore, it is grossly unethical to inflict pain without a verdict of guilt. Torture, however, has been part of the Western legal system until as recently as two hundred years ago.

What are the origins of "official" torture? According to historical sources, many ancient governments engaged in the practice. We have found papyrus documents suggesting that ancient Egyptians may have used torture to coax information from accused criminals. The Greeks of the classical age definitely employed torture as an information gathering tactic in their judicial proceeding. Because it was assumed that the Greek citizen was honorable and that his oath could be trusted, the Greeks confined their use of torture to slaves and foreigners, and tortured them only to elicit information from them, not as a punishment. In Aristophanes's *The Frogs*, we are given a laundry list of Greek torture techniques. The playwright tells us that the accused might be hung up by their wrists, have their flesh ripped with sharp instruments, or have rocks piled on their chests to summon answers from them. Perhaps the most unusual punishment was to hang the victim upside down and pour vinegar up his nostrils. In any case, the Greeks not only portrayed these methods in their "comedies," they used them.

The Romans also used torture; the same practices obtained—at least in the early days of the Republic—as had been the custom among the Greeks. The Romans only tortured slaves, it being assumed that the Roman citizen's oath was a guarantee of his truth-telling. In the Acts of the Apostles (22: 22-30), we read the account of St. Paul, leader of a persecuted sect, who was about to be tortured by Roman authorities. Paul, unafraid, had something up his sleeve. He raised himself up to his full height (which, we understand, wasn't very tall) and said the magic words: "*Civis Romanus sum*"—"I am a Roman citizen." The centurion who was about to flog him stopped cold on the brink of striking a Roman citizen, a crime worthy of serious punishment. As Rome became an Empire, however, torture began to spread from the ranks of the slaves to the lower orders of Roman society. And in the late Roman empire, torture was widely used against Roman citizens. The Romans, of course, created the ancient world's most sophisticated legal system; they established juridical principles which continue to guide us today. It was the Roman Emperor Trajan who stated what is still the basic principle of Western law: it is better that a hundred guilty men go free than that one innocent man be unjustly punished. But the Romans instituted a legal system based on a systematic search for the truth through tangible evidence, and torture was one of the means they used to this end. The rack, the pulley, branding, flogging, confining prisoners in a very small space called the "evil house"—all of these methods of extracting information from the accused were used in the Roman judicial system, and they were legal.

As Rome's rule in the west was supplanted by that of the Germanic tribes, the sophistication of western law declined. The barbarian tribes that overwhelmed Rome had little understanding of the principles of Roman law. However, they had a strong sense of the honor of a free individual; it would have been repugnant to them to torture a German warrior to gather evidence. They decided cases in a far different fashion. If an accuser came before one of the chieftains accusing a warrior of a crime, the chieftain, acting as a judge, would assemble the principals in the case and ask the accused person to take a compurgatory oath, swearing that he was not guilty. If the chieftain choose to question the oath, he might call upon other warriors, who knew the accused and could vouch for him, to swear an oath that the accused was innocent. Implicit in this is the idea that somehow God would punish those who took a false oath. Belief in a justice meted out through divine forces against false oath-takers discouraged perjury. However, if the defendant was not a free German warrior, someone whose word was not automatically respected, other processes were invoked to adjudicate cases: trial by ordeal or trial by combat. These procedures were also based on a blind faith in divine intervention rather than a rational search for evidence. In a trial by ordeal it was assumed that the guilty party would not survive, in trial by combat that the guilty party would lose. While interesting, these notions were not very sophisticated, and by the twelfth century the western world required something more sophisticated in the way of law.

What happened in twelfth century Europe is that Roman law was rediscovered by Church scholars and applied to the judicial proceedings of both the Church and the State. An important part of Roman law, in its rational search for the truth, was the definition of principles for admitting evidence to a case, that is, standards as to what constitutes adequate proof of guilt. And as Roman law was practiced in medieval and early modern Europe, the general principle was that, to convict somebody of the death penalty, either two eye witnesses or a confession was required. Now, we've all watched enough Perry Mason to know there are very rarely two eye witnesses. You've got one eye witness to the robbery and murder, then you've got somebody else who saw the accused running down the street with the victim's purse in one hand and a bloody knife in the other hand. But that's not two eye witnesses. According to the principles of Roman law, that would be incomplete proof of guilt. The judge, in such a case, would have very strong suspicion that the accused was indeed guilty, but he would not be able to convict and execute. What would he do? He would opt for the next best proof of guilt—indeed, what the medieval lawyers called the queen of proofs: confession. Now, most criminals are endowed with a healthy sense of self interest, so they don't readily confess. Well then, how do you get a criminal to confess to a crime? The answer is, you help him along: you torture him. And this is where torture enters medieval jurisprudence, to get the confession that the judge needs to convict.

Let us look at this more closely. What we need to understand first and foremost is that torture was conducted openly, formally, as part of the trial—not in a back room on the sly. To emphasize that, let me describe the actual process. If we are in France, the judge puts on his red robe with the ermine trim; he goes down to the torture chamber followed by a scribe; he proceeds to administer torture to the accused. The scribe records the event in precise detail, paying special attention to the words of the accused. A typical entry might read: "At two o'clock on the afternoon of October fifth, in the year of our Lord, fifteen hundred and seventy-three, [the accused] was placed on the rack; the crank was turned two times. [The accused] cried out, 'Mother of God, it hurts like the fires of hell!' The judge asked: 'did you kill [victim] on the fifteenth of August of this year?' [The accused] responded: 'I did not.' The rack was turned twice more. [The accused] cried out: 'yes, yes, I did it!'"— the accused finally giving out the information necessary to convict him. Such accounts are on record; there is nothing hidden. The whole register is available for study—the questions that were asked, how many times the rack was turned, and so forth. It was an official and legal part of the trial.

In most European countries, the defendant could be tortured at least twice in the course of a trial. In France, the process was referred to as the *Question* and it was divided into the *Question Préparatoire* (Preparatory Question), and the *Question Préalable* (Preliminary [to the execution] Question). The first question occurred when the judge had incomplete proof and sought to extract a confession from the accused. Assuming an incriminating answer to the first question, the second round of torture sought the names of the criminal's accomplices. So the poor guy was tortured twice, and then sent out to be executed.

Now, given that torture was legally a part of the trial, certain protections obtained for the defendant. Torture was only applicable in capital cases. Torture came only as a last resort when the judge had tried every other way available to him. In some countries, France for example, judges could only torture after an appeals court had ratified the decision to do so. Torture could not be administered on Sundays or Holy days. Certain people were exempt from torture: pregnant women, youths under the age of twelve or fourteen (depending on the country), the aged, and the infirm. In many countries, aristocrats were exempt; clergymen were always exempt.

And, of course, we all know who wrote the law codes, so anybody with a law degree was exempt from torture as well. A physician's examination was a regular part of the torture process to determine whether the accused could withstand the pain. If the physician opined that the torture would kill the accused, it could not be administered. We need to emphasize that torture was not intended to kill; the intent was merely to inflict sufficient pain in order to get a confession.

As part of the regular procedure of torture, the judge had to first threaten it. Generally that meant not only menacing words, but that the judge would take the accused on a tour of the torture chamber of the local court as a kind of psychological weapon to force the accused to panic and confess. This is the stage of the torture procedure experienced by Joan of Arc.

On May 9, 1431, Joan's judges ordered her taken from her cell to the torture chamber in the keep of the castle at Rouen. There she was shown the instruments of torture. According to custom, the executioner charged with the task was present to suggest his readiness to employ the tools of his gruesome profession. Joan's recorded response was: "Truly, if you were to have me torn limb from limb and send my soul out of my body, I would say nothing else. And if I did say anything, I should always say that you had made me say it by force." Joan's statement reveals, perhaps, some knowledge of the law on her part: a confession under torture had no validity unless it was repeated without torture under oath. Clearly, Joan refused to offer that possibility to her judges. Those magistrates returned Joan to her cell after the visit to the torture chamber, and she was left to dread the possibility of torture for three days. Nevertheless, she refused to make the judges' task easier with a "confession." Finally, on May 12, 1431, the judges in her trial voted eleven to three against torture, with one jurist commenting that they had sufficient evidence to convict her without torture. Thus St. Joan experienced only the preliminary stage in judicial torture. However, although Joan was not formally tortured but only shown the instruments, she was allowed to suffer "persecutions" and "torments" while in prison. Her jailers "mocked and derided" her and, above all, "attempts were made to violate her." Participants in her rehabilitation trial mentioned the "chains loading her body" and also "an iron cage made on purpose too small for her to lie down in..." although no one had actually seen it used.[2]

Had Joan been formally tortured, what means would have been used? Joan's comments, "torn limb from limb," suggest a rack, or perhaps a strappado, which was a widely used method at this time in France because it was cheap. All that was needed was a heavy pulley, attached to a ceiling beam, with a long rope running through it. The hands of the accused would be tied behind his back and attached to the pulley rope. He would then be lifted off the floor and let hang. The pain would have been excruciating so, hopefully, he would talk. Thumb screws and leg screws were also used. Sleep denial was favored in some countries. In Austria, they liked to shove the feet of the accused into the fireplace to see what he might have to say. All this done in the name of the truth.

An interesting note here: in most legal systems up to the seventeenth century, if the accused withstood the torture and did not confess, he was regarded as innocent and had to be released. It was a sort of a trial by ordeal. This seems rather illogical to us; it favors the hardy criminal with a high pain threshold over the innocent man with the low pain threshold. If you put me on a rack and started stretching me or stuck my feet in the fireplace, I'd probably swear on a stack of Bibles that elephants are purple—or that torture had never existed in any country at any time. Anything to stop the pain.

While the idea of torture is repugnant to us, it was not so in the view of our ancestors. By the standards of the twelfth and thirteenth centuries, torture was understood as a step forward in terms of criminal procedure: at least judges were finally looking for evidence rather than divine intervention.

By the way, torture was seldom used in England because of the nature of English law. There, a jury decided the facts of the case and all that was needed was enough evidence—either circumstantial or eye witness—to convince the jury that the person was guilty beyond a reasonable doubt in order to convict him. Not so in the Roman law countries such as France, Spain, Italy, Germany, where judges needed two eye witnesses or a confession to convict in capital cases.

Torture was used widely on the European continent by both the Church and the State through the eighteenth century; in that century, however, it began to die out. Why did this happen? The traditional answer given by historians is that, by the eighteenth century, the thinkers of the Enlightenment, particularly Voltaire and Beccaria (the great Italian legal thinker), were openly critical of such brutal elements of justice, pressing their governments to reform the system. I don't think that theory holds water any more. For one thing, we have enumerated acts of torture in French records and have found that torture began to diminish before Beccaria ever left law school in Pavia. It was already passing out of use in the early eighteenth century because the law was beginning to change. Legal scholars advised their kings to change the laws to make it possible to convict people with less than complete proof (admittedly not to the death penalty but to penalties lesser than death). And new penalties were being devised by the eighteenth century to punish crimes without execution. The British, for example, got rid of their law-breaking population by shipping them to the American colonies. Work houses were instituted, providing a sort of intermediary punishment between death and simply flogging somebody and turning them loose. As the law of proof changed and new punishments emerged, the need for torture diminished. Gradually, then, torture became passé in most of the Western world.

Of course, torture has been "rediscovered" in the twentieth century by totalitarian regimes, but its use is radically different than that which I have described. No regime admits to the use of torture today. Three hundred years ago, governments not only admitted it, they kept written records of it.

Notes

1   *Joan of Arc in Her Own Words*, ed. trans. Willard Trask, (New York: Books & Co.,1966), 132.

2   Marina Warner, *Joan of Arc* (New York: Alfred A. Knopf, 1981), 27.

Joan of Arc: Saint or Symbol?

John D. McCabe

Déchin, Chinon

"Joan of Arc: Saint or Symbol?" There was an idea behind this title before there was a paper to follow it. The idea was essentially this: most of the notions I had acquired about Joan I had derived from reading modern treatises or from watching contemporary productions. My image of Joan was a blend of Ingrid Bergman and Julie Harris: a confused collage of magnificent peasant nobility with the winsome impudence of adolescence. My quick perusal of the late greats who wrote major plays or studies about Joan included Mark Twain, George Bernard Shaw, Maxwell Anderson, and Virginia Sackville-West, to name only those writing in English, a curious collection of emphatic public atheists and skeptics, united in their common cause of celebrating Joan as a symbol of something or other, but always something secular. Now my study of things medieval has over the years engendered in me an equal skepticism about the exaggerated claims of modernity. And when the moderns simply rebuff medieval claims about sanctity, or ignore them with an embarrassed silence, or, worse still, appropriate them as symbols of something more modern, more profound, more secular, well, it gets my dander up.

Dr. McCabe teaches English at Marquette University.

Hence the title: "Joan of Arc: Saint or Symbol?" It could well have been "Joan of Arc: Medieval or Modern?"

One of my professional interests is the literature of England of the fourteenth century, that is, the poetry of Geoffrey Chaucer and his contemporaries, the authors of *Piers Plowman*, *Sir Gawain and the Green Knight*, and a poem entitled *Pearl* — an exquisitely wrought poem wherein the dreamer/narrator holds a conversation with a young girl he once knew who is now dead and who walks radiantly with the 144,000 virgins in the company of the Lamb and who speaks with absolute authority on the mysteries of grace and forgiveness and redemption It is a poem about the communion of saints. But I get ahead of myself. My primary focus has always been on the poetry of Chaucer, and Chaucer died in 1400. In my view of history, western civilization abruptly went into a decline in 1400, entering a downward spiral from which we have yet to recover. Joan, as you know, was born in 1412 or thereabouts, a dozen years after the death of Chaucer, just too late to catch my attention—born, so to speak, on the wrong side of that great dividing line. It wasn't that she was French that was the problem—it was that she belonged to the fifteenth century. A friend of mine who can claim some talent as a wit suggested that I title my presentation: "Chaucer's View of Joan," as one might mount a parody of a scholar's study of Lincoln's opinion of Teddy Roosevelt, or JFK's influence on FDR. Actually, this is not as absurd as it may seem, given the liberties that historians now take in reconstructing and de-constructing historical records. I heard just the other night an account of a scholar of considerable reputation who has put forth the view that Joan wasn't burned at the stake at all; no, some hapless village girl was made to stand in for her while Joan ran off and married well and lived a decent matron's life on the fringe edges of the aristocracy. What are the limits of credulity? Why not have Chaucer's view of Joan? One's fancy is as good as another's, and besides, Chaucer has the right credentials. He, after all, among all the medieval poets, showed the widest range of sympathetic portrayal of women, some good and some no better than they should be: Criseyde, the Wife of Bath, the anguished Dorigen, the long-suffering Griselda, and the martyr Cecilia. Yes, Chaucer wrote a narrative account of the life of St. Cecilia, little known outside a relatively small circle of devoted readers of Chaucer, but in my judgment worthy of a much larger audience. It is one of Chaucer's finest poetic achievements, lean and spare in style. The tale is unabashedly hagiographical; it recounts and celebrates the life of Cecilia as that story had been preserved and handed down for more than a thousand years of Christian memory. Here are some of the essential features of her life as Chaucer tells it:

1. *Her dedicated virginity.* Indeed, on her wedding night, she declares to her aston
   ished husband: you lay one hand on me and the angel who is always at my side
   will slay you on the spot.

2. *The unexpected consequences of her dedication.* Her husband, Valerian, is converted
   to the faith and brings with him his brother, Tibertius, and later their prison
   guard, Maximus.

3. *Her familiar converse with the angels.* They guide her with counsel and lavish her
   with roses and lilies.

4. *Her unshakable trust in the Church* and in Pope Urban, in spite of the difficulties
   this may bring.

5. *Cecilia's confrontation with the tribunal.* Before the power of the state, she is clear of
   eye and firm of speech. Her speeches there are pointedly Trinitarian and
   Christocentric.

6. And finally, *she is sent to the flames,* though, in this instance, the flames do not
   consume her and she must be dispatched by the sword.

Thus the Cecilia of Chaucer offers a remarkable range of parallels with the life of
Joan, parallels that enable us to discern a kind of paradigm for sanctity, or at least
for hagiography, a paradigm of a distinctly un-modern kind. I will have some sug-
gestions to offer about these parallels and paradigms, but first I must acknowledge
some major differences.

The details of the life of Cecilia belong to tradition. What we know of the life of
Joan is a matter of historical record.

For his source for Cecilia, Chaucer turned to a compendium of the lives of the
saints that went by the title *Legenda Aurea*, or the *Golden Legend*, which was enormously popular throughout Christendom. What we can verify historically is pretty
limited. Cecilia died in the year 230 or thereabouts; it is said that she was buried in
the catacombs of St. Calixtus and that her remains were removed to a church named
in her honor by Pope Paschal in 821. When this Church was rebuilt in 1589, her
coffin was found there. The original burial site of Cecilia was uncovered in excava-
tions in 1851. The Church deals with the saints over centuries.

The details of the life of Joan are better known, at least over the span of the last
two years of her life, from her setting forth for Vaucouleurs to seek out Robert de
Baudricourt, in February 1429, to her meeting with the Dauphin in Chinon a
month—and some three hundred miles—later, through the delivery of Orleans

under her banner in May of that year, to the coronation of Charles VII at Reims on July 17, 1429. The public career of Joan is only five months old, with a spring and summer radiance. What follows is that long winter of 1429-30 with one disappointment after another: the failure of the army to take Paris, the vacillations of Charles, the capture of Joan by the enemy that spring, in May 1430, which marks the beginning of a year of imprisonment leading to condemnation and her death by fire on Wednesday, May 30, 1431. What we know of Joan we know primarily through the testimony of eye (and ear)-witnesses to these events delivered at the process of rehabilitation of Joan twenty-five years later. And nearly five hundred years later, on May 16, 1920, Benedict XV proclaimed Joan a saint. The Church deals with the saints over centuries.

The accounts of the lives of Cecilia and Joan show a difference also in the manner of their deaths. There is no question that Cecilia is accorded the martyr's palm in her death. She died in defense of the faith, at the hands of those who militantly denied the tenets of faith. The same may not be said of Joan, as Fr. Tavard reminds us here in his remarkable account of the depths of the spirituality of St. Joan. Those who sent her to her death, however cruel or vengeful they may have been, did not do so in denial of or hatred for the faith, a condition for martyrdom. But that distinction, it occurs to me without meaning to sound irreverent, may have seemed a cold comfort to Joan as she was bound to the stake.

Did Joan know the outlines of the life of the martyr Cecilia? I don't know. I'm not aware that Joan ever mentioned her. But Joan did have an easy familiarity with the saints, and given the popularity of Cecilia throughout the medieval period, it is rather more likely than not that she knew about her. But that is not to my point: I am more taken by the parallels, by the paradigm. Though separated by some twelve hundred years, Joan shares with Cecilia:

—a dedicated virginity
—an easy communication with the angels and the saints
—a loyalty to the Church under the shepherding of the Pope, at whatever cost
—courage in confronting magistrates given authority for granting life or death
—revealing before their respective tribunals an account of their faith that is re
    markably Trinitarian and Christocentric. (I am again indebted to Fr. Tavard
    for his analysis of the Trinitarian dimension of St. Joan's spirituality.)
—clear-eyed purposefulness and a single-minded sense of mission
—compassion
—fidelity even to enduring a violent death.

Are these coincidences? Or are they indications that there is something etched in the lives of the saints that we are called upon to notice. In the extremities of their actions and their judgments, we are scandalized; most of all we want to explain them away, as do the detractors of Joan: Joan wasn't burned at the stake at all, or the records of testimony at the rehabilitation have been falsified, or her canonization was strictly an adroit political maneuver. Or perhaps we are compelled the other way, as are so many contemporary admirers of Joan, to translate anything so remarkable as her life to a more remote, disembodied, and manageable symbolic order, to reduce her life to an idea, or even an ideal, such as "The Natural Man" or the "Life Force" or the "Vitalist Spirit." But the fact about the annals of the saints is that they press in on us, giving testimony of living persons, in real historical moments and human situations, persons being in the world and acting in the world, but acting in such a way that nothing in the world, nothing we could have thought or imagined or dreamt, can explain.

From the parallels in the lives of these two young maidens, called to their deaths in their youthful prime, I draw a paradigm. For centuries, St. Cecilia had a profound influence upon the piety and imaginations of faithful Christians. They were stirred by her audacity. In our own age, Cecilia has faded from our collective memory, but St. Joan has risen to prominence and, especially in the last century, has attracted the interest and devotion of believers and non-believers alike, and for a similar reason, because we are stirred by her audacity. The image of Joan, the "wee one," as Fr Tavard has nicely dubbed her, standing before the powers of church and state, mobilizing armies, freeing cities, crowning kings, noble in defeat, courageous in death: it is too much and she becomes the icon. By what means can we reclaim for her the accolade of saint? If we measure sanctity in human terms, then it makes good sense to canonize her for her audacity, for her self-possession, for her spunk. But if we read the words of Joan that have come down to us, and try to discern therein her own understanding of herself, we do not find her claiming her authority in her spunkiness—we find her always claiming only the authority of the counsel that had come to her. She is a saint not because she was audacious but because she was prudent: and I mean prudence here with the force that St. Thomas brings to it in his description of prudence as an infused cardinal virtue. Prudence is simply doing what God asks one to do; prudence is surrendering oneself entirely to God; prudence is becoming (in another excellent phrase of Fr. Tavard) fully "available to God." And that is what Joan did. And how do we know it? By reading the record, by hearing Joan's own voice:

—When I was thirteen, I had a voice from God to help me to govern myself. The first time I was terrified…There was a great light all about.

—Above all, St. Michael told me that I must be a good child, and that God would help me…. He told me that St. Catherine and St. Margaret would come to me and that I must follow their counsel; that they were appointed to guide and counsel me in what I had to do…for it was at Our Lord's command.

—And when I have made my prayer to God, I hear a voice that says to me: 'Child of God: go, go, go. I shall be with you to help you. Go.' And when I hear that voice I feel a great joy. I would that I might ever be in that state.

—My counsellors are three. There is the one who remains with me always, another comes and goes and visits me often, and the third is he with whom the other two take counsel.

—I do best by obeying and serving my sovereign Lord, that is, God.

—I believe as firmly as I believe that our Lord Jesus Christ suffered death to redeem us from the pains of hell that they are St. Michael, and St. Gabriel and St. Catherine and St. Margaret, whom Our Lord sends to comfort and counsel me…That Jesus has failed me I deny.[1]

Prudence, in Aquinas's account of it, is attending to good counsel, being well-advised, and then living by it. The infused virtue of Prudence is the operation of grace in nature.[2]

I am fully aware of the irony in calling Joan prudent. The charge most frequently levelled against her was her recklessness, and with some good reason. Was it reasonable to risk life and limb for that ninny-dauphin? I am reminded of a line in Robert Bolt's *A Man for All Seasons*, when Thomas More comes to realize that he has been betrayed by a young Thomas Cromwell: More turns to Cromwell, saying that he understands ambition, but adds "For Wales, Thomas, for Wales?" As we might say to Joan: "For Charles, Joan, for Charles?" But again, such is to miss the point: she didn't do it for herself; she didn't do it for Charles; she didn't even do it for France (though one can say that there was justice on her side in standing up against oppression); politics was not her motive. She is crystal clear on this point: she did what she did "for her sovereign Lord, that is, for God." She did what she was asked to do.

The manifestations of the virtue of prudence—doing God's will —in the life of a saint is moment of coalescence: in it we can see coming together the full rational, volitional, and affective powers of the soul fused in one act. Prudence in a single act encompasses understanding: it looks to the past, is circumspect in attending to the present, is prescient with regard to the future. Prudence is teleological, directed to an end, informed by faith, sustained in hope. The judicial side of this virtue is complemented by what we can call the executive side: the quick dispatch of action (*solertia*), alert, prompt, firm, swift, animated by charity, disposed to kindness. Such are the virtues we discern in Cecilia and in Joan.

Such are the lineaments of a saint, not a symbol; but to come full circle and close this off, let us link this saint to a symbol. Jean Anouilh uses the symbol of the lark to concentrate the qualities he uncovers in Joan. That's fine, but I am mindful also of another fowl in flight, "The Windhover" of Gerard Manley Hopkins, wherein Hopkins sees in the abrupt change in the pattern of flight of the bird, in that instantaneous motion, a breaking forth of the beauty of his chevalier, of Christ our Lord:

> Brute beauty and valour and act, oh, air, pride, plume, here
> Buckle! and the fire that breaks from thee then, a billion
> Times told lovelier, more dangerous, O my chevalier.[3]

Notes

[1] The words of Joan cited in this paper are drawn from *Joan of Arc: In Her Own Words*, ed. and trans. Willard Trask. (New York: Turtle Point Press, 1996).

[2] St. Thomas Aquinas' discussion of Prudence may be found in the *Summa theologiae*. IIaIIae, Q. 47-56.

[3] *Poems of Gerard Manley Hopkins*, (Mt. Vernon, New York: Peter Pauper Press, n.d.).

A Psychosocial Case Study:
Joan of Arc as a Marquette Student

Dr. Sherri Coe-Perkins

Mercié, Domremy

The Dean of Students has asked me to address you, as the members of the Student Conduct Board, regarding the mental health of one of our students. I appreciate this opportunity and do not envy you the task of advising the dean about whether this student should be retained or dismissed from our University.

As a psychology professor and psychotherapist in the University Counseling Center, I consult with others when asked to develop an evaluation of a student. So what I share with you this evening is the result of sustained discussion with my faculty colleagues and the entire Counseling staff of psychologists, social workers and a consulting psychiatrist.

I stand before you tonight and state the case of the student in question, one Jeannette Darche. I have been asked to address these issues in her regard: What is the status of Jeannette's mental health? Should she remain at the University? If she is retained, what treatment plan would be suggested? I have the student's written permission, as well as that of her parents, to review all particulars of this matter with you.

Dr. Coe-Perkins is former dean of Student Affairs at Marquette University.

Background

Jeannette Darche is a single, eighteen-year-old Caucasian female, of average height and weight, with brown eyes and black hair; she lives in Cobeen Hall, where she seems happy and comfortable. She is an Arts and Sciences student who has not decided on a major, although she is inclined toward theology; she is uncertain about a career, but has shown an interest in our Army ROTC program.

The first in her family to go to college, subject is from a strict, Catholic, middle income family, who resides in a rural community in upstate Wisconsin. Her father—clearly the dominant parent—and her mother are farmers; both have transmitted the importance of hard work and moral values to their children. Jeannette has two brothers, one of whom is older than she, and one older sister. Jeannette was an academically average high school student, with a few close female friends. She reports to me that she has never dated and that she is a virgin. There is no history of drug or alcohol abuse or mental illness in the family, and Jeannette was never subject to serious physical illness or injury. She seems easy-going and personable, although her parents indicate she has been more introspective since the age of about twelve, often preferring to spend time "daydreaming," in a field on the family's property. Otherwise, Jeannette observed a usual family routine and enjoyed her life on the farm.

Psychosocial Functioning

During the last six years, since she was about twelve years old, Jeannette has experienced voices and visions on an almost daily basis. She believes the voices are those of certain saints, one male and two female, sent to her by God, who come to her as great entities of light. She only recently told her parents about these phenomena and has also confided in her roommate and a few floor mates. At Marquette, the visions and voices have continued, most often when she is sitting on the lawn of central mall near the Joan of Arc Chapel or when she is actually in the chapel. The voices instruct her to be a good person, to talk to God daily, to serve others, and to assume leadership roles.

Accordingly, the student now attends church daily instead of weekly; engages in personal reflection twice daily; participates in service activities through University Ministry, which she performs three or four times a week; and is formally investigating our Army ROTC program. She has also joined the planning committees for Fr. Wild's inauguration and the Joan of Arc Celebration, asking to assist with the arrangements for the historical reenactment of the crowning of the dauphin as Charles

VII. Furthermore, she has just become president of Cobeen's Hall Council and she has taken a special interest in helping her RA with various organizational duties and providing unsolicited input on agenda items for floor meetings, which she occasionally attempts to lead. She aspires to become the first sophomore elected president of the student government association.

Over the last year, the voices have also begun to tell her about events before they happen. For example, at home during her senior year in high school, she was told about the death of a teacher one month before the teacher was in a car accident and passed away. On campus, she was informed on the first day of Orientation that a particular Cobeen woman would drop out of school on the first day of classes five days later, which, in fact, happened.

Some of Jeannette's actions and self-reports have been disconcerting to others: the parents of those with whom she lives, who are afraid for the welfare of their daughters and have complained to the Dean of Students and the residence hall staff, who have had to re-direct Jeanette's interest in taking charge of the floor and monopolizing meetings. Moreover, a few faculty have observed Jeannette talking to herself while sitting on the grass of central mall and Public Safety officers have noted that she asks for access to the Joan of Arc Chapel when it is closed. Most recently, subject has cut her hair, has begun to wear men's clothing and has started fencing classes at a fitness center. In addition, she wants to bring her horse to the Milwaukee area and has called a County office to find out about boarding stables accessible to Marquette through her UPASS card.

She has also reported new messages from her voices, to the effect that something very remarkable and frightening will happen to her next year when she turns nineteen. Nevertheless, she continues to express her intention of being faithful to her voices and the belief that God's saints will serve as her "navigators and guides" even if some horrendous event should occur.

Diagnosis

In a lengthy case conference, we first reviewed the results of two psychological tests administered to the subject: the Minnesota Multiphasic Personality Inventory, which did not support the existence of traits commonly characteristic of disabling psychological abnormality, and the projective tool known as the Rorschach Inkblot, which failed to demonstrate a significant relation between its scores and relevant criteria for a diagnosis of concern. These results, in combination with an analysis of my case notes from over eight hours with the subject, led us to conclude that Jeannette is not suicidal, nor does she pose a risk to others.

We also reviewed several possible diagnoses. The worse-case scenario is that Jeannette is at the start of a *schizophrenic process* as suggested by these behaviors: a change in her social interactions beginning at age twelve, aggression in pursuing leadership roles, daydreaming, a religious fixation, hallucinations, delusions, and feelings of grandiosity and paranoia. But each of these symptoms may be otherwise explained and she has not exhibited other key symptoms of this disorder, such as fundamental disturbances in reality relationships, a lack of coherence in associative and thought processes, emotional blunting, a pronounced inward orientation, a lowering of moral standards, or a deterioration in habits of personal hygiene. We therefore eliminated this diagnosis.

We also considered the possibility that Jeannette may have an *obsessive-compulsive* disorder, as exemplified in three particular ways: her ritual of establishing time for reflection twice a day, her irresistible need to be in or near places of worship, and her preoccupation with leadership roles. But since these actions are not necessarily irrational, we have also discounted this diagnosis.

We further reviewed a psychological stress reaction known as *identification,* when individuals identify themselves with others who are most like themselves or who possess the qualities which they most desire. This ego defense mechanism, which we all use to some extent, allows us to experience vicarious achievements and feelings of adequacy, such as when our Golden Eagles win a game. In the matter before us, however, Jeannette's identity seems to have been inordinately influenced by the life of a religious figure; specifically, it is as though her identity has become blended into the identity of Joan of Arc.

Although identification may not explain everything, it may have some relevance to our final diagnosis: we believe that Jeannette Darche is experiencing a *developmental or adjustment disorder.* Human development tends to follow a definite schedule, not only in terms of physical and motor development but also in emotional, intellectual and social development. At each stage of the life span, specific tasks must be mastered if one is to maintain a so-called normal course of development. In Jeannette's case, recall that she was first visited by the voices and visions at about age twelve, the onset of puberty, occurring toward the end of the stage known as middle childhood. Tasks at this stage include building wholesome attitudes toward oneself and understanding one's gender assignment. Is it possible that the emergence of Jeannette's voices and visions is related to her failure to resolve these tasks?

A similar question may be asked about Jeannette at age seventeen, when the voices began informing her about events in the future. In this stage of late adolescence, tasks include establishing a clear sense of identity, accepting one's physical and psychological changes, and understanding one's sex role. And now, at age eighteen, Jeannette is faced with sets of tasks from two previous stages, in addition to those of early adulthood, which center around integrating the various maturational tasks and traits into an harmonious whole.

We also question Jeannette's apparently undifferentiated sexuality and if she is fearful about expectations that accompany the formation and expression of her sexuality and sex role. She seems to have suppressed various aspects of her sexuality as indicated, for example, in her change of appearance and lack of involvement with the opposite sex. Moreover, her strong belief in Catholicism may be a significant intervening variable.

Consider again the defense mechanism of identification as juxtaposed onto the adjustment process. Jeannette may subconsciously aspire to reflect the life of Saint Joan, who, as we all know, cut her hair, wore men's clothing, joined the army, became a leader of others, rode horses, handled swords, and was a virgin country girl from a devout Catholic family with a strict paternal figure. She also, from age twelve, had visions, heard the voices of saints and, according to historical accounts, later developed an ability to foretell events. If this is so, one wonders what lies ahead for Jeannette next year, when she turns nineteen, the age that Joan was tried, convicted and executed for heresy, sorcery, idolatry and blasphemy.

Despite all of this, however, Jeannette continues to function successfully at Marquette, as detailed in reports I have from her professors and peer group members. She has even curtailed some of her aggressive actions in Cobeen Hall.

Recommendation and Proposed Treatment

We in the Counseling Center recommend that Jeannette Darche be permitted to stay at the University. There is absolutely no evidence to suggest that she is psychotic or dysfunctionally neurotic. To separate her from Marquette at this time would be ill-advised, unnecessary, and illegal. The University needs to support Jeannette, perhaps more intentionally and intrusively than has already been the case; we need to be mindful of the American Disabilities Act, which prohibits discrimination based solely on a physical, learning, or psychological disorder.

We suggest the following treatment plan, each part of which will require the subject's consent and cooperations:

First: Since Jeannette is comfortable in University Ministry, she should enter into counseling with a lay minister or Jesuit so she may discuss aspects of her faith and talk freely about her visions and voices.

Second: Her pastoral counselor should eventually facilitate a referral to the Counseling Center so Jeannette can explore key developmental tasks needing resolution and her mental health progress may be monitored through on-going therapy.

Third: Identify a faculty member or an administrator who would mentor Jeannette, help her get involved in some of our leadership development programs, and assist her in integrating her learnings from counseling with selected leadership roles.

Fourth: Offer support and guidance to Jeannette's roommate and floor mates, so that they and their parents will be reassured that Jeannette is not a danger in the community and they will be relieved of some of the responsibility they currently feel for her welfare.

And *fifth:* The treatment team of the Jesuit, mental health practitioner, and mentor should meet periodically to coordinate their efforts and refine the treatment plan as necessary.

Conclusions

We in the Counseling Center have determined that Jeannette Darche is experiencing an adjustment disorder characterized by a failure to resolve key developmental tasks in previous stages of her life resulting in an inability to express her full and integrated identity as a young adult. She defends against these adjustment problems by identifying with a religious figure whose non-traditional life serves to justify Jeannette's non-normative behaviors and enhance her self-esteem. Her voices and visions are perhaps functional in nature and we believe she poses no threat to herself or others.

Our considered conclusion is that Jeannette Darche has a right to her voices and visions if she is doing well academically and socially. Consider other students who persistently and zealously pursue leadership roles, those whose patterns of service are so exceptional that they are nominated for the Aruppe Award? Are we concerned about students with green hair and earrings in their noses? Are there not those in our midst who, like Jeannette, are celibate, dress differently, hold firm religious beliefs, reflect daily, pray a lot, and talk to God?

Let us remember that standards of mental health are based on what *most* people think, feel, do, and look like most of the time in our culture. But research cautions us to adjust our theories for those who may be gifted or otherwise different. Whether Jeannette Darche is "gifted" or just "otherwise different," she follows our University Ethos Statement and she is successfully negotiating her way through our academy. Who are we to censure this student because of her unquestioning faith and rather remarkable spirit in transforming her beliefs into actions? To penalize her because her experiences may defy our tests of reason and rules of normalcy?

My own clinical intuition is that there is something quite special about Jeannette, although I am unable to capture and communicate it adequately. While in some ways childlike, she projects a certain inner strength and spiritual maturity. While seemingly innocent, there is something all-knowing about her. I have actually begun to believe that she may be destined to achieve something great, although I know not when or how. I have the impression that, if brought before this Board today, Jeannette would address you with something out of a modern day movie or play about the life of Joan of Arc; she might say, "What I am, I cannot denounce. What I have done, I do not deny."

And so let us respect the way this student has chosen to pursue excellence, to find God in all things, and to become a woman for others as a leader-in-service. We do not have the right to demand that she follow our blueprint for how she should conduct her own self-actualization process. I have confidence that Jeannette will eventually find the meaning of her voices and visions and unfold her identity. So let her be free to discover her best Self in her own way. Let her be free to live out her faith. Let her be free to keep her head tilted to the sky, where she looks everyday for counsel, comfort, and direction. Let her be free like the lark—the tiny European bird known for its unique song and for its steep upward flight toward the heavens.

Respected members of the Student Conduct Board, we urge you to retain Jeannette Darche as a member of the student body at Marquette University.

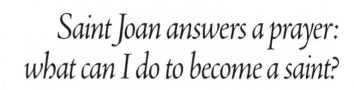

Saint Joan answers a prayer:
what can I do to become a saint?

Embrace solitude.
Hear the music in your soul.

Work for the transformation of yourself and your world.
Welcome suffering so you can shed tears for those who suffer.
Nurture a passion for justice; act even beyond your ken for the sake of others.

Know Christ's love in your heart that you may be inspired to greater love of others.

Wear your heart ever on the outside,
wear your "warts" there as well;
let others see you're a bit mad,
as you know yourself to be.

Bury yourself in God.

Dr. Mary E. Feeley

Dr. Feeley is director of University Ministry at Marquette University.
Drawing by Alice Pollack.

Joan of Arc: A Brief Life

Mary Elizabeth Tallon

Domremy, the place of Joan's birth, lies in the Meuse valley in northern France. Here, where the river flows gently, the valley fans out between the wooded hills of Lorraine to form a remarkably peaceful landscape. In the small village of only fifty houses, the home of the d'Arc family stands today, as it did when Joan was born in 1412, immediately adjacent to the church whose bells tolled the daily prayers of the villagers. Here Joan spent her early years, sharing the life of a peasant farmer with her father, Jacques d'Arc; her mother, Isabelle Romée; her sister, and her two brothers. An apparently ordinary young girl, Joan spent her days spinning or shepherding the animals. On village feast days, the young girls wove garlands and danced around the "faerie tree," a wide-branching beech that was the legendary gathering place of fairies. Joan often danced and sang with her friends, but not always. She preferred sometimes to disappear to a tiny chapel in the pathless woods—a dense stand of ancient oaks at whose edge the "faerie tree" stood—to pray. Later in Joan's life, a prophecy that had been spoken by Merlin and Venerable Bede would be remembered: France would be lost by a woman and saved by a virgin from an ancient forest.

One summer noontime, in 1424—Joan was about twelve years old then—she heard a voice coming from the direction of the church amid a blinding white light. The voice made itself known to her as St. Michael. His first message was simple: "Be a good girl; God will help you." When he came again, he gently advised her that she needed to prepare to come to the aid of France. Soon, Saints Catherine and Margaret joined St. Michael. Joan's early uneasiness in their presence gave way to joy and then to confidence that they were truly God's messengers; she later described them as beautiful and clean smelling, with melodious voices. Thereafter, the saints—she called them her voices—came to her often, especially in the church bells and when she prayed in the woods. Joan told neither family nor friends, afraid that she would be forbidden to obey her voices which, with increasing urgency, were telling her that she must leave home to go to the aid of her country. In 1428, in Joan's sixteenth year, the voices became insistent: France was in grave danger. The French and English had been in a state of intermittent war since 1337 over the right to certain territories and to the French crown. In 1420, the Treaty of Troyes, signed by France's "mad" king, Charles VI, declared Henry V of England heir to the French throne; Charles's son, the dauphin and lawful heir, was barred from royal succession with the complicity of his mother, Isabelle, who suggested that he was illegitimate. Many considered Queen Isabelle to be the "woman" of the ancient prophecy who would "lose" France.

Joan left Domremy in May of 1428 to enlist the help of Robert de Baudricourt, the governor of Vaucouleurs. She entered his audience chamber in her patched red dress, curtsied politely, and asked him to send a message to the dauphin from her Lord, saying that she would lead Charles to be crowned. "Who is your lord," he asked? "The King of Heaven," she answered. Baudricourt was surprised and amused, then sent her home to her father for a thrashing. That winter, pressed by her voices, Joan went again to Vaucouleurs. She left Domremy after Christmas, as though for a short while, but was never to return. This time, Baudricourt took her more seriously. The city of Orléans was under seige by the English; if Orléans fell, the French cause was lost. Baudricourt listened to Joan, impressed with her honesty and sense of purpose. Still, he promised nothing. Then, on February 12, a date Baudricourt would remember, she pushed her way into his chamber: "You have done ill to delay in sending me! This very day, near Orléans, a great disaster has taken place!" A few days later, Baudricourt and a priest visited Joan; he had just received word that the devastating Battle of the Herrings had taken place on February 12, and Joan could have had no knowledge of it except by supernatural means. Baudricourt needed to know if she was a witch or, indeed, a messenger of God. Joan's devout humility in the priest's presence convinced him; he sent word to the dauphin and prepared Joan for her journey to Chinon.

Disguised as a page, in the company of several soldiers, Joan left Vaucouleurs late in the afternoon of February 23, 1429. As the 350 mile journey to Chinon lay within enemy territory, they were obliged to travel by night, their horses' hooves wrapped in rags to dull the sound of their steps. They stayed at monasteries when they could, slept on the ground when they had to, but Joan never complained about pain or fatigue. Joan's arrival at Chinon caused quite a stir, the townsfolk curious to see this girl who insisted on seeing the dauphin. After three days of questioning by Charles's ministers, Joan was summoned into the great hall of the chateau—a room filled with more than three hundred curious nobles and courtiers. Charles Valois, the dauphin, was poor, homely, and overwhelmed with his royal responsibilities. His melancholy lassitude had encouraged his power hungry advisors, notably Georges de la Trémouille, to usurp his authority. Treated like a fool, Charles often acted like one. Legend has it that Charles was persuaded to hide behind several courtiers in order to test Joan. To the crowd's amazement—Joan had never seen Charles—she went directly to him and knelt: "Gentle dauphin, I am called Joan the Maid. The King of Heaven sent me to you." She made Charles three promises: to raise the seige of Orléans, to crown him King of France, and to drive the English from French soil. He asked her for proof that her message to him was indeed from God. What Joan said in confidence to the dauphin is not known, but what she told him changed him. Charles became animated and focussed, vowing to give her what she needed to achieve her goals. An army was raised, commanded by the duke of Alençon; Joan was given a squire, a chaplain, a suit of armor, and a standard of her own design. She refused Charles's offer of a sword, however, saying she wanted the one that was buried behind the altar of the church of St. Catherine in Fierbois. No one knew of such a sword. But because of his faith in Joan, an armorer went to look. The sword was indeed there and, as centuries of rust fell from it, five crosses were revealed on the blade, just as Joan had described them. Joan's new weapon was thought a miracle—as miraculous as the new weapon of the gathered army: hope.

When Joan started for Orléans, in April of 1429, the city had been under seige for nearly six months; the battle between the English and the Orléanais had settled into periodic skirmishes and the French were losing heart. Joan's troops approached Orleans from the southeast, across the Loire river, but a strong wind prevented their crossing. Joan went quietly aside to pray, and, to everyone's astonishment, the wind suddenly changed. In the following days, the French routed the English, taking St. Loup, St. Jean le Blanc, les Augustins. During the fierce, fifteen hour battle for Les Tourelles, Joan was wounded—as her voices told her she would be. She had purposefully worn armor that left her face and neck unprotected so her soldiers could always recognize her. An arrow pierced her shoulder near the neck and passed completely through her body, and she fell from the scaling ladder. The English cheered (they knew her reputation and feared her); the French trembled. But Joan rallied. One of her captains, Jean Dunois, severed the tip of the arrow and Joan herself pulled out the shaft. She raised her standard and rushed back into battle, her men behind her. The English, retreating over a bridge whose timbers were burning, plunged into the river and were dragged down by their armor. The next morning, Joan and her captains rode out of the west gate of Orléans to watch the retreat of the remaining English army. Amid the wild rejoicing, Joan prayed for the English dead. She had achieved an important victory, strategically and symbolically; now she was ready to keep her second promise to the dauphin: to have him crowned at Reims.

Ever since Clovis, the first Christain king of the French, was annointed there in 496, Reims had been the traditional place of crowning for a French king. Although the road from Orléans to Reims passed through enemy territory, victory followed Joan and her army. They won many battles, notably at Patay, when a whole English army fled; in some cases, the keys of enemy cities were handed to them peacefully. In July of 1429, less than five months after Joan left Domremy, she arrived in Reims with the dauphin. The English had stolen the crown of Charlemagne and the book containing the coronation ritual. What really mattered, however, was the ceremony itself and the holy oil, said to have been brought from heaven by a dove for Clovis's annointing. Early in the morning of July 17, a procession wound its way through the city; the Abbot of St. Rémi, in the company of priests and nobles, was bringing the holy oil to the cathedral. Charles was first knighted and given the spurs and belt of chivalry by his cousin, Alençon. Swearing to defend his people, he was annointed by the Archbishop of Reims, who crowned him and led him to the throne chanting, "Noël, noël, Long live the King." The cathedral vaults echoed with the crowd's response. Joan, who had stood beside Charles, placed higher than any noble of his kingdom, knelt before him and wept. She, and France, now had a rightful king to lead them; the Treaty of Troyes had been broken. Among the those who celebrated with Joan that day was her father, Jacques d'Arc; he had been invited as the city's guest of honor and had been given, by the king, freedom from taxes for himself and all the citizens of Domremy. Later, Charles would confer nobility on the d'Arc family, giving them the name of du Lys.

Joan had now kept two of her promises to Charles. Her last task lay before her: to drive the English from France. To this end, she needed to free Paris. But Joan's enemies were many and not just English. Several of Charles's closest counsellors were in the pay of the English; many wished to feather their own nests; some wanted peace at any cost. Charles listened to the pacifists as he was more interested in savoring his late victories than continuing the struggle. But he knew how Joan felt— that the only answer was war—so he kept secret a treaty he made with the Duke of

Burgundy (an ally of the English), who promised to surrender Paris in two weeks. So they waited. Joan was troubled; her voices were ever more pressing: "daughter of God—onward, onward, onward." Finally, as Burgundy still held Paris, Alençon convinced Charles to attack the city. At this time, two events occurred which were taken as bad omens: Joan had, from the first, commanded her soldiers to give up swearing, thievery and loose women: those wenches who traveled with the army, sometimes dressed in armor to disguise themselves. As the French armies assembled outside of Paris, Joan ordered these woman to leave the camp. One refused. Joan, striking her, broke her blade in two. Although Joan insisted that it was not the sword of St. Catherine, the French were uneasy. Also, Joan decided to attack Paris on September 8th, the Virgin Mary's birthday; this, too, was seen as a dangerous sign. Joan and Alençon attempted to breach Paris defenses from the north, but the moat was too deep. Then Joan's leg was struck with a bolt; her squire, reaching to help her, was killed, and her standard fell to the ground. Meanwhile, although a bridge had been built for the troops on the south, Charles had it dismantled during the night. He said he preferred peace. So the French army left Paris without another skirmish.

During the next few months, Joan stayed at La Trémouille's castle at Sully, perhaps as a prisoner. Meanwhile, her army disintegrated. Joan pressed Charles, but he would not listen; he made further truces. In mid-April, 1430, Joan rode north; the treaty with Burgundy was about to expire and La Trémouille wanted her to prepare for war. During the battle of Melun, in which Joan was victorious, her voices told her: "Daughter of God, you will [soon] be captured." A few weeks later, at the battle of Margny, although the French took the offensive, the English were quick to counter-attack. As the French retreated across the river to Compiègne, the drawbridge was raised. Stranded outside with a few soldiers, including one of her brothers, Joan was captured.

Throughout the summer and fall of 1430, Joan was moved from prison to prison, gradually farther north and west into English held territory. She ended up in Rouen on Christmas day of 1430. While it was the custom for important prisoners to be offered for ransom, Joan was an exception. The English wanted her out of the way. Many French churchmen were pleased with her capture as well; she had insulted them by listening directly to her voices rather than to their counsel. An ecclesiastical court was summoned to try her in January of 1431. The chief judge, Pierre Cauchon, bishop of Beauvais, was a bitter enemy of Charles; he was also in the pay of the English crown and understood very well the English wishes regarding Joan. The trial dragged on for almost five months. Although Joan answered honestly and wisely and no crime was proven, her words were twisted and the most minute facts of her life—the innocent childhood dances around the faerie tree, for example—were used against her. It became apparent that the judgment had preceded the trial. Joan was not tortured, but she suffered greatly in prison. Foul-mouthed English soldiers threatened her chastity, she was chained to a cot matted with sodden straw. But her greatest torture was being kept from receiving the Eucharist. On May 24th, a year and a day after her capture, Joan was taken out of her cell, publicly admonished for her sins, and threatened with burning—while an English crowd roared their death wish for her. Worn down, promised the sacraments, a church prison, and a woman guard, Joan recanted. The document that was read to her—one admitting her sinfulness—and the one she signed—stating that her voices were from the devil—were probably different. But as she couldn't read, she didn't know what she had signed. She was returned to an English prison and languished in misery for five days. On May 29, Joan told her guard to summon Cauchon and the judges. She denied her recantation—and the English made ready for her burning.

The following morning, May 30, 1431, Joan was brought from her cell to the marketplace of Rouen, where a huge crowd had gathered; she was placed on a high platform surrounded by bundles of faggots. Joan asked for a cross. A sympathetic English soldier lashed two sticks together and gave them to her while her confessor, Martin Ladvenu, ran to a nearby church for a crucifix which he held up for her to kiss. The pyre was lighted; the flames hissed and rose. After a short time, Joan cried out "Jesu, Jesu," and died. At that moment, many believed they saw a dove circle out of the fire and fly south toward France. Joan's ashes were thrown into the nearby Seine, along with her heart which, one soldier swore, would not burn. Her executioner sobbed, "I am damned, I have burned a saint."

By the end of 1450, nineteen years after Joan's death and after more than a century of fighting, the English had been entirely driven from the soil of France. In 1456, in response to a plea made by her mother for a new trial, Joan was declared innocent, her earlier trial invalid. In 1920, Joan of Arc was proclaimed a saint.

Joan of Arc Celebration

OPENING CEREMONY

In the late fall afternoon, a fanfare of trumpets as the fleur de lis ripple in the breeze, faerie trees glimmer, and the statue of Joan of Arc is unveiled in a moment of solemn prayer dedicating the celebration to her. (Rev. Grant Garringer, S.J.)

Sunday, September 29, 4pm, Joan of Arc chapel garden

SPECIAL EVENTS

Solemn High Mass honoring Saint Joan. (Rev. Robert Wild, S.J.)

Saturday, October 5, 4:30pm, Gesu church

Production of *The Lark* by Jean Anouilh, adapted by Lillian Hellman, directed by Debra Krajec. The story of Joan of Arc, told from the viewpoint of recorded history as well as through her own eyes.

October 2–October 20, Wednesday through Saturday, 8pm; Sunday, 2:30pm, Helfaer Theatre

Medieval Faire: in the ambiance of a medieval village—games, entertainment, food, merriment. (Kelly Miller)

Saturday, October 5, 11am to 4pm, south campus grounds

LECTURE SERIES

Opening lecture: "The Many Faces of Joan"

Dr. Ronald Zupko

Introduction: Dr. Thomas Hachey

Commentator: Dr. Phillip Naylor

September 29, 5pm, Weasler Auditorium

Jesuit lecture: "The Spirituality of Joan of Arc"
Rev. Dr. George Tavard, A.A.
Introduction: Rev. John Laurance, S.J.
Commentator: Rev. Thomas Hughson, S.J.
October 6, 7:30pm, Helfaer Theatre

Haggerty Art Lecture: "Changing Images of Joan of Arc"
Dr. Linda Seidel
Introduction: Dr. Curtis Carter
October 3, 6pm; October 4, 2pm; Haggerty Museum

Law Debate: "Joan of Arc, Saint or Terrorist?"
State of the Question: Dean Howard Eisenberg
Representing Joan: Atty. Michael Gillick
Representing the Church: Rev. Joseph Perry
September 30, 7:30pm, Law School Auditorium

Curtain Talks: Lively, brief talks given before performances of *The Lark*
"A Psychosocial Case Study: Joan of Arc as a Marquette Student"
Dr. Sherri Coe-Perkins
October 2, 7pm, Helfaer Theatre

"Right or Left, Who Owns Joan of Arc?"
Dr. Brigitte Coste
October 3, 7pm, Helfaer Theatre

"Closing Argument: A Lawyer's View of the Trial of Joan of Arc"
Atty. Michael Gillick
October 4, 7pm, Helfaer Theatre

"What Do I Do to Become a Saint?"
Dr. Mary Feeley
October 5, 9:30am, Cudahy Lecture Hall

"Church Heresy Trials and the Inquisition up to 1215"
Dr. Ronald Zupko
October 5, 11am, David Straz 106

"Torture in Medieval Justice"
Dr. Julius Ruff
October 5, 11am, David Straz 106

"Her Spirit in Stone: Marquette's Joan of Arc Chapel"
Dr. Curtis Carter
October 5, 7:30pm, Cudahy Lecture Hall

"Joan of Arc and Charles de Gaulle"

Dr. Phillip Naylor

October 6, 1:30pm, Helfaer Theatre

"Saints as Poetry: Joan of Arc Between History and Myth"

Dr. Daniel Maguire

October 9, 7 pm, Helfaer Theatre

"Joan of Arc: Saint or Symbol?"

Dr. John McCabe

October 10, 7 pm, Helfaer Theatre

"Homasse!: Joan of Arc as a Feminist Model"

Dr. Helen Sterk

October 11, 7pm, Helfaer Theatre

"The St. Joan Theme in Film"

Prof. Dominique Paul Noth

October 12, 4:30pm, Helfaer Theatre

"Architecture of the Middle Ages: the Coronation at Reims"

Dr. Lawrence Hoey

October 10, 7:30pm, Helfaer Theatre

"The Devil's Tool: An English View of Joan of Arc"

Dr. Carol Devlin

October 13, 1:30pm, Helfaer Theatre

THEATRE

Coronation procession: costumed representatives of the Marquette and
Milwaukee communities, on foot and horseback, accompany Joan and the dauphin
to the "Cathedral of Reims" for his coronation. (Michael Price)

October 5, 10 am, south campus grounds

Crowning of Charles VII: historical reenactment. (Tom Bruno)

October 5, 10:30am, south campus grounds

Medieval dance/music demonstration.(Leslie Corvo)

October 5, 11am, central mall stage

Medieval battle techniques: combat demonstration. (David Krajec)

October 5, 12:30pm, 4pm, Tory Hill

Medieval battle machinery: catapult demonstration. (Cory Reinbold)

October 5, 2pm, Tory Hill

"The folk of Joan's world": spoken biographies of "real" medieval individuals as
they appear in authentic dress of the period. (Beth Armatoski)

October 5, 3pm, Helfaer Theatre

"Light My Fire": Medieval Game Show featuring the d'Arc family pitted against their adversaries: history, costumes. (Beth Armatoski, Lisa Remby)

October 7, 7:30pm Helfaer Theatre

Debate among historical characters: Joan, Cauchon, the Inquisitor, Warwick.

October 8, 7:30pm, Helfaer Theatre

ART
"Images of St. Joan in 19th and 20th Century Works of Art." (James Scarborough)

Opening: October 3, 6pm, Haggerty Museum

MUSIC
Brass fanfare and orchestral suite composed for the Joan of Arc celebration by Dr. Nicholas Contorno, played by the University orchestra. (Nicholas Contorno)

September 29, 4pm, Joan of Arc chapel garden (Opening ceremony)

Collegium Musicam: medieval music. (Connie Sleger)

October 3, 5pm, Haggerty Museum; October 5, during the faire; October 10, 3pm, Joan of Arc chapel

"Giovanna d'Arco, Jean of Lorraine, the Maid in Music."

Christine Thomas, soloist

October 4, 7pm, Haggerty Museum

University Chamber Choir: medieval chant. (William Ross)

October 5, 10:30am, south campus (Coronation ceremony)

Carillon concerts, tours. (William Geisheker)

October 5, throughout the day, Marquette Hall bell tower

Strolling medieval singers. (Cathleen Morris)

October 5, throughout the faire

University Chorus: Church music of the 13th and 14th centuries (William Ross)

October 5, 2pm, Weasler Auditorium

FRENCH
Course: "St. Joan in Literature and Film."

Dr. Steven Taylor

Fall semester, 1996

Scènes de L'Alouette (The Lark). (Josh Kauffman, Marie Fossier, Joan Navarre)

October 5, 1:30pm, Helfaer Theatre

October 10, 3pm, Helfaer Theatre

French Mass celebrated in medieval vestments. (Rev. William Kelly, S.J.)

October 10, 4pm, Joan of Arc chapel

FILM

"Joan of Arc," screenplay by Maxwell Anderson; starring Ingrid Bergman.

> October 2, 4:30pm, Cudahy Lecture Hall

"The Passion of Joan of Arc," screenplay by Carl Dreyer; starring Renee Falconetti.

> October 9, 4:30pm, Cudahy Lecture Hall

"Saint Joan," screenplay by G.B. Shaw, Graham Greene; starring Jean Seberg.

> October 16, 4:30pm, Cudahy Lecture Hall

ONGOING EVENTS

Multi-media installation with images and information about Joan and her life and historical/military background including examples of music, art, architecture, costumes, everyday life in the late Middle Ages. (Bill Schulz, Lisa Remby)

> Cudahy lobby; Union information lobby; Memorial Library lobby

Special tours of Joan of Arc chapel. (Irene Wesoloski, Tom Stasiewicz)

> September 30 - October 12 (Sunday excepted) 10am to 4pm

Electronic bibliography of materials on Joan of Arc in context. (Susan Hopwood)

> http://www.mu.edu/

Special exhibit: "The Spirit of Joan of Arc." (Irene Wesoloski)

> Memorial Union, upper lobby

Exhibit of archival materials on Joan of Arc chapel. (John LeDoux)

> Memorial Library, south lobby

Vade Mecum: "Medieval newspaper." (Nik Raffin)

> distributed at the Medieval Faire, Saturday, October 5, south campus

Joan of Arc at the University. Published by Marquette University Press

CLOSING CEREMONY

A prayer service, liturgical dance, and medieval chant solo will remember Joan of Arc's death and commemorate her living spirit; the banners will be furled and the faerie tree lights wink out, but as the statue of Joan burns, the iron cross within it remains as a permanent memorial in the chapel garden: "the tomb of heroes is the heart of the living." (Rev. Grant Garringer, S.J., Alice Pollack, Clare Tallon)

> October 13, 5pm, Joan of Arc chapel garden

DONORS

American Litho

Mr. Joseph Becker III

Mr. Les Blum

The Frank Crivello Family

The Fox Company

Heiser Rent-a-car

Professor Richard Leonard/Breezewood Stables

Lithoprint Company

Mark Miskimen/ACME Production

Dr. and Mrs. Robert Pavlic

Mr. Stephen Pouliot

The Sternke Family/Mainstage Theatrical

SPONSORS

Wisconsin Humanities Council

National Endowment for the Humanities

Marquette University

    Alumni Association

    ASMU

    Division of Academic Affairs

    Division of Student Affairs

    College of Communication

    English Department

    Haggerty Museum of Art

    Instructional Media Center

    Instructional Media Center—Graphics

    Marquette Tribune

    MU Press

    Rec Plex

    Theatre Department